Rethinking Communication Geographies

RETHINKING HUMAN GEOGRAPHY

This series is a forum for innovative scholarly writing from across all substantive fields of human geography. The series aims to enrich the study of human geography by promoting a cutting-edge approach to geographical thought and analysis. Academic scrutiny and challenge is an essential component in the development of human geography as a field of study, and the act of re-thinking and re-examining principles and precepts that may have been long-held is imperative.

Rethinking Human Geography showcases authored books that address the field from a new angle, expose the weaknesses of existing concepts and arguments, or 're-frame' the topic in some way. This might be through the introduction of radical ideas, through the integration of perspectives from other fields or even disciplines, through challenging existing paradigms, or simply through a level of analysis that elevates or sharpens our understanding of a subject.

Rethinking Communication Geographies
Geomedia, Digital Logistics and the Human Condition

André Jansson

Department of Geography, Media and Communication, Karlstad University, Sweden

RETHINKING HUMAN GEOGRAPHY

Cheltenham, UK • Northampton, MA, USA

© André Jansson 2022

All rights reserved. No part of this publication may be reproduced, stored in a retrieval system or transmitted in any form or by any means, electronic, mechanical or photocopying, recording, or otherwise without the prior permission of the publisher.

Published by
Edward Elgar Publishing Limited
The Lypiatts
15 Lansdown Road
Cheltenham
Glos GL50 2JA
UK

Edward Elgar Publishing, Inc.
William Pratt House
9 Dewey Court
Northampton
Massachusetts 01060
USA

Paperback edition 2023

A catalogue record for this book
is available from the British Library

Library of Congress Control Number: 2022932885

This book is available electronically in the **Elgar**online
Geography, Planning and Tourism subject collection
http://dx.doi.org/10.4337/9781789906271

ISBN 978 1 78990 626 4 (cased)
ISBN 978 1 78990 627 1 (eBook)
ISBN 978 1 0353 2916 8 (paperback)

Printed and bound by CPI Group (UK) Ltd, Croydon, CR0 4YY

Contents

List of figures		vi
List of tables		vii
Acknowledgements		viii
1	Rethinking communication geographies	1
2	Dwelling under geomedia	33
3	The culture of streamability	60
4	Transmedia travel	92
5	Guidance landscapes	116
6	Geomedia *as* the human condition	151
References		168
Index		188

Figures

4.1	Activist ground media, River North Art District (RiNo), Denver, Colorado, 2019	114
5.1	The relationship between guidance landscape and logistical accumulation	135

Tables

2.1	Typology of the relations between activity types and media affordance registers	52
3.1	Uses of music-streaming services via smartphone in Sweden 2019 – depending on gender, age and education level (row percentages)	79
3.2	Three orientations in music listening in Sweden 2019 (factor analysis)	80

Acknowledgements

The original idea of this book was to write some kind of introduction, or invitation, to media and communication geography. As I started to put together the key perspectives and arguments, however, I soon realized that many of the discussions I wanted to pursue were too far-flung to fit an introductory textbook. I wanted to go further. I'm thus very grateful to the editors at Edward Elgar, who suggested that I submit a book proposal to their *Rethinking* series. This allowed me to write a book that elaborates new perspectives on our mediatized world, yet at the same time describes what this transdisciplinary field is about. There have been occasions during the writing processes when I've regretted that I didn't go for the original idea (which doesn't mean that it is an easy thing to write textbooks), but I now feel confident that this is the right time for putting "geomedia" to the test – largely because of the way our digital society develops, but also because I believe there is a need to open up new spaces for transdisciplinary dialogue.

At Edward Elgar, I want to thank especially Matthew Pitman and Alexandra O'Connell, who supported and worked very efficiently with this project from the start. I also want to thank the three anonymous reviewers for providing valuable feedback on the proposal, as well as for their general enthusiasm for this book project.

My warm thanks go to my colleagues at the Centre for Geomedia Studies at Karlstad University, and to friends within our affiliated international networks, a rather unique transdisciplinary platform where many of the ideas that led up to this book were shaped.

I'm very grateful to the Swedish Research Council for the Humanities and Social Sciences (Riksbankens Jubileumsfond) for funding a ten-month research sabbatical in 2021. The sabbatical was vital to the completion of this book. I want to thank Maren Hartmann at the University of the Arts, Berlin, who kindly hosted me as a visiting researcher as part of my sabbatical in September–October 2021 and with whom I've had many inspiring conversations throughout the writing process. During this period, we've also co-edited a special issue of *Space and Culture*, entitled "Gentrification and the Right to the Geomedia City," which may be considered an intellectual sibling of this book.

Likewise, I want to thank the colleagues I've worked with in the research projects *MECO (Music Eco Systems Inner Scandinavia)*, funded by the

European Union Interreg programme, and *Measuring Mediatization*, funded by the Ander Foundation. These projects have been essential to the gathering of empirical data as well as to the development of theoretical ideas that are embedded in this book (as specified in Chapter 1). My thanks go especially to Linda Ryan Bengtsson, Stina Bengtsson, Karin Fast and Johan Lindell.

While this book is written as a coherent monograph, some parts of the text have appeared in other publications. Parts of the article "Beyond the platform: Music streaming as a site of logistical and symbolic struggle," originally published in *New Media and Society* (Jansson, 2021), have been reworked and incorporated into Chapter 3. Parts of the article "The transmedia tourist: A theory of how digitalization reinforces the de-differentiation of tourism and social life," originally published in *Tourist Studies* (Jansson, 2020), have been reworked and incorporated into Chapter 4. Parts of "The mutual shaping of geomedia and gentrification: The case of alternative tourism apps," originally published in *Communication and the Public* (Jansson, 2019), have been reworked and incorporated into Chapter 5.

My heartfelt thanks go to two respected colleagues, Paul C. Adams and Jenny Sundén, who read the whole manuscript and whose sharp and constructive comments helped me strengthen the argument and fill in certain blind spots. Any weaknesses that still remain in this book are entirely due to my own limitations.

Finally, a very special thanks to Karin Fast, my partner and colleague, who has continuously commented on various parts of the manuscript and contributed to inspiring discussions on different topics, also far beyond the scope of this book.

André Jansson
Karlstad, October 2021

1. Rethinking communication geographies

At the time of writing this book, e-scooters seem to be everywhere. They are part of a new, and still quite experimental, infrastructure provided by start-up companies claiming they want to save the planet and improve the traffic situation in cities all over the world. In the town where I live, e-scooters were for several years obtained only as private gadgets for getting to school or to work in an "efficient," "cool," "stylish" and "environmentally friendly" manner.[1] They were stored and charged at home. There were no app-based services for micro-mobility until 2021. Then, suddenly, the situation changed. There are now several competitors on a limited market – just like in hundreds of other towns and cities around the world. E-scooters are lying around on street corners and in parks when not used for transportation or play. According to reports from other cities, many of them also end up in the water, in canals and rivers, unreachable for the "hunters" and their trucks roaming the streets in the evenings to collect bikes to charge.[2] Digital tracking systems do not help. The discarded underwater vehicles become electronic litter for the municipalities, to take care of, sometimes via specialized contractors. The life-length of an e-scooter is just a couple of months, we are told, indicating a not very sustainable transport solution after all.

The popularity of the e-scooter seems somewhat paradoxical and is thus an ideal subject of debate. In the media, new voices are raised on a regular basis for and against this new technology and business model.[3] Protagonists of market-led innovation and "smart" solutions meet more sceptical environmentalists, critics of the gig-economy and urban planners who struggle with new kinds of traffic problems. In October 2020, the politicians in Copenhagen, Denmark, decided to ban e-scooters in the central parts of the city because the municipality needed space for other purposes.[4] Meanwhile, in several French cities, climate activists were sabotaging so-called *trottinettes* (e-scooters).[5] In Paris, people protested against "anarchy in the streets," as well as against foreign business ventures and digital capitalism colonizing their city and their public spaces.[6] Around the same time, a radio reporter interviewed ordinary people in the streets of Stockholm, Sweden, asking them about why they rent e-scooters. Most of them described the e-scooter as practical, fun and good for the environment. It also made them feel closer to the urban buzz than if they had been in the subway or glancing at the street-life through a bus window.[7] As a radio listener, one is left bewildered. Are these people betrayed by the green-washed advertising campaigns of urban start-ups, or just eager to embrace the culture of digital micro-mobility? Or, do e-scooters after all represent a pathway to more liveable cities?

The e-scooter is not just a symbol of the digital platform economy, the "smart city," and the marriage of environmentalism and entrepreneurialism. It has also become a nodal point in our public culture, something to defend or criticize, test or detest, analyse or make jokes about – a key reason being that it *takes place*, and *takes up space*. Whether we ride them, stumble upon them, or just see them crossing our field of vision, the e-scooter engages our feelings for and moral judgements of our life environment. During the COVID-19 pandemic, this tendency was further accentuated and fed into a new kind of moral geography, related to whether and how to get around in the city without spreading the disease. To many people, the e-scooter provided a practical alternative to crowded buses; among others, the impression of urban disorder and over-consumption grew stronger. While this is not a book about the e-scooter – and the future of this new infrastructure remains uncertain both as a business model and as a solution to environmental problems – the phenomenon and the controversies around it highlight a number of issues that I want to discuss. In one sentence, these issues have to do with the rapidly changing form and substance of *communication geographies* under the regime of *geomedia*, and what these changes mean to the *human condition*.

On the one hand, e-scooter services are *reliant on*, and blend into, a complex amalgamation of old and new communication infrastructures. Without road networks, traffic signals, mobile networks, global positioning systems (GPS) and online transaction systems the rentable e-scooter would be unthinkable, at least in its current shape. To be even more precise, its arrival in cities around the world is intimately bound up with the fact that most people nowadays walk around with smartphones in their pockets. This is not to deny that the e-scooter's popularity may also have something to do with the public awareness of climate change and the need to reduce carbon dioxide emissions (or reduce the spread of COVID-19). But nobody would have come up with the idea of establishing entire fleets of rentable e-scooters if the infrastructural preconditions – the ability to efficiently track, maintain and charge micro-mobility – were not in place. In this way, the e-scooter reinforces and adds another layer onto existing communication geographies, just like other technologies have done in the past.

On the other hand, the e-scooter should be seen as a material and social *intervention*. While it consolidates people's habit of using their smartphones to manage most kinds of everyday practices, it also brings about change, even ruptures, in the urban texture. City dwellers, as we saw, may alter their commuting routines and encounter the urban landscape in new ways. Tourists may organize e-scooter tours as an independent form of sightseeing. Unemployed people may alter their day-to-day movements altogether, as they get out in the streets to earn money from collecting and charging geo-tagged e-scooters. Activists may demonstrate to stop the intrusion of venture capital into public life. In addition, all these activities may spark the appropriation of additional means of communication, such as navigation and guidance apps, and give rise to new online communities and networks for coordination and discussion (for or against the e-scooter). The e-scooter is an intervention into the *streams* of people, things, money, information and, not least, data.

As such, the consequences of, as much as the preconditions for, the expansion of e-scooter networks are largely *logistical* in nature. This may seem like a truism, given that the very purpose of transit systems is to organize traffic as efficiently as possible. As the Wikipedia entry on "logistics" tells us: "In a general business sense, logistics is the management of the flow of things between the point of origin and the point of consumption to meet the requirements of customers or corporations."[8] However, if we consider the e-scooter phenomenon from a communication geographical perspective, it points to a broader shift that warrants critical analysis. While the e-scooter per se is promoted and adopted foremost as "mobility as a service," that is, a transport solution, it also articulates the general expansion of the platform economy – predicated on the circulation of digital data – and the coming of geomedia as an *environmental regime*. Geomedia refers to the social normalization of certain media technological affordances, especially those enabled and driven by datafication, *and* to how people's relations to their life environments are in the same process redefined. This is also what popular notions like "smart technology," "artificial intelligence" (AI) and "the Internet of things" refer to. The fact that people are constantly connected to the Internet through mobile devices and use digital apps whose offerings are automatically tailored to the user's online engagements, geographical position, and so forth, means that everyday life is digitally entangled. People increasingly dwell and orient themselves *with, on* and *across* platforms whose operations are woven into the life environment, and by which they are also algorithmically *steered*, instead of dedicating their time, space and attention to separate distribution technologies like newspapers, television and other traditional mass media. This is why we currently witness an explosion of platform reliant services – "X as a service" (X standing for "transportation," "security," "banking," etc.) – whose purpose it is to extract economic value through the logistical management of people and their data. This is, in short, what I will call *logistical accumulation*.

Smartphones and other connected devices have obviously contributed to this dialectical transition. They have made it easier for people to find their way and coordinate activities in physical and other spaces; represent and construct visions of space, and, ultimately, appropriate, manage, (re)configure and create (new) places and territories. As such, geomedia can be seen as a regime that expands the logistical capacities of human beings, fostering a sense of spatial ease, even expertise, that was hardly thinkable just a few decades ago. At the same time, these new capacities are unevenly distributed in society. They are conditioned by, and produce, industrial forms of flow management and data mining that tie people closer to the new systems of circulation, as we saw in the case of the e-scooter. People's dwelling with and in geomedia environments becomes a form of *logistical labour*, a means of value creation, that looks different and means different things depending on who you are. While some groups are deeply reliant on the new technologies and social imperatives of geomedia as part of their livelihood – not least many of those working in the new gig-economy, charging e-scooters or delivering fast food – others gain social influence and recognition, even the power to influence the production of environments *in which other people dwell*, through their handling of geomedia. The latter pertains to anything from the day-to-day creation of domestic streaming environments to more professional initiatives related to the platform economy.

Therefore, a key purpose of this book is to explore the negotiations and struggles over logistics that follow in the wake of geomedia. This is partly a matter of showing and explaining what the shift from mass media to geomedia is all about and how new possibilities for spatial mastery are linked to social power relations. But I also want to go deeper. In contrast to the techno-centric, or data-centric, views that have thus far guided most research on digital geographies, I am concerned here with how the regime of geomedia affects the *human condition*, following Hannah Arendt's (1958/1998) classical work. What is it to dwell in, with and, ultimately, *under* geomedia? How does it feel? What kinds of frictions and frustrations do humans experience beyond the comforts of a geomediatized life environment? There are many circumstances that complicate the dominant picture of increasingly capable individuals, that is, people turned into "ordinary logistical experts." Like other technological systems, and in spite of their growing ordinariness, the infrastructures of geomedia are full of glitches, bugs and contradictions; they are imperfect, incomplete and in continual transition (e.g., Berlant, 2016; Pink et al., 2018; Sundén, 2018; Leszczynski, 2020a; Paasonen, 2020). As humans, we must handle this state of technological "brokenness" on a day-to-day basis – emotionally, morally and practically.

Let us consider another example – the case of the mobile parking app, or, what might be called "parking as a service." In Sweden, arriving by car to a new town or city, even a new neighbourhood, often means that you have to install a new parking app on your smartphone. This procedure, in turn, involves a registration process that links the service to a particular vehicle and a particular credit card. In order to pay the right fee, you must also disclose your location.

While this system allows for greater flexibility in day-to-day life, as you can extend or shorten the parking time depending on circumstances, it also causes frictions and annoyances. Many people consider the binding nature of digital services *in general* as a threat to privacy and autonomy; and among occasional visitors and tourists, the request to download a site-specific parking app may seem superfluous and much less convenient than using a globally valid credit card. Mobile individuals will obviously have to keep numerous apps.[9] It can also be quite stressful to download an app before paying the parking fee, especially if the registration procedure is slow or does not work (which happens), or if you are not an adept smartphone user. There are numerous examples of malfunctioning parking apps, and apps that refuse to download. In Stockholm, a new parking app (developed by a new service provider) was introduced to roughly 570,000 users in October 2020. After the introductory week, its average rating on Google's App Store was 1.1. The overarching reason for the bad rating was that users could not see why the previous parking app had been replaced by one that did not work; it did not communicate well with credit cards, did not identify the right taxes, did not allow for flexible time adjustment, and, for many Android users, did not work at all.[10] On top of such practical hassles, users of parking apps may have to pay app-related extra charges that are not evident from the start (unless you take the time to read all the details of the user agreement).

This example, trivial as it may seem, bespeaks the human underside of geomediatized life environments, not least in relation to platform urbanism (e.g., Richardson, 2015, 2020a; Barns, 2020; Leszczynski, 2020a; van Doorn, 2020). It touches upon the ordinary, yet sometimes unexpected, toil and trouble that perforate people's ambitions to "go with the flow." This is related to what Whiting and Symon (2020: 1079) call "digi-housekeeping," work that is required (but still does not count as proper work) "to maintain the digital tools that enable flexible working, and incorporates the tasks of clearing, sorting, preparing, provisioning and troubleshooting." The ability to lead a *flexible life* is not entirely predictable, not even to the digitally skilled person, and those who are not at ease with geomedia will be systematically disadvantaged, experiencing continuous interruptions and misunderstandings. Several new notions have recently been presented in the research literature to capture different aspects of such experiences, for example, "digital resignation" (Draper & Turow, 2019), "digital irritation" (Ytre-Arne & Moe, 2020), "privacy cynicism" (Lutz et al., 2020) and "digital unease" (Fast et al., 2021). And behind all this, we must not forget, are material infrastructures that require continuous, professional maintenance from people whose labour is most often invisible to the ordinary user of digital services. As Stine and Volmar (2021: 10) put it in their introduction to a volume on media infrastructures and digital time: "Behind and beneath our real-time interactions with on-demand media and services is a temporal geography as uneven as our social and political geographies, in which slowness and waiting are produced and distributed alongside every advance in convenience and speed."

This is why we should think of geomedia as an expanding environmental regime whose human consequences are ambiguous. Whether we speak of e-scooters, parking apps or location-based dating services, inasmuch as these phenomena enter into the ordinary lifeworld, or "the digital mundane" (Maltby & Thornham, 2016; Leszczynski, 2020b) – for functional, social or other reasons – they have differential impacts on how humans go about and feel about their lives and their co-existence with others.

Against this background, this book advances three ways of rethinking communication geographies. First, it presents a systematic and critical account of *geomedia* as the environmental regime of everyday dwelling. Second, it addresses the *struggles over logistics* to which geomedia gives rise. Third, it scrutinizes how geomedia affects *the human condition*, especially people's ways of making place and existing together in a geomediatized culture and society – that is, their "digital throwntogetherness" (Leurs, 2014), or "digital thrownness" (Lagerkvist, 2017).[11] While this focus on humans and their lifeworld is guided by Arendt's (1958/1998) classical exploration of the three variants of the "active life," the *vita activa* – namely, *labour*, *work* and *action* – it also implies a re-actualization of theories from the humanistic, phenomenological strands of human geography, as well as from cultural studies. Ultimately, the book seeks to reformulate the emancipatory agenda of humanistic research (e.g., Buttimer, 1999) in relation to geomedia and the coming of a *logistical society*. Emancipation here implies a double concern with human autonomy – notably the possibility to act meaningfully not just with(in) digital platforms but also beyond and against their entangling forces – *and* security, that is, to protect the boundaries of the self, permeable as they are, especially among those groups that are most vulnerable to the exploitative power of "surveillance capitalism" (Zuboff, 2015). In the sections that follow, I introduce the three cornerstones in turn. After that, I present an outline of the book and its chapters.

UNDERSTANDING GEOMEDIA

The concerns of this book are positioned at the centre of a research field called "communication geography," or, "media and communication geography." While this label may seem to denote a subfield of geography (the geographical study of media and communication) it should be understood as an interdisciplinary endeavour aiming to build *bridges* between core concerns of human geography *and* media and communication studies (Adams & Jansson, 2012).[12] It means that communication geographical research applies media and communication theory to gain deeper understandings of spatial phenomena, and vice versa. Similarly, as I try to "rethink communication geographies," I am interested in the *mutual shaping* of space/place, on the one hand, and media/communication, on the other. In a previous publication (Jansson, 2007a), I formulated this matter as a dialectical question; *how does communication produce space, and how does space produce communication*? This is precisely the dialectical relation that geomedia enters into and reshapes. As already mentioned, geomedia refers not merely to technological change, that is, alterations in media technology (even though such developments are vital), but to an environmental regime that ultimately blurs the boundaries between spatial and communicative processes. It is a notion that reflects the enhanced tendency of space to become communicative, and of communication to become spatial (locative) (cf. Thielmann, 2010), or, as Fast et al. (2018a: 7) puts it, a condition "where human subjectivity, media and space/place are co-constitutive of one another." To understand more concretely what this means, and before we stake out the theoretical properties of geomedia, we must clarify what the basic components of the dialectical formulation stand for in this book. I will deliberately keep this clarification on a rudimentary level.

If we look at the "communicational side" of the formulation, first, it should be stated that media is here understood as *means of communication*. Communication is thus the broader of these inseparable terms. Given that communication refers to the social processes whereby "something is made common to many" (from Latin: *communicare*), media should be understood as the resources people use for sharing or disseminating thoughts and meanings amongst themselves. They entail material resources like clay, paper and electromagnetic waves; technological resources like pencils, typewriters and smartphones; as well as institutional resources, including organized, even industrialized, modes of sharing and disseminating information such as broadcasting companies and social media platforms. Simply put, a certain material is turned into a media technology when it is deliberately shaped to communicate meaning through a shared semiotic system. As so conceived, paper becomes a medium when it is formatted according to culturally recognized standards, such as a letter, a tabloid, or an A4 sheet. Following John Durham Peters' (1999: 6–10) conceptual framework, media as means of communication pertain to "the project of reconciling self and other," that is, to *cultural life*, rather than to transportation. This is not an easy distinction to sustain, however, and a key feature of geomedia is that such demarcations are destabilized. This issue will be addressed throughout the book.

If we turn to the "spatial side" of the question, it is important to acknowledge the basic distinction between space and place. Whereas place refers to a socially demarcated and culturally meaningful location, akin to a social region, we should think about spaces as more open-ended constructs established through relations and interactions that traverse or join different places (e.g., Adams, 2009; Cresswell, 2015). For example, while the physical places of the e-scooter can be identified in the streets of Stockholm or Hamburg, the wider phenomenon of the e-scooter, not least the platform (Richardson, 2020b), also actualizes a variety of more loosely demarcated spaces, such as the discursive space of social media; the flow-spaces that appear when micro-mobility is digitally charted and represented in mobile apps, as well as the device management and mobility tracking spaces accessible to the service provider – which, in turn, play into the production and coding of particular places and environments in the city or elsewhere. Spaces may also lack material, geographical bonds altogether, as with purely communicative or imaginative worlds. This does not rule out that there exist socially recognized *places in media*, notably online (e.g., Zook & Graham, 2007; Adams, 2009). From a phenomenological perspective, however, places tend to be associated with the socially and materially bounded domains where humans dwell. As Yi-Fu Tuan (1974) shows in his work on *topophilia*, that is, the "love of place," people's attitudes towards the environment and their ways of setting down roots at particular locations are largely informed by their senses and ongoing tactile engagements with the world around them. This includes media, both as material things and as carriers of content (sound, vision, text, and so forth) (see, e.g., Adams, 1992; Moores & Metykova, 2010).

This leads us to the final key term in the aforementioned formulation; "produce." To speak about "production" is to indicate that media and communication, as well as space and place, undergo mutual change. Metaphorically speaking, to study communication geographies is not to draw a fixed map. Rather, we must deal with material, symbolic and imaginative terrains that are continuously contested, moulded by social, economic and other forces. As the terrain changes, the map must be redrawn, and what was once taken as a convenient mode of communication may fall into obsolescence as new technologies emerge and people start expecting new things from their life environment. One of the theoretical foundations of this processual view is Henri Lefebvre's (1974/1991) theory of the production of space; a theory that explicates how the power, and struggles, over space, whether we speak of very specific places or entire cities or regions – including their "mediaspaces" (Couldry & McCarthy, 2004) – are played out along different spatial dimensions. As such, the production of space relies on processes pertaining to representations, myths and lived experiences of space and place, as much as it stems from material conditions. Lefebvre's model cogently exposes the inseparability of spatial and communicational processes, as well as their morally and ideologically imbued nature. We will dig deeper into these critical issues in Chapter 2. At this point, we should instead consider how geomedia fits into the equation.

Three Registers of Media Affordances

A theoretical premise of this book is that the properties of different media can be meaningfully described in terms of three basic affordance types: *connective*, *representational* and *logistical* affordances. These affordance types, or *registers*, define how different media typically sustain communication, or, at least, what people under certain historical and cultural circumstances have agreed that media are good for (and not). Following James J. Gibson's (1979/2014) original, ecological approach to affordances, we should not think of affordances as essential or pregiven capacities of technology. They are better understood as conventions that evolve through people's continuous interactions with, and communication about, different resources in the environment (whether or not conceptualized as "technology"), which guide people to certain ways of appropriating and using these resources. This does not mean that affordances are stable or equally offered to every individual or group. As people's life conditions change and as specific challenges are to be mastered, a particular resource may prove to possess previously unnoticed, even unimagined, affordances and enter into new patterns of use. The same affordances may remain hidden, or inaccessible, to other people and thus hinder them from certain (inter)actions. As subsequently argued by Ian Hutchby (2001), this holds for media technologies as much as for other resources in the environment. While affordances tend to consolidate over time, there is always a margin of freedom, a space for improvisation and for the unexpected to happen, as well as a potential for exclusion and discrimination. For current purposes, we should thus deploy the three above-mentioned affordance types as relatively flexible registers that undergo change and may play out differently in different contexts. As they help us unpack what different means of communication are generally (thought to be) good for, that is, how they contribute to communication as the "reconciliation of self and other" (Peters, 1999), they can also assist us in carving out the contours of geomedia as an evolving environmental regime.

My key point, which I will now develop, is that *geomedia implies the intermingling of connective, representational and logistical affordances in digital communication, and the budding supremacy of logistical affordances over the other two types.*[13]

Connective affordances, first, refer to the *linking together of people*, and thus respond directly to the human desire to get in touch and stay in touch with others. While the archetypical set-up for sharing ideas and information is human co-presence in time and space, connective media affordances can be understood as potential bridges to overcome geographical, social and other distances between human beings. While most media in history have been reliant on supplementary technologies like ships and railroads, as well as human labour and animal power, to transport a message from point A to point

B, certain media systems carry connective affordances in themselves. For example, the expansion of the global telegraph system in the late 19th century had a revolutionary impact on society due to its capacity to convey information instantaneously over large distances.

Representational affordances, in turn, refer to the perceived capacity of a certain technology to *provide engaging and/or adequate representations of people, places, events and ideas* through which human beings can make sense of the world and other people. As such, there is no communication without representation. While the photograph obviously does not attain the connective affordances of the telegraph, it is an outstanding tool for depicting anything from the inner life of human existence to events in the world. In its "pure" form, as Roland Barthes (1977: 17) famously pointed out, photography is the only medium that communicates "a message without a code." In other media, we encounter a variety of representational techniques, or modalities, such as sound, text and moving images. The combination of such techniques is often institutionally defined, determined not only by technological possibilities but pertaining to genre and audience. The newspaper format, for example, has been continually adapted to changes in society and culture (including other media) and thus refined its way of combining text and image in ways that provide lucid representations of the world to its audience – most recently, via various digital remediations.

The last register, logistical affordances, is the one that has been discussed and analysed the least in media and communication theory. Yet, to our understanding of media and communication *geographies* and the normalization of geomedia as an environmental regime, this register is even more important than the other two. Some thinkers (e.g., Peters, 2008, 2013, 2015; Case, 2013; Rossiter, 2015, 2016) have posited "logistical media" as a separate category of media. The function of such media, according to Peters (2008: 40), is to *"arrange people and property into time and space"* (emphasis added). In contrast to connective media, logistical media do not establish any direct links between people. Rather, they constitute *infrastructures* that *sustain* communication in as much as they help people orient themselves in the world and in relation to others, and thus pave the way for meaningful interactions. Good examples are clocks, time-tables and maps. While I agree that the infrastructural aspect is crucial for understanding what logistical affordances "do," I would refrain from speaking too categorically about "logistical media." For analytical purposes it is crucial that we take into account that there is in each medium always a mixture of affordances. This means that if we want to grasp the growing prominence of logistics in our contemporary media culture, related above all to the platform economy, we cannot look only at the things we normally associate with "infrastructure." There are, as we will see, logistical affordances also in other kinds of media. In particular, representational and logistical affordances are difficult to tell apart, since obviously most media are representational in one way or another. What marks the difference, still, is that while representational affordances invite people to understand the ideas, feelings and lifeworlds of others, logistical affordances *guide*, or steer, human beings towards those arenas where further communication can take place (Rossiter, 2015). As such, the logistical register encompasses affordances that often blend with other resources of the environment, constituting a largely taken for granted "material substrate of culture" (Siegert, 2013: 51). However, as we will see later in the book, this basic statement also needs to be problematized under the regime of geomedia (see especially Chapter 4).

When presenting and thinking about these registers it is obviously easier to use historical examples than to engage with our contemporary, convergent media landscape. Older media most often attained a clear *bias* in favour of one of the three above-mentioned affordance types (cf. Innis, 1951). In a specific sense, we might say that media like novels, telephones, music recordings and photos are "purer" than the digital technologies and platforms of today. Still, there are classical examples of how different registers blend within one media form. The modern newspaper with its variety of contents can be seen as a forerunner of today's media in the sense that representational affordances were supplemented by logistical ones – partly because of content types like economic and cultural announcements, partly due to the newspaper's propensity to structure the daily and weekly routines of its readers according to its distribution schedules and modes of delivery. Under geomedia, as we will see, such intersections are the norm.

The three affordance types describe not only how different media sustain communication in society; they also expose different registers of the complex relations between communication and space. They represent three approaches to our study of how communication produces space, and vice versa. Connective affordances characterize media that enable communication to *transcend* space and *link* different places together. Representational affordances sustain communication *about* spaces and places, and are as such vital for *understanding*, *envisioning* and *producing* space and place. Logistical affordances, as we saw, help people to *orient* themselves in space as well as *coordinating* and *orchestrating* various activities and flows in and across spaces and places. In Chapters 3–5 I will deploy each of these registers, in turn, as entry points for exploring the significance of geomedia as an environmental regime. In order to set the scene for these discussions, however, we should now sketch the contours of geomedia.

GEOMEDIA

I assert three things about this new regime. First, geomedia arises through technological transitions, enabled by digitalization, that change the ways in which each of the three affordance types is articulated. Second, geomedia implies that connective, representational and logistical affordances amalgamate within digital media technologies and platforms. Geomedia thus points to the extended consequences of media convergence (Jenkins, 2006). Third, geomedia signifies the growing prominence of logistical affordances in human affairs *and* as a driver of the platform economy. This makes it possible to speak of a more general *logistical bias* of contemporary media environments and to envisage the coming of a *logistical society*. Let us now briefly consider what is going on within each affordance register, and in this way also grasp the broader trend.

Connective affordances are today pervasively moulded by the logics of social media platforms, or what José van Dijck (2013) prefers to call connective media (see also van Dijck & Poell, 2013). The logics of such platforms, which increasingly also saturate other branches of the media industry and beyond, is to extract value from the management and computation of *digital data streams*. Simply put, connectivity today means that media users are connected through networks that enable many-to-many communication with instantaneous feedback in different modalities (text, image and sound) *and* that the circulation of content is customized according to the user's previous and anticipated engagements. In the "front-end," the user's connections with other people, places and events in the surrounding world are mediated through various *content streams*, ranging from the real-time streams of social media platforms and digital news outlets to audio- and video-streaming services (e.g., Weltevrede et al., 2014; Burroughs, 2019). At the same time, the customization of front-end streams relies on the continuous aggregation and managing of "back-end" streams of user-generated data, in order to *predict* the users' responses and behaviours (e.g., Zuboff, 2019: 16–17). The industrial imperative to generate and manage streamable content resonates with a cybernetic model of accumulation, meaning that the activities of users, down to their slightest expression of engagement or affect (Karppi, 2018), automatically generate data streams that sustain algorithmic user profiling and prediction, and thus feed into the composition of additional content streams (including recommendations, advertising, user-generated content, and so forth). Thus, our key term here is *streamability*. Connectivity in this new shape produces a representational space whose end it is to guide, steer or stream human subjects – as digital subjects generating data (Goriunova, 2019) – in the directions most profitable to the industry. As Andreas Bernard (2019) asserts, people also *internalize* this logic through voluntarily setting up user profiles and tracking their whereabouts through various online applications (see also Berry, 2012; Ruckenstein, 2014). Hence, as we will discuss in Chapter 3, this emerging culture of streamability involves a logistical drive that penetrates deep into human life environments, affecting people's dwelling "online" as well as "offline" (to the extent that it is meaningful to maintain this distinction).

Representational affordances, in turn, are increasingly shaped by the rise of *transmedia* as a normalized mode of cultural circulation (Fast & Jansson, 2019). Transmedia implies that cultural texts (understood in a broad sense) circulate across different devices and platforms to be reworked, remixed and re-contextualized throughout the processes. The term was introduced in the 1990s to describe "world building" in popular culture (Kinder, 1991) and later elaborated in relation to new forms of interactive storytelling (Jenkins, 2006). It has since been applied in a variety of areas where media users are actively involved in media circulation (for an overview, see Freeman & Gambarato, 2019). This does not mean that texts are always drastically altered. The notion of transmedia applies to all those cultural techniques that enable users to comment upon content, add additional elements, *and*, most importantly, re-circulate material. Today, transmedia thus reaches far beyond popular culture. People share, amend and circulate texts – images, documents, news, videos, and so forth – as a matter of routine, and often for practical everyday purposes. In a previous study, Karin Fast and I applied the transmedia approach onto the world of work and labour, showing how transmedia affects anything from how work tasks are carried out and work places designed, to how the boundaries of work and leisure are drawn and what kinds of jobs are even available to people (e.g., within the expanding "gig-economy") (Fast & Jansson, 2019). Similar things can be said about a wide range of contemporary life domains, including consumption and travel, which is the theme of Chapter 4, where online systems for searching, ordering and rating various services enable, and *direct*, people to dwell and coordinate their activities across time and space. This, again, highlights the logistical bias of geomedia and shows how transmedia feeds into the logic of streamability, as the circulation of texts is also the circulation of profitable meta-data about users and their activities.

Logistical affordances, finally, are altered mainly through the development of *locative media*. The latter term has been given slightly different meanings by different authors, but refers broadly to "media of communication that are functionally bound to a location" (Wilken & Goggin, 2015: 4). As Wilken and Goggin argue, locative media today entail much more than location-based services based on the combination of cell-phones and global positioning systems (GPS). Place-contingent news streams, check-in services and geo-tagging are today standard ingredients of mobile apps – turning locative information into the norm (ibid: 5). Likewise, as I will discuss in Chapter 5, a whole range of "platformed" services, especially those linked to the urban platform economy and the "smart city" (e.g., Sadowski, 2020a, 2020b), provide social and spatial *guidance* and respond to the user's online activities in ways that depend on where the device is located. These developments, it should be noted, are reliant on the embeddedness of digital networks into our everyday environments, including digital media and sensors placed in for example transit systems, cars and shopping malls, producing what Kitchin and Dodge (2011) call "code/ space." The abundance of spatial information and digital access points available to anyone with a connected device makes life in general, and practices of orientation and coordination in particular, easier – in the everyday as well as when moving about in foreign terrains. Electronic tickets can be booked on the go; transactions can be carried out instantaneously; time-tables are available at one's fingertips. Whereas many people appropriate these resources to develop a form of *ordinary logistical expertise*, however, locative media also allow for pervasive forms of surveillance and monitoring of human activities in space (see, e.g., Rossiter, 2015; Andrejevic, 2019; Bernard, 2019; Iveson & Maalsen, 2019). Again, the more profound human consequences of geomedia are ambiguous.

As given by this schematic outline, I take geomedia to represent a fundamental, still ongoing, shift in how communication produces space, and how space produces communication. As the prefix *geo-* suggests, our media today, our digital means of communication, are increasingly embedded into – and *re-*embedding – our everyday life environments, whether we speak about the domestic setting, the shopping mall or the city, whose character is increasingly responsive, manageable *and* prescriptive due to digital mediation. We may here think of Google Maps as a concrete and particularly pervasive example (see, e.g., McQuire, 2016, 2019). While this digital embeddedness reminds us that all media are basically in and of the earth, as Peters argues (2015) in his work on *elemental media*, and that spatiality may be thought of as "always-already mediated," as Leszczynski (2015a: 729) holds, geomedia is a regime that furnishes our media/environment with hitherto unseen forms of connective, representational and logistical affordances. We may conceive of these furnishing processes and their moral and political implications, that is, the social *normalization* of geomedia, as *geomediatization* (see also Fast et al., 2018a). I will offer a more detailed account of what this means in Chapter 2.

At this point, it is also important to acknowledge two antecedent accounts of geomedia to which the current investigation is indebted, and in some regards also differs from. First, my approach is acquainted with Tristan Thielmann's (2010) idea that geomedia represents the coming together of mediated localities and locative media, through which a seamless realm of spatial information is established. Geomedia, in Thielmann's view, is thus a *relational construct* that sits *in-between* space and communication and is *enacted by humans*, rather than just another type of technology.[14] This is an important point, and a perspective that resonates with the basic idea of affordances (see also Nagy & Neff, 2015). Still, the approach I advance here is more concerned with the human and social consequences of geomedia than with how geomedia "works." In this sense, secondly, my approach is also related to Scott McQuire's (2011, 2016) work on geomedia. McQuire (2016) understands geomedia as a *technological regime* marked by four trajectories: media convergence, real-time-feedback, location-awareness and ubiquity. These technological trajectories have a profound impact on life conditions today, especially in larger cities, as McQuire shows. They also make much sense in relation to the three affordance registers advanced here. Still, an environmental regime is not the same thing as a technological regime. In contrast to McQuire's technological characteristics, the three affordance registers constitute *bridges* between media/technology, space/environment and human subjectivity – what Leszczynski (2015a) in her work on "spatial media" calls "socio-spatio-technical relations" – that are not particularly tied to the digital era. As theoretical bridges, they are relevant over time and across social, geographical and technological contexts, which means that they can help us delineate more enduring processes of media-related social change. One such longer-term process of change, I argue, is the coming of a logistical society.

LOGISTICAL STRUGGLES

Let us look back a couple of decades. In 1990, in the aftermath of the political uprisings in Eastern Europe and the fall of the Berlin Wall, Scott Lash diagnosed the coming of what he called a "semiotic society" (see also Wexler, 1990). According to Lash, the political transitions at the time, referring especially to the so-called Monday Street demonstrations in Leipzig, were representative of a society no longer dominated by industrial capitalism but steering towards an updated, semiotic version of capitalism where "social practices [...] find their regulating principle in signs" (Lash, 1990: 146). Among the street protesters in Germany, Lash discerned two fractions of the semiotic struggle, which were both distinctively "postmodern": a "spectral" fraction (the dominant one) celebrating atomized and individualist consumerism, and a more "organic" social movement proclaiming ecological, communitarian and localist values. While heading in different directions, both fractions represented a critique of industrial modernization as a process of cultural differentiation. They represented postmodernization, de-differentiation and the coming of a semiotic society.

A few years later, Lash and Urry (1994) developed and contextualized these ideas in their book *Economies of Signs and Space*, which draws the contours of a society where the circulation of *representational goods* (signs) has taken over from *industrial goods* – which in the 19th century had taken over from *agricultural goods* – as the key driver of social and economic life. Electronic media, computerization and expanding digital infrastructures powered this transformation whereby semiotic expertise once confined to the cultural industries was adopted in a growing number of sectors of society. Industries were to an increasing extent managing information and symbolic meaning rather than raw material. Images, brands and designs became more important than products per se – they *became* the goods. One might say that Lash and Urry's analysis "sociologized" pre-existing, and more radical, depictions of postmodern society as a condition where material concerns gave way to semiotic desires, and where reality imploded into a realm of mediated simulacra (copies without originals) (see, e.g., Baudrillard, 1983).

Why is this important to the current discussion? Simply put, the semiotic society (if we subscribe to the general argument) highlights two important things. First, it depicts the significance of *mediatization*, that is, the growing social reliance on media and communication technologies, in the rise of post-industrial social structures. While mediatization certainly did not begin with electronic and digital media – its history is much longer (see, e.g., Couldry & Hepp, 2017) – semiotic society represents the point in history when media technologies moved to the very centre of social and economic life. Second, inasmuch as mediatization processes led to the semiotic society they attained a *representational bias*. This is obvious not just on the production side of the economy and in various "promotional cultures" (Wernick, 1991) – what Lash and Urry (1994) refer to as "reflexive accumulation" – but in human affairs at large. The mounting technological capacity to engineer and circulate sign-value, now in the hands of lay-people as well as experts, describes the triumph of representational media affordances.

A central argument of this book is that the semiotic society is now gradually transforming into a *logistical society*. This is still a capitalist society. It is also still a deeply mediatized society, and a society in which the circulation of representational goods is intense. Yet, in certain respects it is a very different society. The logistical society manifests a version of capitalism that is even more ephemeral than "semiotic capitalism." The logistical bias of geomedia, as we will see throughout this book, implies that the tailoring, manufacturing and provision of representational goods become secondary to the management of those movements, or *streams* – of people, goods, capital, information, and so forth – that generate calculable data. While data can be understood as a very particular kind of simulation, thus underscoring the extended relevance of postmodern theory, the economic focus has now moved beyond representational goods. Just like in previous shifts, we are witnessing how means are turned into ends. The shift from agricultural to industrial accumulation saw an explosion of economic growth linked to the provision of machines, tools and other appliances needed for the production of agricultural and other types of basic goods. The semiotic (or post-industrial) shift, in turn, saw how the representational means once developed for circulating industrial goods to expanding masses of consumers were gradually turned into essential resources autonomously generating value through economic circulation. This is what Lash and Urry (1994) termed reflexive accumulation, or what might also be thought of as semiotic accumulation. Now, the logistical shift implies that the controlled, generative *movement* of various types of representations becomes more significant than representations per se. While business-oriented logistics has always been a matter of making circulation more profitable, a form of "monetization of time and space" (Hepworth, 2014: 1121) through minimizing delays, excess space, turnover times, and other frictions, data capitalism means that streams *as such* generate economic value. I call this *logistical accumulation*. Of course, this dialectical view is much simplified and should be interpreted cautiously. It is given here as a schematic backdrop to the discussions that follow later on in this book, notably in Chapters 5–6.

Until now, relatively little has been written about the logistical society and its reliance on different types of media technology. This might seem like a strange verdict given the exponential growth in literature on subjects like big data, connective media and digital geographies during the last decade. Still, while this body of literature has a strong bearing on the arguments put forward here – and parts of it will be implemented in the book – it rarely takes logistics as its focal point and most often leaves aside the wider social and human implications of technological environments biased toward the management of streams (including the movement of human bodies, goods, capital, information and, ultimately, *data*). Likewise, while there is a growing interest in logistics within sociology and human geography, problematizing not least the transformations of global trade, labour migration and politics of (regional/urban) place in the wake of increasingly powerful, computerized, flow-architectures (see, e.g., Cowen, 2010, 2014; Neilson, 2012; Kanngieser, 2013; Hepworth, 2014; Chua et al., 2018; Mezzandra & Neilson, 2019; Hesse, 2020), the penetration of logistics into the fabrics of everyday life via various media platforms has so far rendered little attention. If one enters the search term "digital logistics" into Google Scholar, the publications that come up concern the digitalization of industry related supply chains, rather than the logistical implications *of* "the digital" *across* social domains.

We can discern a similar limitation if we look at the literature that explicitly discusses *logistical media*. The notion of "logistical media" has been developed most consistently by media theorists John Durham Peters and Ned Rossiter, as well as by Judd Case (2010, 2013) in his work on the history of radar. It is difficult to determine exactly when and where the term was coined. Peters referred to logistical media in a couple of shorter texts (Peters, 2008,

2012, 2013), where he stressed the overlooked role of media in organizing and orienting people and property in time and space. It was only later, in his book *The Marvellous Clouds: Toward a Philosophy of Elemental Media* (Peters, 2015), that he expanded on the concept and incorporated it into a theory, and *history*, of media as elements of the human environment – including anything from calendars and meteorology to contemporary search engines. This is where we find the link to geomedia, as presented earlier. However, while Peters' work is fundamental to the analyses of geomedia, especially to understand its infrastructural aspects, it has relatively little to say about how life conditions change under this regime. Rather, Peters' theorization comes close to the German research tradition on "cultural techniques" (e.g., Siegert, 2015), which allows us to think about most kinds of material constructs, even the natural elements, as media that organize life (see also Young, 2015). I will come back to these discussions in Chapter 2.

If we turn to the work of Rossiter, who advocates the development of a "logistical media theory" (Rossiter, 2016: 4–6), we encounter a perspective that mainly concerns the logics of infrastructures, including algorithmic architectures and automated governance of global transport systems (see also Rossiter, 2014, 2015; Zehle & Rossiter, 2016). While Rossiter's (2016) book *Software, Infrastructure, Labour: A Media Theory of Logistical Nightmares* addresses important questions of labour in the wake of new cybernetic software – including how such software impacts on academic knowledge production and labour practices at various international ports – it is somewhat detached from the lived experiences of those who are actually involved in, and affected by, logistical processes. For instance, Rossiter depicts the "logistical city" as "a city of peripheries […] occupied by intermodal transport terminals, warehouses, IT infrastructure, container parks, and shipping ports" (Rossiter, 2016: 35). The logistical city is located somewhere beyond the ordinary places of most people's day-to-day life, as something that few people encounter but which "ticks along in the background as we get on with our busy daily lives" (ibid: 36). In other words, Rossiter advances a theory of (global) media infrastructure that needs to be adapted to relate to people's ordinary media practices, even though vital questions of platform(ed) labour are part of the discussions (see especially Kanngieser et al., 2014; Zehle & Rossiter, 2016).

While the works of Peters and Rossiter have influenced the ideas presented in this book – along with other writings on logistical media, infrastructure and cultural techniques (e.g., Case, 2013; Siegert, 2013, 2015; Berlant, 2016) – my take on logistical society is largely shaped by a different set of concerns and thus results in a different picture. In particular, the picture I want to advance is *contemporary* and *socially oriented*. It is about ongoing transformations related to geomedia and aims to represent the everyday lives of people entangled in weaves of mediated logistics. My focus is on the *logistical struggles* that unfold at the intersection of people's values, moralities and behaviours, and the material – economic, technological, infrastructural – forces of geomedia. This should not be reduced to a struggle among certain people who want to liberate themselves from some kind of evil techno-capitalist apparatus. The relations are more complex and, most of the time, quite mundane, as we saw in the examples with e-scooters and parking apps. Logistical struggles play out *within*, rather than against, geomedia. This means that while geomedia supports people in their day-to-day orientation in, and mastery of, space, it also sustains industrial and other interests in organizing and *steering* the very same human activities for the sake of data extraction and economic profit (logistical accumulation).

Even before the rise of the platform economy, Julian Reid (2006) professed the coming of "logistical lives" predicated on continuous human disciplining "under the duress of the command to be efficient, to communicate one's purposes transparently in relation to others, to be positioned where one is required, to use time economically, to be able to move when and where one is told to" (Reid, 2006: 20). Logistical accumulation takes this condition to a new level, as recognized in critical analyses of digitalization and datafication (most often without discussing the concept of logistics). Shoshana Zuboff (2019) argues that the spread of surveillance capitalism as an economic order has led to "an involuntary merger of personal necessity and economic extraction, as the same channels that we rely on for daily logistics, social interaction, work, education, health care, access to products and services, and much more, now double as supply chain operations for surveillance capitalism's surplus flows." Along the same lines, McQuire (2019) discusses the power of Google Maps as an everyday navigational tool. The social normalization of this particular tool via various other platforms that people have on their smartphones turns Google into something of a colonial force – an agent of what Couldry and Mejias (2019a, 2019b) call "data colonialism." Moving through space with Google is also to be steered; a form of consumption and self-surveillance. A similar point is made by Mark Andrejevic (2018) in his work on "drone cartographies," where he highlights that "the drone takes on some of the logistical characteristics of the tower, with the added element of a detached, and thus mobile, verticality" (Andrejevic, 2018: n.p.). Understood as a networked, dynamic interface, drones contribute to the merging of map and database; the production of digital maps as "profiling machines" that not only represent space but "read" their users. This is a rather precise illustration of what logistical struggles might look like in a not-too-distant future:

> The map and territory converge in new digital configurations: the space itself can tell you where you are and how to get where you want to go. It may well know in advance of your query where you want to go – or, taken to the limit, in advance of

your desire: your very ability to form the query in the first place. (Andrejevic, 2018: n.p.)

Prediction is thus turned into *prescription*, which means that new forms and infrastructures of guidance-through-surveillance exploit people's need to orient themselves in the world. The boundaries of human agency, between steering and being steered, become increasingly fuzzy. A similar point is made by Andrejevic and Volcic (2021) in their analysis of facial recognition technology, so-called "smart camera systems." According to the authors, public and shared spaces are now turned into "perceiving spaces," that is, spaces that automatically process information and as such contribute to social sorting and control. The social implications of this development, especially if we consider a future scenario where smart cameras are integrated in most public spaces and where interactive maps and AI have become even more advanced and commonplace, are dubious. As Iveson and Maalsen (2019) argue, the power to steer people's movements and actions (exercised by public as well as commercial disciplinary institutions) may operate on several levels at the same time, including direct surveillance of individuals as well as indirect control whereby people adapt their behaviour in the face of future risks associated with excessive data collation. Ultimately, as Amanda Lagerkvist (2020: 19) puts it in her account of "anticipatory media," as AI becomes an inevitable part of our lives it "not only sits on but seemingly also closes the horizons of futurity."

The critical questions that should be asked here concern to what extent, in what ways and under what circumstances different individuals and groups are able to explore and make use of new technological opportunities for logistical agency and, conversely, to what extent geomedia, via logistical accumulation, constitutes a regime of further segregation and exploitation of daily human life (see, e.g., Leszczynski, 2016; Elwood, 2021). While it is relatively easy to identify the disciplining and sometimes direct force of geomedia in relation to particular sectors of activity, such as the gig economy, where food couriers and other precarious labourers are inevitably and literally steered by their platforms, this does not rule out that there can also be frictions and various forms of "counterlogistical" tactics in such environments (e.g., Chua et al., 2018; Goods et al., 2019; Richardson, 2020a; Andersson, 2021). If we turn to more leisurely activities, such as music listening (Chapter 3) or tourism (Chapter 4), it gets even more difficult to assess whether, how and on which premises people are empowered or exploited under the current regime. As a general rule, it seems, enhanced logistical capacities come at the expense of further digital entanglements and further logistical control. They also come at the expense of labour and environmental extraction taking place elsewhere that logistical platforms tend to hide from the everyday consumer (Hill, 2020). The addressing of such critical issues, I argue, calls for a logistical turn in the study of media and communication geographies. Such a turn would imply that we paid closer attention to the logistical affordances and implications of digital media in general, and everyday platforms in particular. This is not enough, however. If we want to get at the deeper, socially embedded nature of logistical struggles, we also need to develop a humanistic perspective based on insights from social and critical phenomenology.

THE HUMAN CONDITION

Most research on how geomedia shapes the human condition stems from the relatively new field of digital geography, or digital geograph*ies* (noting that geomedia is rarely explicitly applied). Most of the above-mentioned examples of how digital technologies in general, and datafication in particular, alter the meaning of space and what it is to inhabit space, can be associated with this field. While presented as a "turn" within human geography (see Ash et al., 2018), digital geographies transcend disciplinary boundaries and resonate with intellectual trends in media studies, such as software studies and surveillance studies. As told by the edited volume *Digital Geographies* (Ash et al., 2019), the field concerns such main themes as governance, public space, urbanism, infrastructure and mapping techniques. While the themes cover important aspects of human life conditions, the presence of any "real people" in these texts is quite limited. By "real people" I mean human subjects that in various ways, depending on social background and life situation, try to manage, orient themselves, and feel at home in geomediatized life environments; subjects that are affected in different ways and have different, often ambiguous, feelings towards the "digital geographies" they inhabit; subjects that combine different roles in their day-to-day lives and as such have to adjust their attitudes to technology according to practical needs, whether at home or at work, alone or with friends, in the city or in the country, and so forth. In short, there is some work to be done to expose the geomediatized human condition *from within* and at *different sites* of human activity.

The lack of human-oriented perspectives in digital geographies is somehow expected given that much inspiration to the field comes from theoretical strands like post-phenomenology, post-humanism and actor-network theory (ANT). To some degree it is also reasonable. The embedding power and interactive nature of digital technology – especially in times of artificial intelligence and machine learning – is such that it calls for perspectives that from the outset conceive of objects and environments as active rather than as "simple tools that humans use to complete pre-existing aims and goals" (Ash & Simpson, 2016: 63). Also, as the same authors note, the post-phenomenological approach is not about abandoning phenomenological insights, but "about refiguring and expanding phenomenology's analytic and conceptual boundaries" (ibid: 63).

Yet, the eagerness to avoid anthropocentrism in accounts of our new digital life environments has so far resulted in analyses marked by social detachment. Digital geographers, including many media scholars and researchers from the digital humanities, have focused on abstract streams of data and affect rather than lived experience; the logics of algorithms rather than of social difference and habitus; practices within rather than beyond the technological architectures of platforms; dividuals rather than individuals. As such, some of the critical potential of the field is lost, as well as the prospects of understanding social change.

Couldry and Mejias, two media scholars, argue in their book *The Costs of Connection* that it has been "fashionable to forget […] the 'special' moral status of human beings" and to apply language and analogies from computing in accounts of the relations between humans and digital technology. Such approaches, the authors argue, "may divert attention from the human costs of capitalism's new social order" (Couldry & Mejias, 2019b: 158). This "non-human" bias is also recognized by Rossiter (2016) in his account of the digital humanities, as well as by Gillian Rose (2017), who stresses that the agency of humans is often undertheorized in post-humanist research on digitally mediated environments. Similarly, Eden Kinkaid (2021), writing from a feminist and queer perspective, formulates a critical response to the post-phenomenological trend in human geography that goes beyond digital geographies. It revolves around two problems.[15] First, the author argues, post-phenomenology has constructed a view of human subjects that is not commensurable with what it is to be human. Post-phenomenology goes too far in its problematization of human intentionality and in its creation of an ontology that places "non-humans" and humans at the same level. Second, Kinkaid argues, post-phenomenology overlooks social difference, which makes the perspective unfit for social critique. The anthropocentric perspectives of social phenomenology that influenced humanistic geography in the 1970s did, after all, entail a propensity to *understand* the situatedness and contextuality of human life, which paved the way for subsequent developments of critical phenomenology. Here, Kinkaid refers particularly to situated analyses that undertake phenomenological description from the perspective of "minority subjects," such as Sara Ahmed's (2006) work on "how non-white and queer bodies disrupt space and are constantly called into question," based on the premise that these (inter)subjectivities are "necessarily sites of politics" (Kinkaid, 2021: 308; see also Kinkaid, 2020). It is also in research that looks at our connected lives through such critical lenses, dealing for example with feminist, race or queer digital geographies or with the precarious undersides of platform urbanism (see, e.g., Richardson, 2015, 2020a; Chun, 2016; Tudor, 2018; Nash & Gorman-Murray, 2019; Paasonen, 2020; Sundén & Paasonen,

2020; Elwood, 2021), that we find some of the more promising ways forward when it comes to excavating geomedia *as* our human condition.

Following these important remarks, I want to advocate a humanistic (re)turn in media and communication geography. It does not imply a wholesale subscription to anthropocentric ideals that were in some respects overly romantic already at the time they were formulated, especially with regards to such things as "place," "home" and "belonging" (see Cresswell, 2006). Yet, my ambition is to elaborate an approach that reactualizes the critical mission of humanistic research and brings it into dialogue with our contemporary logistical society. As Anne Buttimer (1990: 2) puts it in her essay "Geography, humanism and global concern," "humanism is defined as the liberation cry (*cri-du-coeur*) of humanity, voiced at times and places where the integrity of life or thought was in need of affirmation." While this statement may sound a bit bombastic, it highlights an ethical stance that necessarily follows from any situated engagement with fundamental human concerns. It speaks directly to the question of *relevance* in humanistic research (see also Buttimer, 1999) – the fact that deeper understandings of spaces, communities and ideas that are suppressed or trying to resist dominant norms are crucial to uphold our vision of an emancipatory society. It also resonates with Kinkaid's two points of critique, which in a good way summarizes how I envision a humanistic (re)turn. Let us consider them in turn.

To capture "humanness," which is the first point, we should acknowledge key insights from the humanistic tradition of human geography, especially those grounded in social phenomenological thought. In their introduction to the landmark volume *Humanistic Geography: Prospects and Problems*, Ley and Samuels (1978) identify two characteristics of the humanist position. First, it is *anthropocentric*. As mentioned, this is now a starkly contested position, especially given the increasingly advanced technological systems in which humans and other species are entangled, and the environmental crisis affecting the world, beyond humanity. Yet, anthropocentrism does not have to be a flawed position in itself. It depends on what kind of questions one asks as a researcher, and how one conceives of the general role of humans in the world. In a book concerned with how human subjects experience and relate to the extension of media technology into, and across, their lifeworld, anthropocentrism is close to inevitable. It even serves as a reminder of the cultural agency exercised by the researcher in his or her construction of the world (Ley, 1978). A classical thinker that will play a key role in this book is Hannah Arendt (1958/1998), whose work on *the human condition* (in the book with the same title) provides the scaffolding to how I approach human activities and their relations to our mediatized, capitalist society. Arendt's view is anthropocentric, concerned with whether and how humans can find meaning in their everyday toil and trouble, their labouring activities, and communicate ideas to find common solutions to problems in the world they inhabit. Here, she recognizes not just the forms of exploitation to which human labour has been historically exposed, not least under industrial capitalism, but also the paths to emancipation and social change that the so-called *active life* (*vita activa*) entails. While Arendt's work helps us see the fragility of our human existence and how structural conditions play into the continuous oscillations between growing human capability and fractured agency, it also exposes the social and environmental responsibility that comes with the active life. In Chapter 2, I will elaborate upon and situate these ideas in relation to geomedia and the logistical society.

The second characteristic of humanism is *holism*, meaning that the relations between humans and their environments are seen as dialectical and contextual. Here, Ley and Samuels refer to the classic works of Robert Park and the Chicago school of urban sociology that conducted situated analyses of the reciprocal development of humans and the city (see, e.g., Park & Burgess, 1925/2019). In this spirit, Ley and Samuels (1978: 12) see "reality as a social construction but one that acts back upon its subject, sometimes in ways that may remain unseen and taken for granted." This is to say that humans are inseparable from their environments – a socio-phenomenological view that in (spite of) its anthropocentrism is not as naïve as some critics have insisted upon (see also Kinkaid, 2021). Furthermore, if we think of human/environment relations, or subject/world relations, as reciprocal and largely unpredictable, this raises ethical concerns pertaining to how humans could lead their lives responsibly, and, conversely, how to make environments as liveable as possible. When humanistic geography expanded in the 1970s it was actually much acquainted with a broader movement of humanistic critique of modern society, including existentialism and phenomenology as well as (neo-)Marxist thought, which in turn went back to an ethical tradition of renaissance humanism that "sought to defend the variety and the integrity of human existence" (Ley & Samuels, 1978: 3). In other words, while the mission of humanism is a timeless endeavour, it should resonate in a meaningful way with the social challenges of particular societies and the life conditions of different groups.

This brings us to Kinkaid's (2021) second critical remark, concerning social difference, stratification and power. Whereas the digital, post-phenomenological turn in human geography has still much to prove in this respect, as noted, a humanistic (re)turn must also compensate for the blind-spots characterizing most 20th-century humanistic geography. In a progress report from 1981, David Ley stated the following:

> In retrieving man from virtual oblivion in positivist science, humanists have tended to celebrate the restoration perhaps too much. As a result values, meanings, con-

sciousness, creativity, and reflection may well have been overstated, while context, constraint, and social stratification have been underdeveloped. (Ley, 1981: 252)

Until that point, while humanistic geographies had been empirically concerned with micro level spatial arrangements – *place* in particular – they had also tended to search for general principles that applied to humanity at large. Social structures and cultural differences were overlooked. Ley thus called for a bridge between humanistic geography and "alternative materialist positions," such as those developed by the Birmingham School of cultural studies. In his own work, where he analysed the role of culture and aestheticization in early gentrification processes in Canadian cities (e.g., Ley, 1996, 2003), he showed the prospects of such a bridge. Deploying ethnographic methods, Ley described, for example, how in-migrating artists and cultural entrepreneurs led to the semiotic upgrading of previously under-privileged, working-class neighbourhoods. He thus expanded the humanistic ideal of situated understanding to get at the broader socio-cultural dynamics of urban regeneration.

This type of work, reminiscent of the Chicago school and the cultural materialisms developed by scholars like Pierre Bourdieu (1979/1984, 1980/1990), Raymond Williams (1980) and Beverly Skeggs (1997), is instructive about how studies that basically deal with people's daily lives can further our knowledge about social difference in general and geo-social segregation in particular. We may here recall Bourdieu's (1980/1990) understanding of *habitus* as a mechanism of social reproduction – a socially inherited predisposition guiding individuals on a day-to-day basis to things they are structurally expected to desire. This approach, which Bourdieu developed to overcome the epistemological division between phenomenology and the structural social sciences (or, "social physics"), is crucial to our exploration of geomediatization as a socially structured and structuring process.

Besides the critical issues related to human subjectivity and social difference, there is also another important (and interlaced) problem attached to the digital geographies approach, at least if we follow its post-phenomenological trajectory. This is the problem of *agency*. As I mentioned before, the turn to such perspectives as actor-network theory is understandable in times of interactive media and increasingly responsive environments. The very idea of "objects acting back" upon humans (which, as we saw, was not alien even to humanistic geographers in the 1970s) has become increasingly tangible. In its extended form, however, this approach not only reduces human lives to something less than they actually are, but also tends to splinter composite life environments into "objects" (with agency) related to one another in "networks" – which is, after all, a rather paradoxical outcome of an approach intended to do justice to the complexity of material environments. As Tim Ingold (2011) argues, thinking of the environment in terms of networks where different objects are somehow functionally related to one another is based on a false premise that there are clear divisions between things and substances. In fact, as recognized also by Gibson (1979/2014) in his theory of affordances, they spill over and leak into one another. Ingold goes so far as to argue, in a paper programmatically entitled "Bringing Things to Life," that we should envision an *environment without objects* (EWO):

> I suggest that the problem of agency is born of the attempt to re-animate a world of things already deadened or rendered inert by arresting the flows of substance that give them life. In the EWO, things move and grow because they are alive, not because they have agency. And they are alive precisely because they have not been reduced to the status of objects. (Ingold, 2010: 7)

The world we inhabit, according to Ingold, is a world of becoming that looks little like a network with clear connection-points. It is more like a *"meshwork* of entangled lines of life, growth and movement" (Ingold, 2011: 63, emphasis in original). As humans we are thoroughly *in* this world, part of its becoming, rather than occupying it. Through our everyday dwelling we are part of weaving the textures that make up the world through which our lives can materialize (see also Ingold, 2008).

There is an interesting parallel here between how Ingold describes the becoming of things and environments and Bourdieu's thinking around properties and life trajectories in social space.[16] While putting the accent on different aspects of the human condition – materiality versus sociality – Ingold and Bourdieu share one concern, namely to reveal the entangled nature of things/properties and thus to transcend (or eliminate) the division between those perspectives treating the material environment ultimately as a product of the human mind (phenomenology) and those trying to build models of how objects influence each other ("social physics") or operate together as units of a network (ANT). In Bourdieu (1997/2000), we find intermediary concepts like *habitus* and bodily *hexis* that articulate the fact that social and material conditions *inscribe* themselves into things, as well as into the human body, which become properties of an entangled socio-material environment. This is also, according to Bourdieu's cultural materialist view, how things, practices and people alike – as properties – become meaningful to other human subjects, and enter into mutually constitutive power relations that shape entire lives.

Ingold's view of entangled, and entangling, environments, and how we as humans inhabit the world, is fundamental to how I conceive of a life with media, or *in* media (cf. Deuze, 2011, 2012; Moores, 2012). As with other substances of the environment, the "thingness" of "geomedia technologies" makes them inseparable from other things. They do not have agency but are "brought to life," to paraphrase Ingold, through their interweaving with other things and properties (including humans) and their life trajectories. This is also what Wendy H. K. Chun (2016) suggests when she describes digital media – especially as they are no longer "new" but habitually incorporated into day-to-day life – as lively, leaky, even "promiscuous," and thus difficult to fit into the dominant model of "networks."

But how can we reconcile this environmental view of the human condition with the humanistic, phenomenologically oriented (re)turn suggested above? My point is that these views are in fact complementary (which is not to say that they can be joined without careful consideration). They provide answers to different questions. While I consider Ingold's approach to the material (geomediatized) world of human habitation much more meaningful to the current analysis than, for example, actor-network theory, I also maintain that the human perspective is of great relevance. If our life environment is undergoing rapid change, it is important to understand not just how this new environment is constituted, for instance in terms of digital geographies, but also how different people relate to it; what it means to inhabit it, and how it feels to be "woven into" the social and material textures of geomedia. Here, Ingold remains as silent as the post-phenomenologists (but for a different reason). We need to look elsewhere, to critical and social phenomenology and to the cultural materialisms of Bourdieu and Williams, as well as to Arendt, as mentioned, to find the right analytical tools for addressing such things as human desires, lived experience and social subordination under the regime of geomedia. These perspectives underpin my general diagnosis that everyday dwelling under geomedia is increasingly turned into a form of *logistical labour*, while the opportunities to problematize, resist and counter this regime are at the same time growing from within the regime itself. There are not just infrastructural frictions built into the system, so to speak; there are also humans that feel anxious, irritated, estranged – in short, vulnerable – in the face of escalating surveillance and exploitation, *and* are capable of acting with, upon and against the system in ways that may open up new, more emancipated (autonomous and secure) spaces for human co-existence. It is my wish that the following chapters will demonstrate how such a diagnosis of the human condition is possible, and at the same time stake out some new terrain for the field of media and communication geography.

RESEARCH CONTEXT AND STRUCTURE OF THE BOOK

The ideas presented in this book will unfold through a dialogue between theoretical elaborations and empirical observations. There is always a challenge to make theoretical arguments touch ground, making them at the same time meaningful and valid. Similarly, our academic world is over-saturated with empirical data and details that too often fail to be cohesively integrated into books or other theorizing overviews. While this book certainly has its limitations and blind-spots too, it is my hope that the discussions that follow do justice to the research directions to which I refer. Also, while the breadth of our interdisciplinary research field makes it impossible to find and make sense of every relevant piece of research, I hope that my efforts to grasp the main trends in a cumulative way have resulted in a meaningful condensation. Again, the most important thing is that the interweaving of "high theory" and empirical detail leads to a strong and sustainable end-product. One factor that speaks in favour of this ambition, at least, is that the key ideas that eventually led up to the writing of this book have evolved through a rather extensive process, roughly a decade, and are the fruits of studies and discussions that took place within a series of research projects, networks and other intellectual contexts. I am particularly indebted to continuous conversations within the framework of the Geomedia Research Group at Karlstad University.

There are also two research projects that have a direct empirical bearing on the analyses that follow. One important data source is the EU-funded Interreg project *Music Ecosystems Inner Scandinavia* (MECO) (directed by Dr Karin Fast and Dr Jenny Karlsson, 2018–2021), which among other things analyses how digital media (re-)configure music consumption and experiences. The project entails several sources of data, among which this book primarily makes use of six focus group interviews conducted in Sweden in 2019. The interviews concern people's everyday music listening habits, with a special focus on the handling of new streaming platforms, and how these are related to media and lifestyles at large. The focus groups gathered altogether 48 interviewees. Each interview was conducted in a specific geographical setting (provincial village, regional centre, etc.) and gathered a specific constellation of people in terms of age and gender. While some groups were demographically mixed, others were more homogeneous. The interviews were conducted in municipal, semi-public venues and lasted for approximately two hours each. In collaboration with another project, *Measuring Mediatization* (directed by me, and funded by the Ander Foundation, 2017–2025), MECO also gathered data via a national survey, conducted by Kantar-Sifo in February–March 2019. The survey asked questions about, for instance, perceived media reliance (see Bengtsson et al., 2021; Jansson et al., 2020) and uses of different audio technologies. It covered a representative sample of Swedish citizens in the age span of 18–90 years. The online questionnaire was sent to 12,481 individuals, out of which 3,904 answered, leaving the response rate at 31 percent. I refer to these data sources especially in Chapter 2, where I elaborate how streamability alters the articulation and perception of connective media affordances. A few additional examples from the projects are given in other parts of the book.

The aim of this chapter has been to set out the cornerstones of the argument I want to pursue in the book and point out the direction of the discussions that follow. Chapter 2 is entitled "Dwelling under geomedia," where the word "under" is chosen to signify the status of geomedia as an *environmental regime* (in contrast to technology). This is where I develop the theoretical framework in closer detail. The chapter begins with a discussion of "media life" (Deuze, 2011) and how digital media technologies are woven into the human life environment. I argue that while this deeply mediatized environment calls for media ecological approaches that account for the "elemental" nature of media (Peters, 2015), notably their infrastructural significance, we must also consider the human efforts, and frictions, involved in the appropriation of media. Thus, I elaborate upon Ingold's (2008) "dwelling perspective," which emphasizes the co-constitution of human practices, things and environments, to argue that geomedia is today the environmental regime of dwelling. However, it should not be understood simply as a structure of environmental resources, or affordances, but as an ever-incomplete, obstructive and entangling cultural-material force that conditions people's lives differently. In the final part of the chapter, I introduce Arendt's (1958/1998) view of the "active life" – encompassing labour, work and action – as a way of capturing how dwelling under geomedia oscillates between, and entwines, vulnerability and capability, and exploitation and emancipation.

Chapter 3, "The culture of streamability," discusses how connective affordances are transformed under geomedia and what this means to the human condition. The key concept here is streamability, which basically refers to the industrial logic governing cultural circulation in the digital platform economy. The strive for enhanced streamability means that all kinds of platformed businesses compete to spur, harvest and compute digital data streams that are as rich, combinable and computable as possible in order to improve their offerings to target groups. This logic reaches beyond the so-called connectivity industry, or social media (van Dijck, 2013). It also reaches beyond the culture industry and the expanding sector of streaming media. In the chapter, I outline the logic of streamability and explain how it translates into a cultural shift, as the maximization of streamability brings along the need to monitor, predict and steer people's attitudes and behaviours (the very sources of data streams), which are in turn adjusted to handle streams on a day-to-day basis. This mutual relationship, reminiscent of cybernetics, leads us straight to the core of logistical struggles and the tension between *logistical accumulation* and *logistical labour*. To concretize how such struggles are played out in everyday life and how people's ability to navigate in and organize various streams, that is, their *ordinary logistical expertise*, affect social relations, I conduct an analysis of audio streaming. The analysis moves beyond people's direct interactions with streaming platforms via an interface, to show how the handling of everyday infrastructures and environments in a much wider sense underpins complicit forms of logistical dominance and translates into symbolic violence.

Chapter 4, entitled "Transmedia travel," turns to representational media affordances and discusses how transmedia reinforces *de-differentiation* in the realm of tourism. The analysis revisits the post-tourism thesis (e.g., Feifer, 1985; Lash & Urry, 1994), which held that tourism had become such a commonplace mode of encountering the world that it was impossible to unravel from social life at large. The proponents of post-tourism argued that the distinctions between home and away, the ordinary and the exceptional, the real and the simulated, were dissolving, not least due to the phantasmagoria of popular media. My point is that the open-ended circulation of media representations (broadly conceived) across platforms and devices enhances this condition, not just via extended phantasmagoria but also through logistical labour attached to transmedia circulation. The chapter introduces the notion of *transmedia travel* to highlight the new intersections of tourism and labour. Such intersections are related, first, to "virtual travel," where transmedia contributes to turning *travel planning* into a continuous everyday activity (especially via mobile platforms) and bringing the *tourism activities of others* into the ordinary lifeworld (especially via social media). Second, intersections are related to ongoing corporeal tourism practices, which are increasingly difficult to shield from various transmedia streams emanating from the world of everyday labour. Finally, tourism activities are themselves turned into a form of logistical labour due to the socially and commercially invoked obligation among tourists to circulate certain types of representations while travelling (and not just the occasional postcard). In this connection, I zoom in on the selfie spot as a logistical device and discuss transmedia travel as a site of logistical struggle.

Chapter 5 is entitled "Guidance landscapes," and concerns the alteration of logistical media affordances in the wake of locative media. Based on a brief historical exposé, the chapter introduces spatial pragmatics (e.g., Lussault, 2007, 2009) as a framework for analysing how new affordances, notably what I call *locative guidance*, affect people's capacity for orientation, co-ordination and orchestration. Again, a key point is that whereas human beings (some more than others) are increasingly capable of mastering spatial processes, they are also steered, or guided, in ways that feed the system of logistical accumulation. The analytical focus of the chapter is on *platform urbanism*, which is here taken as a particular kind of *landscape* – a *guidance landscape* – that legitimizes and reproduces logistical accumulation via particular discourses and representations of the digital, hospitable city. The landscape constitutes an intermediary realm – a social formation that normalizes certain (capitalist) power relations in society *and* certain ways of seeing the environment (see, e.g., Cosgrove, 1984; Zukin, 1991; Olwig, 2003, 2005). Based on an analysis of alternative tourism apps and videos promoting urban mobility services,

I assess the role of logistical accumulation as a form of landscaping through which geomedia finds its place in society and culture.

In the final chapter of the book, "Geomedia *as* the human condition," I bring together the key arguments of the book in a condensed assessment of how geomedia (re)shapes the human condition and what it would take to challenge its more oppressive tendencies. The discussion is framed by Arendt's (1958/1998) understanding of *action* as the form of human activity through which open-ended spaces of appearance can emerge – pre-political public realms where human beings disclose themselves to one another and gain mutual recognition. I argue that geomedia, after all, entails unprecedented resources for logistical action and as such entails the tools for challenging or subverting logistical accumulation. Some trends in society already point in this direction, not least the kinds of logistical struggle discussed in the book. I also highlight the significance of disconnection and media withdrawal. While such counterlogistical trends are sometimes bound up with commercial interests, they also actualize a reconfigured sense of place – what I call *post-digital sense of place* – that reclaims the human need for *boundedness* and *spaciousness* as the basis for action. I am thus inclined to draw a picture that is not all bleak. Rather, I see reasons to reinstate the humanistic belief in people's capacity not just for adaptive labour and resistance, but also to bring about change.

NOTES

1   The quoted attributes were used by the major retailers *elgiganten.com*, *cdon.com*, and *netonet.com* in their online advertising in spring 2019. The quoted attributes were used by the major retailers *elgiganten.com*, *cdon.com*, and *netonet.com* in their online advertising in spring 2019.
2   See, e.g., *Göteborg Direkt*, 23 July 2020, https://www.goteborgdirekt.se/nyheter/dykare-hittade-19-elsparkcyklar-i-vattnet. As of July 2020, a total of 220 e-scooters had been harvested from the river and canals of Gothenburg. The water clearing company has signed an agreement with one of the e-scooter networks, Voi, to return the rescued vehicles for recycling.
3   E.g., Swedish Radio (SR) P1, 17 October 2019; full version in "Prylarnas pris," SR P1.
4   See *Dagens Industri Digital*, 9 October 2020, https://digital.di.se/artikel/kopenhamn-rensar-bort-elsparkcyklarna-fran-gatorna.
5   *Thelocal.fr*, 9 December 2019, https://www.thelocal.fr/20191209/extinction-rebellion-activists-sabotage-electric-scooters-in-french-cities.
6   See, e.g., *The Independent*, 22 June 2019, https://www.independent.co.uk/news/paris-scooters-lime-electric-trottinettes-accidents-a8955561.html.
7   "Prylarnas pris," SR P1, 17 October 2019.
8   Wikipedia accessed on 3 May 2021.
9   According to a preliminary overview there are "at least 17 different parking apps" in Sweden (Swedish Radio, 27 November 2019).

10   The explanation from the municipality was that the testing period had been too short and that the problems were to be solved as soon as possible. Retrieved from *Dagens Industri* online, 10 October 2020, https://www.di.se/bil/ny-parkeringsapp-totalsagas-vi-hade-kort-testperiod.

11   The meanings of "digital throwntogetherness" and "digital thrownness" are partly overlapping, but where Leurs (2014) mainly builds on Massey's (2005) geographical theorization, Lagerkvist (2017) anchors her theory in continental philosophy, notably the existentialism of Heidegger. While digital throwntogetherness puts the accent on the "politics of encounters" and how people's life trajectories intersect in new, sometimes unpredictable ways online, "digital thrownness" refers to the basic fact that human beings are today "thrown" into a digital existence, whether we consider its mundane aspects or more liminal experiences.

12   The aim of this book is not to present an overview of the field and how it has been articulated within and across the different disciplines. Useful overviews and (re) considerations of the field are provided by, for example, Falkheimer and Jansson (2006), Adams (2009), Adams et al. (2014), Mains et al. (2015), Lindell (2016), Adams et al. (2017), Fast et al. (2018b).

13   In a previous article (Jansson, 2019) I used the term "communicational affordance" instead of "connective affordance." I have reconsidered this terminology and prefer to conceptualize connective, representational and logistical affordances as the key characteristics defining different media as *means of communication*.

14   In certain other contexts, the term "geomedia" refers to a particular combination of media technologies and infrastructures, especially GPS technology, the Internet and mobile devices (see, e.g., Lapenta, 2011). Such definitions tend to coincide with other technologically oriented labels, such as, "locative media" (as described above) and "spatial media" (Leszczynski, 2015a). The latter term, however, opens up a broader research terrain as it refers to "networked spatial information technologies (both hardware/software objects and information artifacts) as 'spatial media' to advance media as an *epistemology* for engaging these presences as both channels for content and as cultural apparatuses" (Leszczynski, 2015a: 729, emphasis added).

15   Kinkaid's article is above all a critique of Ash and Simpson's (2016) work on post-phenomenology and human geography.

16   There are interesting commonalities between Bourdieu's and Ingold's work, especially if we consider Bourdieu's ethnographic research on the environmental aspects of social practice (1980/1990) and his subsequent analyses of embodiment and movement (Bourdieu, 1997/2000). Ingold discusses Bourdieu's approach to practice and skill in his essay "Culture, perception and cognition" (Ingold, 2000; see also Lizardo, 2011; Moores, 2012).

2. Dwelling under geomedia

It is June 2020 and the COVID-19 pandemic occupies our lives. Different regions in the world are in different stages of the pandemic, but we all have to handle the direct consequences and lingering threat of the virus. Many of us are working from home. As an academic, I am reluctantly conferring with colleagues and students via digital platforms. I spend time in "breakout rooms" and look at the tedious sight of my own pixeled face within a frame. I try to get used to a situation where the family's domestic space, our home space, is redefined. While the dining area has turned into our main video conferencing unit, digital labour can take place anywhere. Anyone who enters the house during office hours must be cautious not to make any noise or open any door without first checking whether this door leads to a regular room (as we knew it) or to a digital elsewhere inhabited by strangers. I have also volunteered to use a special app to help society fight the virus. Every morning I receive a push notice in my smartphone, instructing me to update my health status and disclose some of my whereabouts. At least it does not track everything I do, and it does not gather data automatically. In that sense, it is a very friendly app compared to many others I am using to organize my daily life.

In these times, speaking of "media saturated lives" has turned into something of an understatement. We are in the midst of what seems like a huge digitalization experiment. Some analysts predict that "after COVID-19" many workers will not go back to their offices again – not because they may have lost their jobs, but because they, as well as their employers, have found that much work can be done without a permanent office. Many corporations have retooled their organizations and updated their routines to accommodate the large volumes of staff working from home during the pandemic. Thus, "the heyday of the office is probably over," as Johan Javeus, Chief Strategist at the Nordic financial services group SEB, puts it in an analysis of the situation: "Since working from home has become so popular, employers that for different reasons decide not to offer that opportunity will have a hard time competing for the best workforce."[1] There is also an opportunity for employers to cut costs. If the market for office space continues to cool down, that would come as good news for companies spending large amounts of money on keeping representative working environments at good locations. Still, for many workers, turning the "home office" into a permanent solution – an office that may not even have a designated place for itself – would not be a particularly pleasant transformation. The experience of being fully at ease with one's everyday home environment would come under threat and social interactions that now occur spontaneously at work would require continuous planning. In addition, the pressure on individuals to adapt to new digital systems would intensify – a process whose ambivalent nature the COVID-19 pandemic has already exposed to us.

This chapter is not about COVID-19. But it deals with underlying structures that the pandemic, with its associated lock-downs and digitalized quarantines, has made visible (like any good experiment). Learning how to live with media does not come easy, especially not if transformations are imposed from the outside and one lacks the skills or resources to appropriate new technology. I am thus sceptical of any theory that underplays the *human efforts* involved in digitalization. While we, as humans, have indeed incorporated a steadily growing number of media within our lives, especially during the digital era, there is no rule stating that every new device or software will become a natural life companion, or an extension of our minds and bodies, and eventually "disappear" (cf. Deuze, 2011). On the contrary, we often feel frustrated with the labour it takes to *make things work*, that is, to make technologies fulfil their given purposes as tools, or, alternatively, to make them withdraw from our immediate attention and blend into the life environment. The following anecdote, taken from a focus-group interview with women in a Swedish countryside village, reveals much of the irony in our endeavours to stay afloat in the maelstrom of new digital technology.

> Ingrid: Most things [with digital technology] are difficult. I recently replaced my smartphone and I think it's boring too. I can't stand it, "oh well, I have to get a new app and…" I use Spotify, but there one doesn't have to choose. Perhaps updating it, but anyhow. I was home alone for a couple of days and we have a Chrome Cast that we got to ourselves and then I thought that "now I will sit down and I'll watch a film from my phone to the computer," and the kids had to write an instruction to me before they left.
> [laughter in the group]
> Ingrid: And so, I looked for that instruction and then it was time to sit down in the sofa. And when I had made all the choices among all the choices, then I went to Netflix and "oops, which film should I chose?" – and it took me an hour and then I gave up and went straight to bed.
> [laughter in the group]

What we encounter here is a laconic description of helplessness, disorientation, and finally resignation (or is it victory?). At the same time, and in light of the celebratory discourses surrounding digital life, the episode is quite disturbing. How many of us cannot identify, at least to some extent, with it? How many of us would not like to resist the forces that make us feel inferior, alienated or stressed? Now, with COVID-19, these questions are pushed to their limits.

How big an effort are we willing to make to keep up with digitalization and what happens if for some reason we cannot, or refuse to, adjust to the "new normal"?

My aim in this chapter is to lay the ground for an exploration of the day-to-day labour that we all pursue just to get by in a geomediatized society and how this labour, and our various *feelings about it*, articulate who we are and the forms of power we assert and to which we are subjected. Following Hannah Arendt (1958/1998), I take labour to be the type of ordinary activities we are involved in just to satisfy our basic material and social needs, that is, to stay alive. Labour, in this understanding, is distinguished from *work* and *action*; the former referring to the deliberate making of durable products and the latter signifying more intellectual endeavours through which we may even problematize and try to evolve the human condition. Through an analysis of people's daily toil and trouble with media, I argue, it is possible to problematize the unevenness of geomedia as an environmental regime – and thus what it means to *dwell under geomedia*. The appropriation and continuous handling of new media is a socially, even existentially, charged process that comes easier to some people than to others. Feeling at home *in* media may constitute a sign of status, unattainable to those who are marginalized or victimized by technological developments. But there are also examples of the opposite, when the ability to instrumentalize and *work* or *act with* or *against* media is what counts – what we may think of as privileged forms of technological de-naturalization.

Before we get to the Arendtian framework, however, it is necessary to clarify what is meant by geomedia as an "environmental regime." I will do this in three steps. The chapter opens with a sympathetic critique of certain environmental understandings of media – approaches that expand the horizons of media studies to include all things that are used by humans to orient themselves in the world. I will in this connection consider especially Mark Deuze's (2011) work on *media life* and John Durham Peters' (2015) more historicizing approach to *elemental media*, which also opens up to our concern with logistical media affordances. I will then turn to the question of dwelling, guided by the works of anthropologist Tim Ingold (e.g., 1993, 2011), but also in dialogue with key figures from phenomenology and humanistic geography. I assert that dwelling constitutes a vital link for us to understand the continuous interweaving of human beings and their technologized (geomediatized) life environments. As Peters (2015: 15) writes, "media are our infrastructures of being, the habitats and materials through which we act and are." Media constitute the underpinnings and moorings of our human existence and thus attain ecological as well as ethical import. Geomedia accentuates and makes this condition increasingly complex. Thus, in the third step, I try to concretize the notion of geomedia as an environmental regime via empirical examples that also point to the *frictions* accompanying people's engagements with media, notably before, but also after they become "elemental." While we are indeed born, or "thrown," into a certain media environment that we take for granted, life is full of disruptions and negotiations (cf. Berlant, 2016; Lagerkvist, 2017). It takes continuous efforts, most of which are highly *instrumental*, to achieve and maintain environments for non-reflective dwelling – in spite of the ideally invisible character of media infrastructure that Deuze and Peters, among others, have described. Another media theorist, Shaun Moores, has emphasized the need to study precisely such moments of everyday friction. Developing what he calls a "linealogy of quotidian cultures," largely inspired by Ingold's environmental anthropology, Moores (2020: 17) recommends that we "explore such moments of unfamiliarity and discomfort" with media, and to ask more broadly about "which kinds of people feel uneasy or maybe even queasy in specific social situations." These are critical questions that will help us understand what kind of regime geomedia is, and under what social premises it can exist.

SOME REFLECTIONS ON MEDIA LIFE

Under the regime of modern mass media, we could clearly see the boundaries of media, or so we thought. By the mid 20th century, the signifier "media" had gradually loosened itself from its earlier meanings, which were associated above all with the natural elements and chemical substances capable of mediating other substances. Smoke could pass through the sky, or the air, and copper could mediate electricity, which in turn became the mediator of light. Up until the modern period, media were seen as entangled elements of natural circuits – sometimes even divine or super-natural as in the case of the aether or spiritual media – and thus fundamental to the human habitat (cf. Gibson, 1979/2014). It was the rise of specific technologies for transmitting and storing text (broadly defined) that eventually gave media its now dominant meaning as a tool, and ultimately an institution, for human communication. Media were envisioned as distinct channels with distinct properties and purposes. This understanding was reinforced in academia, where functionalist researchers like Shannon and Weaver (1949) set the tone for mass media research for decades to come with their influential mathematical study on efficiency in radio transmission (see, e.g., Scannell, 2007).

Since then, the scene has changed drastically. In 2011, Mark Deuze published a defining article, entitled "Media life" (also elaborated upon in a book with the same name, see Deuze, 2012), where he argues that "media are not just the types of technology and chunks of content we pick and choose" but constitute invisible, taken for granted structures that "underpin and overarch the experiences and expressions of everyday life" (Deuze, 2011: 137). Hence, Deuze argues, we should think of our lives as *lived in*, rather than *lived with*, media; and such a perspective "should be the benchmark for a 21st century media studies" (ibid: 137). Now, a decade later, our smartphones contain applications for most types of activities and our life environments are increasingly equipped with sensors for "smart living." It has become more and more difficult to discern where one medium ends and another begins; what is a medium and what is a message; what is media and what is environment. This, in turn, makes it difficult even to grasp when and where we are using media and when or where we are not. It does seem like we live in media and media live in us.

One obvious consequence of "media life" is that the modern understanding of media that once guided the social sciences, also beyond (mass) media studies, has come under pressure. As Deuze notes, media have become to us humans like water to fish, a natural element, or "the invisible interlocutor of everyday life" (2011: 139). What he refers to, then, is the structuring role of media, as outlined by Kittler (2009) in his ontology of media as cultural techniques. The type of media we commonly perceive as "media" – the things we "pick and choose" from on a day-to-day basis to get information, guidance, entertainment, and so forth – is just the tip of the iceberg. Underneath, there is a vast substructure, or *infra*structure, of media that quite literally "stand under" other media and the world. This has also been discussed by John Durham Peters (2015) in his work on elemental media. The modus operandi of infrastructure, Peters notes, is *withdrawal*, "something that seems a more general property of media, which sacrifice their own visibility in the act of making something else appear" (Peters, 2015: 34). It is also this insight that leads him to plead for *infrastructuralism* as a necessary intellectual project for gaining a deeper understanding of all the basic things that make our lives with/in media possible.

The observations of Deuze and Peters serve as useful entry-points to our rethinking of communication geographies, especially since media are understood here as *spatial* from the very start rather than reduced to means of representation. It is also helpful to compare their thoughts to clarify how they can, and cannot, inform our notion of geomedia as an environmental regime. Beyond their shared concern with the invisible, structuring role of media, the intellectual compasses of Deuze and Peters point in somewhat different directions. Deuze seems to hold on (at least implicitly) to the modern view of media as communication technology – albeit inspired by the German research tradition on cultural techniques – and proclaims the emancipatory potential of a digital media life. He even states that "we should not dwell too much on existential contemplations and just go with all the affordances media provide us with and be satisfied with the privilege of our times to use such technologies to make art with life" (Deuze, 2011: 145). Media life is thus an outstanding achievement of our digital age. Peters, by contrast, embarks on a grand historical exploration of elemental media and the human condition that takes us back to the older notion of media as environmental, logistical resources including anything from fire sermons, clouds and stars, to Facebook and Google. Peters (2015: 325) depicts Google as the emblematic example of how "media have shifted from mass media to cultural techniques, not only in theory, but in facts." Google is an extension of the library with its sophisticated metamedia of indexes and catalogues, while at the same time representing "the latest step in the methods of classifying and valuing that deny any transcendental truth or central authority for determining it" (Peters, 2015: 323). Only through this deep historicizing, Peters argues, can we come to terms with the nature of our digital existences. While he does not use the word "media life," one might conclude that from the viewpoint of elemental media anything other than a media life would appear strange. Our digital life conditions have prompted us to rediscover the past and see that life was always lived in media, albeit in starkly different ways.

The theoretical lessons of Deuze's and Peters' works are significant. While my ambition in this book is not to portray the *longue durée* of geomedia, Peters' panoramic view helps us see how affordances that may seem new to media are actually remediations of functions and meanings that existed long before but in social and material settings that typically slipped the scrutiny of media scholars. In particular, this regards logistical affordances. Also, Deuze's insistence on giving up the dead-end notion of an autonomous, non-mediated self is crucial to the arguments of this book, even though I am somewhat sceptical about Deuze's optimistic agenda for agency through hyper-connectivity.

There are two remarks I want to make in relation to Deuze's and Peters' perspectives before we move on to the question of dwelling. The first remark concerns the intellectual history of media studies. It is important to acknowledge that the critique of instrumentalist and text-oriented thinking is far from new. While Peters mentions the culturalist approach of James Carey (1989) as well as the aforementioned materialism of the "German School," there were also many other thinkers around the same period who questioned the idea of rational media users and audiences. Most prominently, in the 1980s, scholars in British cultural studies, spearheaded by figures like Roger Silverstone and David Morley, began problematizing the representational bias of media studies and gradually turned their interest towards other kinds of environmental and social functions as well as material dimensions of media, especially within the domestic sphere (see especially Silverstone & Hirsch, 1992). This intellectual trajectory eventually led Morley (2009) to advance a research agenda for a "materialist non-media-centric media studies." At the core of the agenda is the attempt to challenge the boundaries between media and communication studies and transport geography with its focus on *communications* and logistics (see also Morley, 2017).

My second remark concerns the epistemological implications of the media life perspective (if we use the term that Deuze proposes). As always when there is a "rethinking" of established concepts and perspectives there is also a risk that the pendulum shifts too far to the opposite side. I do not agree that the media life perspective, as thought-provoking as it may be, should (or even could) be "the benchmark for 21st century media studies." The reason is that it implicates a simplification of ordinary life. Even though people to an increasing extent are unaware of the mediations they partake in, especially in their capacity of data-generating digital subjects (Goriunova, 2019), and interact with technologies (devices, platforms and channels) without much reflection (see also Chun, 2016), this is certainly not the full picture of how contemporary media shape the human condition. Probably, the expanding experience of living *in* media, with few chances to exit, is also what has made many people look back with nostalgia at earlier periods and seemingly less hurried lives. Alas, the current condition may not be that invisible, or "seamless," after all. For example, since music became streamable and accessible virtually anywhere and anytime without any limitations or costs linked to the particular cultural product, there has also been an analogue trend (albeit not comparable in terms of magnitude). The interest in vinyl records has grown exponentially and given rise to distinctive "post-digital" cultures, accompanied by polaroid cameras, typewriters and "dumb phones," where tactility and analogue aesthetics are centre staged (see, e.g., Cramer, 2015; Sundén, 2015; Thorén et al., 2019). Likewise, analogue books are bought and read about as much as before, even though the market for e-books and streamable audiobooks is growing (Wallin et al., 2019).[2] These types of media practices reinstate some of the boundaries and sense of finiteness, notably in relation to place, that 21st-century digitalization and platformization have swept away (Jansson & Adams, 2021a). The media life perspective is thus too one-sided and makes it difficult to understand why so many people are concerned about their own media habits.

Similarly, if we turn to Peters and his materialist version of the media life perspective, or what he prefers to call infrastructuralism, there is something overly harmonious about his depiction of humans and their lives with, or in, media. Here, it seems, life *in* media is unavoidable and something that *comes to us* as humans because we are destined to expand our horizons and extend our capacities. Media provide our necessary, elementary support systems. But this concern with the infrastructural nature of media tends to hide other things. While Peters acknowledges the historical role of infrastructural media in, for example, warfare and surveillance, for example in his account of the tower (2015: 233–239), his history is largely one of cultural and technological evolution and the gradual human mastery of a world we also inhabit and obey. If we study mediatization processes from within lifeworlds, however, we find many historical examples of how media have been used as tools for supressing and monitoring people, and how media as such have been forced upon people. The Christian bible is a paramount example, serving to preserve the authority of the Church. Under the current capitalist regime, we are bombarded with digital technology that serves to reproduce our consumer culture and raise our inclination to adapt to further updates of our digital systems. Our dependence on media, especially infrastructures, is largely a result of intrusions and can only persist as long as we are willing to develop our skills and carry out the mundane labour needed to keep the systems up and running. Still, unexpected failures and disruptions within our digital systems regularly remind us about the difference between a life *in* media and a life *with* media (see, e.g., Kaun & Schwarzenegger, 2014; Paasonen, 2015; Sundén, 2018). As Lauren Berlant suggests, we should perhaps think of infrastructure as something quite ambiguous; as "that which binds us to the world in movement and keeps the world practically bound to itself" (Berlant, 2016: 394), *and* as a permanent state of brokenness that requires continuous repair, and thus human attention of some sort, in order "for any form of sociality to extend itself" (ibid: 393).

My point here is rather simple. If we are to understand how the human condition changes with the growing supremacy of geomedia, we need to account for the human perspective as much as for the environmental conditions. While Deuze and Peters (who were taken here as guiding examples) are explicitly concerned with the human condition, in my view, they both perform better in understanding media than in understanding humans. As a result, certain aspects of reality are exaggerated (the symbiotic relations between humans and their media) at the expense of others (coercion, disorientation and disruption). In order to reclaim the human perspective, while still recognizing the environmental embeddedness of humans and their media (to avoid the pitfalls of anthropocentrism), I will now turn to the phenomenological notion of dwelling.

RETHINKING THE EARTH DWELLER

Assessing the human condition is to assess questions of dwelling. *Humanus* literally means "earth dweller," indicating that our human activities are always somehow embedded in earthly matters. As Anne Buttimer (1999) argued in an account of humanistic geography at the turn of the millennium, its raison-d'être stems precisely from its insistence that humans are *of* the earth, but at the same time *for* (or, in the worst case, against) the earth, attending to it and acting upon it. The latter implicates certain moral and ethical responsibilities. The project of humanistic geography, according to Buttimer, is a holistic one, aiming to reconcile longstanding humanist insights regarding the nature of humanity with geographical insights regarding "the earth where humans, among many other life forms, make a terrestrial home" (Buttimer, 1999: 105). In other words, humanistic geographers should have an eye for both the fundamental ethics of humanity in relation to the earth, *and* the vulnerability of humans in their habitats as well as in the grander scheme of things.

As such, dwelling appears to be a suitable term for bridging the troubling divide between intentionalist views of humans and their objectifying uses of the environment, and more ecological understandings of humans as just one of many earth-bound species whose boundaries to the surrounding world are permeable. This duality of dwelling can be noted also if we go back to Martin Heidegger's writings on the matter – the original source of most thinking around dwelling and what Tim Ingold has labelled the "dwelling perspective" (see especially Ingold, 1993, 2011: 9–13). Heidegger's most famous account of dwelling comes from his description of a Black Forest farmhouse, an attempt to capture the essence of the ideal house. "Only if we are capable of dwelling," Heidegger (1971: 160) writes, "only then can we build." He then describes how the farmhouse and its place on the "wind-sheltered mountain slope" had been ordered through "the self-sufficiency of the power to let earth and heaven, divinities and mortals enter in *simple oneness* into things" (ibid: 160, original emphasis). The house even contained hallowed places for birth and death, and thus "designed for the different generations under one roof the character of their journey through time" (ibid). While the people implied here obviously built and designed their dwelling-space through the usage of tools, they were also *in-the-world*, intimately linked to a habitat that was born out of earthly conditions as well as a response to these conditions.

In dwelling, according to my reading of Heidegger, the distinction between intentional activities and the more ecological, even biological, side of our existence is blurred. In dwelling, we often do things with a purpose, but most of the time the purpose is vague, difficult to delimit, and intimately bound up with things in the world that "just happen." As David Seamon (2014: 5), a humanistic geographer, puts it in his phenomenological analysis of place making, "human beings are always already inescapably immersed, enmeshed, and entwined in their worlds," meaning that "one cannot assign specific phenomena to either person or world alone." This is not to deny the existence of interpretation and intentionality; it is to obey the fact that we, as human beings, also inhabit the world *before* interpretation and that most of the time there are no clear demarcations as to where or when interpretation begins. Still, this is not a meaningless existence. When Heidegger presents dwelling as a precondition for building, this suggests a viewpoint from which the world is already apprehended but not reduced to objects. "Things speak to us," as Karsten Harries (1983/1993: 53) notes in an essay on dwelling and architecture, and can only be silenced by "the reduction of things to mere objects, a reduction presupposed by science." This is why the intentionality of building (as seen in

Heidegger's account) is so different from that of science. While both activities attain purpose and direction, building is what connects us to earth. It occurs because we are "earth dwellers" and has as its purpose to secure the continuity of dwelling. Science, by contrast (and like certain other types of activities, as we will see), sets us apart from dwelling and thus from the earth.

The main advantage of the dwelling perspective for analysing digital communication geographies, then, is that it provides an account of the human condition without imposing an overly anthropocentric view of the world. On the one hand, it avoids the fallacies that marked some of the early conceptions of humanistic geography, especially in the 1960s and 1970s. For example, in his discussion of the relations between phenomenology and geography, Edward Relph (1970: 196) argued that such a perspective should rest on the basic notion that "man is the ultimate point of reference for all the objects and facts of nature." This meant that "objects of nature are utensils," existing "only through their utility or disutility for man," and that "the world can be understood only in terms of man's attitudes and intentions toward it." It should be kept in mind here, however, that the phenomenological approach was largely advocated as a radical reaction to the longstanding dominance of positivist traditions within human geography. It was crucial for bringing experiential and imaginative aspects of geography into the picture (see, e.g., Lowenthal, 1961).

On the other hand, the dwelling perspective helps us conceive of the interrelations between humans and their surrounding world without imposing strict delimitations between human beings and things. While this was a problem of classical humanistic geography, which viewed nature more or less as a depository of "utensils," it recurs in a somehow paradoxical fashion also in more recent theories that claim the "agency" of objects. As Ingold (2010: 7) argues in his critique of actor network theory, an approach originating from science and technology studies, such thinking can only assert the "agency" of objects after first having reduced the world and its things to objects. The dwelling perspective, according to Ingold (2011: 10), can help shifting the study of material culture "away from the fixation with objects and images, and towards a better appreciation of the material flows and currents of sensory awareness within which both ideas and things reciprocally take shape." Here, Ingold is also inspired by Gibson's (1979/2014) theory of affordances which sees environmental perception as a process that occurs through the whole organism as humans pursue their activities in the material world, rather than through the mind alone. Whereas Ingold criticizes Gibson for not going far enough in rethinking the nature of material surfaces as a communicative interface (e.g., Ingold, 2010, 2011: 21–22), he is generally affirmative to affordance theory as a way of thinking about how people in and through dwelling deploy and evolve their practical knowledge about the environment. As Moores (2012) discusses in his elaboration of the dwelling perspective for media studies, there are also commonalities between Ingold's and Gibson's views and Bourdieu's (1997/2000) understanding of bodily knowledge, or *hexis* (which may pertain to a variety of practices and technologies) as a linkage between "habitat" (normalized material conditions of dwelling) and "habitus" (socially acquired and embodied predispositions). This captures how media affordances are understood in the current work: as part of the taken-for-granted textures of the environment, comprising a felt reality as well as an intersubjectively shared system of meanings upon which humans may purposefully act.

Here, it is important to reflect briefly upon the relation between environment and landscape. In his essay, "The temporality of the landscape", Ingold (1993) argues that while the environment is largely a matter of *function*, and thus resonates with the notion of affordances (as we saw), landscape is about *form*. This does not mean that the landscape should be reduced to a symbolic representation or "signifying system," as some culturalist geographers have insisted on (see, especially, Duncan, 1990). According to Ingold, the landscape is neither "nature," that is, some kind of external reality that humans may observe, nor a cultural, "symbolic ordering of space" (Ingold, 1993: 152). Instead, he argues, "the landscape is the world as it is known to those who dwell therein, who inhabit its places and journey along the paths connecting them" (ibid: 156). As so conceived, the landscape *takes shape* over time through the combination of natural preconditions and events and people's dwelling practices, including things that they build. We could see this in Heidegger's depiction of the Black Forest farmhouse. The farmhouse was located in a way that obeyed the forces of nature as well as the needs of humans, and this location eventually became the defining epicentre of people's dwelling in, and thus co-production of, the landscape.

Ingold's distinction between environment and landscape is important to my subsequent discussions of geomediatization, a process whereby both environment and landscape undergo change (Chapter 5). However, I also see certain problems with Ingold's rejection of culturalist perspectives, in part stemming from his critique of anthropocentrism. While I do concur that we should account for the mutual embeddedness of humans, environment and landscape, we must not forget that the human condition is also defined by *how we communicate about* the world; how we describe it and how certain tropes and imaginations are transferred and translated between and among people across time and space. In these representational practices, which are understated in Ingold's work, lie much of the explanation of how people can actually go on dwelling together with a shared sense of meaning and destiny, even though the world they inhabit undergoes change. While the placing of a house or the design of hollow places, as in Heidegger's example, form part of ongoing environmental processes, such practices are *also* subjected to human conceptions and myths, which are in turn negotiated and adapted over time to suit the dominant conditions of life. As David Lowenthal once put it, our shared world view is *transient*: "it is neither the world our parents knew nor the one our children will know" (Lowenthal, 1961: 245). And the same thing goes for our individual geographical outlooks:

> Whether we stay put or move about, our environment is subject to sudden and often drastic change. In consequence, we must be able to see things not only as they are, but also how they might become. Our private milieus are therefore flexible, plastic and somewhat amorphous. We are physiologically equipped for a wide range of environments, including some of those that we create. But evolution is slow; at any point in time, some of our sensate and conceptual apparatus is bound to be vestigial, better suited to previous than to present milieus. (Lowenthal, 1961: 250)

This is to say that the representational aspects of space – the cultural beliefs and imaginations people attach to space and how these are expressed – are inseparable from the material things among which we, as humans, dwell. While Henri Lefebvre (1974/1991) captures this elegantly in his account of *texture*, the meaningful traces that people (and other species) leave in the environment and which over time turn into more enduring paths and patterns along which others may orient themselves, it is also important not to lose sight of *texts*. The fact that humans communicate about space and develop their capacity to build things and shape environmental conditions to their own needs is essential for understanding why the forms of the human habitat gradually change (which is not the case among other living species) and how these forms may *exclude* as well as *include* other human beings. This is the main point of Denis Cosgrove's (1984) critical approach to the landscape as an ideologically imbued "social formation," which should not be discarded but seen as complementary to Ingold's anthropological approach (as I will discuss in Chapter 5; see also Olwig, 2003; Cosgrove, 2006).

The final thing I want to address before turning to the relations between dwelling, environment and geomedia concerns *emplacement* and *scale*. It may seem odd, in a book about the most recent developments of digital media, to actualize perspectives developed several decades ago that link dwelling to some type of romanticized home-place and to invoke an even older example derived from a philosopher whose ideas ultimately spurred rather dubious ideals of place-bound life forms. Indeed, there are certain things to be sceptical about. Heidegger's thinking around dwelling and building, as well as the arguments of humanistic geographers like Relph, Tuan and Seamon, attain a sedentarist bias that seems to favour lives lived in the local (see Cresswell, 2006: 30–32). This "snug, well-wrapped localism," which led Ingold (2008: 1808) to even question the whole concept of dwelling, is also reflected in Seamon's (2018) recent work, where dwelling is unanimously linked to locality, rest, comfortableness and "at-homeness," and opposed to movement and journeying. The "world of the journey," according to Seamon (2018: 54), "invokes not only travel, sightseeing, and exploration but intellectual, aesthetic, and transpersonal efforts," which move the person "away from his or her secure realm of dwelling" to encounter unfamiliar ideas, places and experiences. While this view of people developing their lifeworlds and sense of place through the interplay between place-bound routines and outward explorations and encounters is empirically grounded and thus captures how people tend to think about their lives (Seamon, 1979), it also rests upon quite rigid dichotomies between self/environment, inside/outside, ordinary/extraordinary, dwelling/journey, host/guest, and the like. Seamon quotes psychologist Bernd Jager who, in an article from 1975, argues that "the journey cut off from the sphere of dwelling becomes aimless wandering, it deteriorates into mere distraction or even chaos" (Jager, 1975: 249; quoted in Seamon, 2018: 54).

Such binary thinking is problematic. As Tim Cresswell (2006) points out, it tends to dismiss life forms that do not conform to the ideals of a stable hearth and a particular place of dwelling as morally suspicious or inferior to what is seen as the general rule. It also overlooks the fact that dwelling may reside in and evolve through movement, whether we speak of corporeal journeys or the forms of virtual wanderings that contemporary media enable – or combinations thereof (see Hjorth & Pink, 2014). The etymological roots of the verb "to dwell" take us back to Middle English meanings like "procrastinate" and "delay," as well as to "linger," "remain" and "sojourn," all of which were common in the 14th century and suggest that dwelling was then understood as a form of pause or slowing down of movement, rather than its very opposite.[3] If we, with Ingold (2011: 10), believe that dwelling is about "the way inhabitants, singly and together, produce their own lives" and thus refers to something that "carries on," we should better think of dwelling as a form of ordinary wayfaring along paths: "Along such paths", Ingold continues (ibid: 12), "lives are lived, skills are developed, observations made and understandings grown." There is both movement and stillness, hurrying and delay. If we return to Heidegger, we should rethink the role of emplacement and also account for the fact that dwelling *entails* and *relates to* movement, whether related to activities in the nearest vicinities (as in the production of rural landscapes) or on a larger scale, which is increasingly the case today.

If we think about the consequences of the COVID-19 pandemic, and consider how the radius of physical activity has shrunk for many of us, not just through the cancellation of long-distance travelling but also, and more significantly, through restrictions pertaining to our mundane movements along well-threaded paths, it is obvious that dwelling cannot be linked solely to the stability and continuity of place. As testified by our enforced experiences of a life in quarantine, affecting some individuals and groups more heavily than others, the freedom to dwell necessarily relies on the freedom to move. While we might be able to connect with acquaintances around the globe, not even the most advanced digital innovations can compensate for the sense of continuity and meaning we derive from such things as going to work, jogging in the park, visiting friends, or going on a Sunday picnic. With Moores (2012: 44–45), I thus argue that we should not give up on the dwelling perspective, but rather try to develop it to fit our mediatized and globalized life conditions. As Larissa Hjorth and Sarah Pink (2014) suggest, based on Ingold's ideas, our mobile media devices, and especially the combination of location-based services and visually oriented apps like Instagram, have turned many of us into "digital wayfarers." As we move and dwell, we are involved in social and visual media practices that both produce and weave us into the surrounding environment (both "offline" and "online"). Likewise, as Magnus Andersson (2021) shows in his analysis of food couriers, mobile platforms can produce an intimate sense of dwelling by taking us *elsewhere*, moving our minds and emotions, as we pause, linger or *wait* somewhere along, or in-between, the paths of mobile life and/or labour conditions. For the food courier waiting for the next order, Andersson argues, the smartphone attains cherished affordances to create a "space of comfort to temporarily inhabit, built on sociality and mental distance to work" (Andersson, 2021: 201), yet being the device that relentlessly steers and paces the individual's movements.

GEOMEDIA AS AN ENVIRONMENTAL REGIME

I began this chapter with a discussion of the ambivalent but important distinction between living *with* and living *in* media. I then suggested the notion of dwelling as a useful frame for grasping how people carry on their lives both with and in environments, which they are thus part of producing. Here, I especially followed Tim Ingold's approach to dwelling, which allows us to rethink dwelling not as an emplaced condition but as bundles of activities pursued *in movement*, along paths. However, the lifeworld that Ingold depicts is altogether "ecological" and as such rather different from the technologized landscapes that surround us in the modern world as well as the non-ecological activities we tend to pursue on a regular basis. In contrast to Ingold, then, I believe that a dwelling perspective must also account for people's *communicative practices* to adequately understand the relations between humans and the environment. Communicative practices necessarily entail moments of objectification – when people talk *about* something – to govern building and other purposeful activities, or just to make sense of the world. In line with Paul C. Adams' (2005) view of the human self as both *grounded* and *extensible*, I suggest that dwelling is a condition where humans continuously alternate between pre-reflective bodily practices and more intentional, not least communicative, acts in relation to other humans as well as things-as-objects.

Dwelling, I argue, is the site *par excellence* where we can study how "the routinized movements of the body and the networking of the self are inextricably intertwined" (Adams, 2005: 7). A similar view, pertaining to our mediatized society, is captured in notions like "digital wayfaring" (Hjorth & Pink, 2014) and "ambient communication" (Andersson, 2021).

As such, I want to claim a dwelling perspective that maintains a fair degree of anthropocentrism in order to take a critical stance on the things people do and to better understand their reasons. In this section, I will carve out a view of what it means to dwell *in* and *with* geomedia environments, which in the next section is elaborated through Arendt's (1958/1998) account of the so-called *active life*. Arendt's categorization of *labour*, *work* and *action* helps us probe the ways in which humans interact with their surrounding environment and with others. Let us first recall the triadic view of geomedia and see how it fits with the dwelling perspective presented above.

As stated in Chapter 1, I understand media technologies to actualize three interrelated affordance registers: *connective*, *representational* and *logistical* affordances. I say "actualize," since affordances are not to be understood as essential qualities of technology. Rather, they emerge, or are discovered, through practice and social interaction. Historically, every new media technology has been biased in favour of any of the affordance registers while at the same time maintaining some significance across all three registers. If we think of the telephone, for example, while it attains a connective bias as well as certain logistical affordances (which can be said about most media inasmuch as they have an effect on how people arrange activities in time and space) it does not in itself represent anything beyond the messages formulated by the human interlocutors. Such a quality could be added with the help of an answering machine. The regime of geomedia stands for a condition marked by increasingly *blurred boundaries* between the affordance registers (spurred by growing media convergence) and an overall *logistical bias* (due to the prominence of streamability, transmedia and locative media).

Given this characterization, I suggest that we think of geomedia as an *environmental regime*. Media technologies and their affordances, if we follow Ingold, belong to the socio-material environment rather than to the landscape (even though geomedia has important implications for the landscape too, as we will see in Chapter 5). Through dwelling, we acquire the necessary practical knowledge not only to get by and feel at home in a world of abundant media resources but also to make use of these resources in ways that support particular needs and desires. Affordances, as held by Gibson (1979/2014), constitute the socially negotiated interfaces through which we engage with the environment in general, and in our case the media environment. What is new about geomedia, then, is that our life environment to a lesser degree contains easily identifiable technologies with clearly demarcated affordances. Dwelling *under* geomedia (as a regime) is to dwell *in* and *with* a volatile environment where media to a greater extent are entangled, even fused, with other materials as well as with our own bodies. If there ever were any clear surfaces between things, these become increasingly permeable and transient. As such, and to evoke Peters' (2015) argument, the regime of geomedia brings out and accentuates the elemental nature of all media.

This is not to say that we should drop the idea of affordances. The three affordance registers are still there. It is just that they have become more difficult to pinpoint and bind to particular devices. Like media, affordances are now scattered in the environment *and* enmeshed within convergent technologies such as the smartphone. While this accentuates the demand on people to be more adaptive, to steadily learn how to orient themselves comfortably in the environment, which largely evolves beyond individual control, it *also* opens up for greater instrumentality and increasingly sophisticated connective, representational and logistical tasks. As a consequence, geomedia brings about greater diversity as to how the environment is experienced and produced by different individuals at different times. Let us consider an example from one of the Swedish focus group interviews to illustrate this point. In the following extract, taken from an interview with men and women living in a smaller town, we are brought into a quite "ordinary," middle-class and mediatized, home environment.

> Eva: If we're eating out on the terrace we have loudspeakers, which I don't quite understand. Sometimes the sound comes from everywhere, the music follows you, sometimes there is different music in the different speakers. But it's Spotify. And in the evening before going to bed, it's not like we play games or any such things, but more Facebook, Instagram or email. Whatever blips by in the moment. Nothing structured, but it's structured that I do it but not what I do. During the weekends these Sonos speakers are on from morning to evening, mixed Spotify lists, no active listening, they are just there.
> Interviewer: Are you choosing the music?
> Eva: Sometimes, but I find it really non-interesting but my partner is more like "change this, change that" and I just want to listen through. It doesn't matter. I also think vinyl is great, to just have the same…
> [...]
> Interviewer: Do you feel that you master all the technologies you need for listening?
> Eva: No, God, no. [...] It's just trial and error every time. If I come home and he has come home with a new loudspeaker again, then I can understand I should download an app and then go in and enter something on the very loudspeaker and select if I want to listen there or what I want to listen to. I try to learn that way, but I don't know what I'm doing and then I get angry.
> [laughter in the group]
> Eva: And then I tell him that "now you have to put something on, 'cause this doesn't work." [...] I feel more and more like my mother who is 75. She sometimes calls me and say "now the telephone has done an upgrading again, now I can't do this."

Then I tell her we're lucky we have similar phones. She once came up with the idea that she wanted to buy an iPhone, but I said "never, then I can't help you with it!"

Eva is a 52-year-old woman, working in the healthcare sector. Basically, everything she describes can be understood as aspects of dwelling, but I want to direct our attention to three things. First, obviously, the quote depicts an everyday domestic environment where media constitute an embedded *resource for* as well as an *outcome of* dwelling. Materials, techniques and texts blend almost seamlessly into one another within the environment that the inhabitants have accomplished through dwelling. The way dwelling unfolds here is akin to what Ingold describes as a *meshwork* (as opposed to network); a woven texture, or a "zone of entanglement," where different lines of becoming intersect (Ingold, 2008: 1807).

Second, the quote casts light on the open-ended distinction between living *with* and living *in* media. This is expressed, especially, when Eva describes her evening media routines as a matter of seizing whatever "blips by in the moment," as "nothing structured, but it's structured that I do it but not what I do." This shows how, in dwelling, we can be in the media, so to speak, while at the same time keeping a certain readiness to turn our focus on *something in particular*. This shift resonates with the phenomenological (Husserlian) description of everyday life as a realm of ordinary, ongoing practice, where the so-called *natural attitude* is occasionally interrupted by events and conditions that deserve particular attention and sometimes problematize pregiven frames of reference (e.g., Schutz, 1932/1967: 36–38). As Berger and Luckmann (1966: 50) argue, while the reality of everyday life is a realm where taken-for-grantedness prevails, it is also "filled with objectivations; it is only possible because of them."

Third, the description of the streamable sound system highlights that a structure that was built by one person, here the interviewee's partner, may be much less meaningful and comprehensible to someone else. In this case, it means that Eva dwells on a daily basis with and in an environment whose handling and maintenance depend on someone else's expertise. To her, the environment's affordances remain diffuse. Her dwelling is torn between a sense of moving through a soundscape that is "just there" to situations where the same environment appears as something that she does not quite understand or must attend to (objectify) even though she is really not interested in it. The regime of geomedia thus materializes as a force of life reassuring texturation *and* coercive entanglement.

This last point actualizes aspects of dwelling that, as far as I can tell, slip the attention of Ingold's ecological view of dwelling. It highlights that what the environment looks like and feels like, which affordances it presents to us, depends on how we are related to it and who we are, which is in turn shaped by a range of social factors. In some cases, this means that the mastery of our shared environments becomes a matter of *expertise*. While Eva is dependent on her partner to manage the digital sound system, she is also trying to help her mother, whose digital skills are even more limited. Buying similar phones is a social tactic to avoid being left alone with one's technical troubles. Here, we are also confronted with the question of who controls, or even owns, the environment. Even though we are woven into it, and thus part of producing it, the built structures we move through in the course of dwelling are not gifts of nature. They are most often constructed with a particular purpose and in the interest of certain industrial actors, or what we may think of as *landlords* (see Chapter 5). Increasingly, the purpose is logistical in nature; to govern, or steer, our "digital wayfaring" (Hjorth & Pink, 2014) in ways that generate measurable data streams (see Chapter 3). Here, geomedia has opened up even more sophisticated opportunities for designing immersive (or, intrusive) environments that enable new forms of surveillance and *exploitation* based on our dwelling-as-labour. The example of the digital sound system gives us just a first glimpse of how such power relations materialize and possibly turn into a logistical battleground.

In the following explorations, I will extend the dwelling perspective to recognize these two forms of environmental, or elemental, power. I will turn first to Arendt's triadic categorization of human activity forms to discuss the question of exploitation. Then, in Chapter 3, I will also implement Bourdieu's theorization of symbolic capital in relation to the question of expertise.

ANALYSING GEOMEDIA WITH HANNAH ARENDT

In "The temporality of the landscape," Ingold (1993) discusses the landscape as an evolving spatial form. It evolves through the successive activities, or tasks, carried out by humans as part of dwelling. As such, dwelling can be seen as a meaningful series of activities, or what Ingold calls a *taskscape*, that produces some kind of outcome, which over time materializes into a landscape. Tasks are defined by Ingold (1993: 158) as "any practical operation, carried out by a skilled agent in an environment, as part of his or her normal business of life," or, in other words, "the constitutive acts of dwelling." By introducing the notion of taskscape, Ingold establishes a way of understanding how dwelling transforms the environment and its relationally defined affordances into a landscape with a certain appearance and feel, something that can be imagined and depicted, beloved or disliked. But what is the nature of these human tasks? How are different tasks related to the production of landscapes, and constitutive of the human condition at large?

As mentioned, Ingold's theorization remains rather silent when it comes to questions of power and dominance. It is difficult, based on his ecological view, to see why different human beings, or what we commonly speak of as "social groups," should have weaker or stronger abilities to influence how the landscapes they inhabit evolve, or to stake out, alone or together, the paths of their taskscapes. To get at these issues, I argue, we need to acknowledge that tasks are different. Some are more reflexive than others. Some are steadily ongoing, while others occur more sporadically. Some are inherently dependent on other tasks while others are more singular in nature. Some are controlled and dictated by other people or enforced by the social environment, while others are more emancipatory and open-ended. In dwelling, such activities co-exist and intermingle. But we should also be aware that there are activities that transcend dwelling; tasks that move us, as human beings, beyond our comfort zone, into the unknown, or radically change our habitat.

Such discrepancies are well captured in Hannah Arendt's (1958/1998) typology of human activities, which distinguishes three basic forms: *labour*, *work* and *action*. While labour refers to activities that are conducted merely to meet our basic biological and reproductive needs, and do not generate any enduring outcome other than life as such, work is the *fabrication* of things that persist over time and thus have an extended import for the human condition. The outcome of work are things, or creations, that are meaningfully linked to the efforts we have put into the fabrication process – whether we work alone or together, whether the things produced are intended for others or for personal use. Action, in turn, refers to the human capacity to appear and communicate beyond mere bodily existence; a capacity through which we, as Arendt (1958/1998: 176) puts it, "with word and deed [...] insert ourselves into the human world." Together, labour, work and action make up the active, or practical, human life, the *vita activa*, which Arendt distinguishes from the *vita contemplativa* of theoretical and religious reflection. While the *vita activa* has been seen as inferior to the *vita contemplativa* ever since the ancient Greeks, and increasingly exploited and suppressed in modern times – through totalitarianism as well as liberal consumer capitalism – it is also through such practices that human beings may assert themselves and, especially through action, initiate new things that may change the human condition.

Arendt's perspective, I argue, can help us establish a conceptual framework as well as a critique of what it means to dwell with, or in, geomedia – a regime that interferes in all three spheres of the active life. While her view is profoundly anthropocentric and might seem incompatible with the ecological thinking of theorists like Ingold and Peters, I would argue the contrary. Arendt's ambition to bring out the human aspects of the human condition, her insistence on thinking human beings as unique and different from other species, even aiming to hierarchize human activities, takes us back to the humanistic ideal of recognizing the responsibility *and* vulnerability of humans in the world (Buttimer, 1999). As Bronislaw Szerszynski (2003: 204) argues in

Table 2.1   Typology of the relations between activity types and media affordance registers

	Connective affordances (Chapter 3)	Representational affordances (Chapter 4)	Logistical affordances (Chapter 5)
Labour	*Connective labour*	*Representational labour*	*Logistical labour*
Work	*Connective work*	*Representational work*	*Logistical work*
Action	*Connective action*	*Representational action*	*Logistical action*

an account of how Arendt's thought may spur critical research on human relations with/in the natural environment: "Her attention is always focused on the way that human beings inhabit the artificial and natural environment around them, an inhabitation that has been disrupted in the modern age, resulting in alienation from both a common, artefactual human world and our embedding in nature." Likewise, while it is impossible in this book to do justice to the depth of Arendt's work, her basic outlook and critical arguments on how different types of human activity are enmeshed and exploited in capitalist society pertain to our exploration of dwelling in geomediatized life environments.

If we combine Arendt's triadic understanding with the three affordance areas introduced earlier, we arrive at a nine-folded instrument (Table 2.1). This, I argue, can help us think through how different media affordances enable, respond to and are defined by different human activities, and assess how the regime of geomedia plays into these relations. The proposed model opens up for extensive historical analyses as well as in-depth accounts of contemporary media life. In the following, I will reflect briefly on each of Arendt's activity forms. The discussions are further elaborated in Chapters 3–5, where I assess how the active life, and ultimately the human condition, is affected by alterations pertaining to each of the affordance registers.

Let us begin with labour. One of its distinctive marks, as Arendt (1958/1998: 87) writes, is "that it leaves nothing behind, that the result of its effort is almost as quickly consumed as the effort is spent." Labour refers to the toil and trouble of just making ends meet and keeping the bodily organism alive. To the extent labour results in any concrete outcomes, such as harvests or in modern society economic incomes, these are meant to be consumed as part of the human life cycle. The productivity of labour lies not in any concrete product, Arendt (1958/1998: 88) notes, but in the human power, "whose strength is not exhausted when it has produced the means of its own subsistence and survival but is capable of producing a 'surplus'." Here, Arendt largely builds on Karl Marx, who defined labour as "man's metabolism with nature" (quoted in Arendt, ibid: 98). While this metabolism can be understood ecologically, underscoring how humans are inserted into open-ended environmental circuits where fertility and generational succession are the ultimate gifts, it also gives us the key to how labour may be exploited.

This exploitation of labour is exactly what expanded under capitalist society and why the hierarchy of labour, work and action, according to Arendt (writing in the mid 20th century) was reversed – turning labour into the most vital human resource. However, this shift actually began with the triumph of instrumental work. Along with the Enlightenment and new forms of systematic experimentation, the fabricating human being, *homo faber*, was elevated as the "measure of all man" and productivity and creativity became the highest ideal. This development entailed a growing focus on nature as a world of objects to be controlled and shaped according to human purposes. Nature thus became a Process, something to be transformed into something else through work, which replaced the concept of Being as the centre of gravitation in human life (Arendt, 1958/1998: 296–297). Gradually, however, the growing importance of fabrication processes, which "disappear into the product" (ibid: 297), also shifted the focus away from utility and the things to be made onto the processes themselves. The rise of consumer society implied that work's instrumentalizing outlook of the world was replaced by labouring as "the highest position in the hierarchical order of the vita activa" (ibid: 306). As Marx (1867/1990) noted in his theory of capitalistic labour and commodity fetishism, the world in which humans oriented themselves started to lack those objects that could be identified as the outcomes of work and was instead furnished with objects from which humans were more or less alienated. As Arendt writes:

> This radical loss of values within the restricted frame of reference of *homo faber* himself occurs almost automatically as soon as he defines himself not as the maker of objects and the builder of the human artifice who incidentally invents tools, but considers himself primarily a toolmaker and "particularly [a maker] of tools to make tools" who only incidentally also produce things. (Arendt, 1958/1998: 309)

How does this distinction between labour and work play out in relation to media? While historically this has not been a common way of thinking about media practices, the rise of digital media and interactive technologies has turned the distinction between labour and work into a major area of debate. In Arendtian terms, speaking of "media labour" refers to the mundane use of media just to "keep life going" or "make a living," that is, activities that do not generate any enduring end-product or use value but rather play into the circuits of consumption. It is even hard to think about such activities before the rise of capitalist societies. While certain media, especially those with a logistical bias, like time-keeping and navigation devices or the making of lists, were already integral to manual labour in the agricultural society, they mainly had a supportive function. The ordinary, labouring use of media became a more prominent part of human dwelling along with industrialization. It also acquired a stronger representational bias, as discussed in critical theory, starting with the Frankfurt School's critique of the culture industry and the perpetual consumption of standardized mass culture (see, e.g., Adorno, 1991), and continuing with various takes on the "audience commodity," referring to how people's everyday labour of consuming commercial media was measured, commoditized, and sold to advertisers (Smythe, 1981). The shift from an industrial to a semiotic version of capitalism in the second half of the 20th century accentuated this representational bias (see Chapter 1), turning symbolic labour into an increasingly common, even mandatory, element of everyday life (Featherstone, 1991). Yet, as we explore in this book, the media-reliant economy of signs, space and attention (Lash & Urry, 1994) is also what paved the way for logistical accumulation and the rise of a new regime of digitally mediated logistical labour.

If we look at "media work," we find a similar accent on representational affordances, which is deeply rooted in the human propensity to build. It is the capacity of media to represent impressions or visions of the world that has made them indispensable to all kinds of construction work, as well as to artistic work. Instances of media work can also be traced to everyday activities that deliberately produced some sort of representational media, for example, through weaving, sculpting, and other types of craft. With new technologies, such ordinary ways of working productively *with* and *through* media have multiplied and typically remediated older forms of activity (Bolter & Grusin, 1996), as seen for instance in recent transformations of photographic practices. Family photography, which was once a cherished way of representing the life of a group and connecting their threads of experience to future generations via photo albums and other domestic archives (Rose, 2010), is today "platformed" (van Dijck, 2013), embedded into a wide range of digital media practices, including sophisticated forms of editing and ongoing sharing processes (see, e.g., Pauwels, 2008; van Dijck, 2008; Rose, 2014; Holloway & Green, 2017).

This is also where the boundaries between media work and media labour (as well as between different affordance registers) get increasingly contested (which is by no means to infer that they were always clear-cut in the past). It suffices here to acknowledge how the field of media studies today is largely defined by the tension between theories of "participatory culture," "user generated content," "produsage," and other types of creative "media work" (see, e.g., Jenkins, 2006; Bruns, 2008; Deuze, 2013), on the one hand, and more critical approaches to "digital labour," "free labour," "play labour" and "interactive surveillance" (see, e.g., Terranova, 2000; Andrejevic, 2007, 2012; Scholz, 2012; Fuchs, 2014; McRobbie, 2016; Gandini, 2021), on the other. Clearly, while the mounting access to digital, computerized media systems has energized (some) people's ability to create things of enduring value, whether we speak of artistic products, self-expressive projects or tools that can be implemented in relation to other types of productive work, such processes are difficult to disentangle from labour.

It is not my purpose in this book to intervene in these political-economic debates, which essentially revolve around the status of different kinds of value creation under digital capitalism (e.g., economic vs. symbolic) (for a useful overview, see Maxwell, 2016). My focus here is on human dwelling and its changing cultural-material conditions. From such a perspective, we can identify two principal instances of media-related everyday labour (i.e., not necessarily related to income-generating content production, or produsage). First, there is the type of labour that is directly linked to datafication, the fact that every platform in a commercially orchestrated media environment is dependent on the continual "engagement" of users to generate digital data streams, regardless of whether or not this "engagement" is part of any purposeful work process. Without such labour, what we might actually think of as relatively estranged "click labour," digital circulation (and thus economic value extraction) would come to an end (see, e.g., Andrejevic, 2012). Second, there is the labour of keeping platforms and their support systems "alive," that is, to continually upgrade and acquire the necessary skills to master new hardware and software. It ranges from platform-specific acts of "digi-housekeeping" (Whiting & Symon, 2020), including routine tasks like "clearing, sorting, preparing, provisioning and troubleshooting" (ibid: 1079), to the wider adaptation and maintenance of material environments *beyond the platform* (as technology) in relation to digital circulation, whether to coordinate domestic media practices (see, e.g., Kennedy et al., 2020) or to facilitate the new services of platform urbanism (see, e.g., Richardson, 2020a, 2020b; Pollio, 2021). While "click labour" tends to be relatively invisible, withdrawing into the background of other elements of media dwelling, the extended labour of digital maintenance and repair can be more troublesome and sometimes, and in certain groups, linked to experiences of disruption and failure. We will study this closer in Chapter 3.

Turning to Arendt's (1958/1998) third category, action, we encounter the type of activities that may have a more direct political or transformative import. Action refers to activities in which the individual *discloses* herself to the world through certain modes of expression and *appearance.* This ability to express and put things into words carries the human capacity to initiate change. While Arendt sees this as the "highest" of the three activity types of the active life, it is by no means marginal or taken as some kind of luxury preserved just to those that have already secured their livelihood through labour and work. On the contrary, Arendt sees action as the activity type "from which no human being can refrain and still be human" (Arendt, 1958/1998: 176). While people may live their entire lives neither labouring (exploiting the labour of others) nor working (parasitizing on what others have produced), a life without action and speech "is literally dead to the world; it has ceased to be a human life" (ibid). As such, this is where we find the deeply rooted *humanistic trait of communication* and may start tracing the significance of media technologies as a means of rethinking, re-valuing and, ultimately, reinventing the world – processes whereby our analysis is gradually *taken out of the confines of dwelling*.

"Media action" is above all a feature of public life, as described by Arendt (1958/1998: 50–58), and what Jürgen Habermas (1962/1989) subsequently called the public sphere. Arendt's notion of action, which entails but is not limited to speech, has much in common with Habermas' (1981/1987) theory of communicative action, whose rationality concerns the willingness among humans to understand one another, that is, a willingness both to *envision* change and to *accept* change under circumstances when such change is convincingly communicated by others. However, as Arendt posits, action is not only dialogical and based on speech acts (in public or in private). Action also unfolds through other types of expressivity, such as, narration, imagery and personal performance, together constituting a *space of appearance* (see also Silverstone, 2007: 38–43). This is basically how communicative action is understood in this book. The role of media in the creation of such spaces of appearance is vital and has become more diversified due to digitalization, as shown for example in studies of social movements and identity politics (see, e.g., Gerbaudo, 2012, 2016; Costanza-Chock, 2014; Papacharissi, 2016; Sundén & Paasonen, 2020). It is also disputed, however, especially since the Internet, according to some thinkers, is seen as "a private, exclusive and fragmenting medium," rather than a platform for plurality and inclusive narration (Silverstone, 2007: 52). Under geomedia, as I will discuss in Chapter 6, media action pertains not only to the construction of a public sphere as a space of communicative connection among citizens (Calhoun, 2013: 70–72), but increasingly also to the problematization and reshaping of the concrete (infra) structures and textures that underpin such (not always desired) communication (see Rodriguez-Amat & Brantner, 2016; Leszczynski, 2020a; Brantner et al., 2021; Hartmann, 2021).

The triadic categorization of media affordances gives us a tool for thinking such activities anew. In relation to classical models of public communication, we may thus schematically distinguish *connective action*, which Bennett and Segerberg (2012: 739) define as a logic "based on personalized content sharing across media networks," from *representational action*, associated with activities that elaborate and expose persuasive representations to foster new ideas and opinions, as seen for instance in political art and culture jamming (see, e.g., Harold, 2004; Carducci, 2006). Of course, it can be difficult to uphold this type of categorical distinction in relation to concrete activities. If we study the online mobilization of public affect via the circulation of subverted, or "pranked," images, for example, we will find that connective and representational affordances are synergistically enacted. Still, the triadic model can help us paint the bigger picture and also include *logistical action* in the analysis.

The latter phenomenon has so far attracted little attention in the literature (especially under this label). We may here think of actions where synchronized flow management is turned into a statement, as well as actions that interfere in the dominant flows of people, goods, information and data. An idiosyncratic example can be gathered from San Francisco, where housing activists in May 2018, as a manifestation against the tech-industries' "techsploitation" of the city, piled up rentable e-scooters to block the way of the Google buses ferrying tech-workers to Silicon Valley.[4] In February 2020, Berlin artist Simon Weckert borrowed 99 smartphones from friends and packed them in a little red wagon that he slowly pulled down the streets, causing false indications of traffic jams on navigation apps like Google Maps, Apple Maps and Waze.[5] The action was part of Weckert's performance project *Google Maps Hacks*, which demonstrates how the city as well as people's lives are shaped by digital platform services.[6] Similarly, Briziarelli (2019) discusses how Deliveroo riders in Milan subverted the logistical, even bio-political, affordances of the platform (and related apps) to co-ordinate street manifestations and town-square occupations to fight precarious labour conditions. Similar forms of logistical action – which should be understood as *counterlogistical* in nature (Chua et al., 2018) – have occurred in places like Hong Kong and Toronto, causing interruptions within the digital ecologies of "smart cities" (Mann et al., 2020). Further examples may include street performances (à la Situationism), house squatting, orchestrated pausing events like Earth Hour, and disruptive media projects. As to the latter, recent studies have looked into various types of "algorithmic resistance," such as art projects challenging algorithms via subversive forms of "repair" that turn the algorithmic tool (e.g., Google) against itself (Velkova & Kaun, 2021) and piracy that intrudes into the logistical ordering of content streams (e.g., the hijacking of Spotify playlists) (Eriksson, 2020). Such activities illustrate, on the one hand, the manifold implications of media that are normally understood as logistically biased (maps, clocks, signposts and so forth) and, on the other hand, how activities that are logistical in nature may bring about analogous affordances in media even though these media are not normally thought of as "logistical."

We are also reminded, again, that affordances cannot be entirely fixed or reduced to a technological asset prefigured by capitalist institutions, or, alternatively, actualized through the intentional acts of "users," "activists" or others. As Agnieszka Leszczynski (2020a) shows (without explicitly using the term "affordances") in her discussion of various "glitches" in the (infra)structures of platform urbanism, affordances are relationally constructed resources. They are actualized through concrete encounters and (non-)usages of different platforms and technologies in relation to one another – and, we should add, through people's *communication about* these things and their use(fulness). Leszczynski discusses the 2017 #deleteUber social media campaign, which urged people to delete the Uber app as an act of resistance against particular events pertaining to the taxi services in New York, and ultimately against "techno-capitalism" at large. While this was indeed a tactical, logistically oriented intervention in, and against, platform urbanism, deliberately enacting the connective and representational affordances of social media, it had been formulated in relation to *mis*information – circulating on Twitter – about the real events. The connective affordances of Twitter had thus spurred a wave of logistical action that was in fact based on false premises. Leszczynski's point is that this type of inherent infrastructural glitch sometimes leads to unexpected outcomes due to the "diffractive encounters of urban denizens, platforms, and spaces" (Leszczynski, 2020a: 199).

Let us sum up. As stated in the beginning of this discussion, I argue that we should think about dwelling, and the unfolding of what Ingold calls the taskscape, as something that *cuts across* labour, work and action. In dwelling, there are elements of all three types of activity, to a greater or lesser extent, even though certain theorists, like Ingold, prefer to see dwelling as a realm of activity that does not entail instrumentalization, or, like Seamon, associate dwelling with the stability of the (taken-for-granted) home-place. At the same time, we must not lose sight of the *ordinariness* of dwelling; it refers to the wayfaring, the habitual everyday movements along paths, through which human beings gain a sense of continuity in their lives. As such, while Arendt's theory of the active life may take us well beyond dwelling (especially via work and action), the analyses of this book start out from *within* the lifeworld, gravitating around those things that people tend to think of as "ordinary," and then move outwards to problematize also the limits of dwelling and the frictions, disturbances, surprises, and extraordinary sensations to which a life under geomedia gives rise.

If we return to the example of Eva and the streaming sound system, from which she feels somewhat estranged, we can already discern how such limits evolve. They do not appear suddenly through the imposition of technological shifts, but more often through conventional habits, everyday repetitions and gradual changes in technology and/or social relations (see, e.g., Chun, 2016). They are not random, but conditioned by structural factors like class, gender and age/generation. If we concretize and "sociologize" dwelling, as I will do in the following chapters, we will discover that different social groups are differently attuned towards labour, work and action and that such attunements include media habits. Only then can we start assessing the differential significance of geomedia across social space, as a source of recognition and assertion as well as a force of entrapment and alienation.

NOTES

1. Quote derived from *Dagens Industri* online, Monday, 10 May 2021 (my translation from Swedish), https://www.di.se/live/chefsstrategens-varning-omfattande-kontorsdod-kanns-oundviklig.
2. This statement refers to the current situation in Sweden.
3. Information retrieved in August 2021 from the Online Etymology Dictionary, www.etymonline.com.
4. Retrieved in July 2020 from *USA Today*, https://eu.usatoday.com/story/tech/2018/05/31/protesters-block-google-buses-scooters-fight-techsploitation/661076002.
5. Retrieved in August 2021 from *The Washington Post*, https://www.washingtonpost.com/technology/2020/02/04/google-maps-simon-weckert.
6. See Weckert's home page at http://www.simonweckert.com/googlemapshacks.html.

3. The culture of streamability

In September 2020, IKEA presented their website and playlist format *Rhythm of Life*. At the website, Spotify users can specify their favourite music and how it is related to their everyday habits and then receive personalized playlists every day adjusted to their daily rhythm. This service is one of IKEA's efforts to deliver more than just furniture. As Per Stolt, marketing director of IKEA, puts it in an interview with a Swedish newspaper, they want to deliver a fully digitalized life environment: "In our vision 'to create a better everyday life for the many people' there is so much more than our products. Together with Spotify, we are now able to help people create flow in their everyday lives, in their homes as well as beyond."[1] IKEA has previously developed connected lightbulbs whose colour and brightness change with the day, as well as smart loudspeakers in collaboration with audio-tech firm Sonos. These innovations in digital home-making are all gathered under IKEA's evolving business area "Home Smart."[2]

Rhythm of Life is supposed to generate a win-win situation for Spotify and IKEA. While Spotify benefit from larger volumes of music streaming, with new lists delivered every day for "Morning," "Lunch," "Kitchen" and "Bedtime," IKEA can steer attention to their series of smart products and overall vision. As a selection device, however, *Rhythm of Life* probably fits just a small segment of the market, and may not work particularly well even for that segment. I tried it myself and found that the concept envisions domestic listening as a strictly individual activity. *Rhythm of Life* is predicated on a particular type of music listener; someone who uses Spotify practically around the clock and wants to associate different types of music with particular time-spaces of the day. Presumably, this listener is also wearing headphones at home or lives in a single household where the choice of audio-streams does not have to be negotiated. When asked about which of my favourite tunes on Spotify matched each of the aforementioned "time-spaces," I found myself quite bewildered in spite of my longstanding interest in music. I rarely listen to music in the morning or at lunchtime, but mostly *when exercising* or *on Friday evenings* or *during the weekend* (none of which was listed as an option). Accordingly, the customized playlists that I began receiving after filling out the online questionnaire turned out to be interchangeable. It was difficult to discern any rhythm to my life.

More surprisingly, given the general sophistication of Spotify's algorithms, my playlists contained several songs and artists I did not like. The algorithms behind the playlists seemed obscure, based on odd criteria. For example, as one of the songs I had been asked to evaluate when setting up the account happened to be German, my first "Morning" list included numerous German tracks that had nothing in common except for being performed in German language. And this "German bias" persisted as more playlists were delivered. The playlists did not contribute to flow but to moments of interruption and estrangement. When played in the sound system at home, the playlists even evoked questions from bemused family members.

Rhythm of Life summarizes key aspects of what I call *the culture of streamability*. Simply put, this culture refers to the naturalization of streaming media as an integral part of our everyday life environments and activities. It is fuelled by dominant commercial discourses that envision streaming media to "seamlessly" blend into our lives, pacing our activities and transposing our minds into a world of perpetual flow. At the same time, and just as important, the culture of streamability entails friction, frustration and alienation. As well as applications and algorithms, entire technological infrastructures may break down or interfere in our lives. People's efforts to realize the vision of a seamless media ecology in their private homes tend to divide social groups based on their ambitions and levels of technological and cultural expertise. Counter to the myth of seamlessness, I argue, we should first of all think of streaming media as *seaming media* (see Nansen et al., 2009: 187). Dwelling under such conditions is largely a matter of *making things work*, that is, a form of *labour* that rarely reaches completion.

In this chapter, my intention is to extend the discussions from Chapter 2 and present a more empirically grounded view of what it is to dwell under geomedia. *Streamability* is basically understood as an industrial logic that extends connective media affordances. It is the propensity to govern activities, objects and relations in ways that do not merely establish as many profitable digital connections as possible, but also generate and respond to data streams as efficiently as possible. At the same time, this logic extends beyond the technological architecture of platforms. Our human existences are increasingly mediated through data streams, automatically geared according to where we are, what we do, and with whom. This means that we should understand platforms as infinite, extensible matters (Richardson, 2020b), and that that streamability gradually translates into a *mindset* and a *cultural condition*. The omnipresence of streams – of various kinds – reshapes our expectations on how the world should respond to our needs and desires, and how our relations to others might unfold through mediation.

A similar relationship between industrial logics and cultural change is outlined by van Dijck (2013) in her book *The Culture of Connectivity*. It explores how connectivity platforms like Facebook and Twitter have become normalized mediators of our social lives and as such have altered the meaning of things like "sharing," "liking," "community" and "participation." In the culture of connectivity, such expressions of social life no longer refer just to interpersonal connections, van Dijck argues, but make up the raw material for commercial datafication processes. The ultimate purpose of our interactions on connective media is to consume things. While this can be seen as a classical example of exploitation, it also represents a broader cultural shift: "The ecosystem of connective media does not *reflect* social norms; interconnected platforms *engineer* sociality using real-life processes of normative behaviour (peer pressure) as a model for and an object of manipulation (popularity ranking)" (van Dijck, 2013: 174, original emphasis). This is to say that the logic of connective media lures people into engaging with platforms in ways that generate as much valuable data as possible – in order to tailor content streams (including user-generated material and advertising) that respond to the computationally extracted preferences of the users (see also van Dijck & Poell, 2013). Today, due to the dominant position of tech-giants like Facebook, Amazon and Google, this harvesting of data reaches far beyond the interactions occurring via the interfaces of these platforms. As people continuously (re)produce their "comfort zone of platformed sociality" (van Dijck, 2013: 173), the culture of connectivity legitimizes a new type of data colonialism "through which life gets newly appropriated by capitalism" (Couldry & Mejias, 2019b: 39).

Van Dijck does not discuss streams even though the logic she identifies depends on the steady provision of computable streams of digital user data. Since she conducted her analyses of connective media, streams have gone from being foremost a technological "back-end" phenomenon (chunks of digital data) to a naturalized part of our connected lives. As a "front-end" phenomenon, referring to how people encounter, consume and imagine media content, *streaming* now feeds into the dominant mythology of immediacy, seamlessness and unlimited access that accompanies digitalization (see, e.g., Mosco, 2005; Fast, 2018). While streaming services like audio and video on demand began to gain traction in the digital market during the 2000s with the emergence of platforms like Netflix (starting their streaming services in 2007) and Spotify (founded in 2008) as well as various "Play" services linked to traditional media corporations, it was during the following decade that streaming became the norm. Now, as Morris and Powers (2015: 107) put it, "streaming is not just a technical form of transmission, but a key metaphor for the flow of information in the digital age." Streaming represents a qualitative *change in connectivity* that alters the appearance of connective media platforms, with recent examples like TikTok (founded in 2016), as much as it affects the film and broadcasting sector. As Burroughs describes in an article about Netflix, the normalization of streaming has affected both viewing practices and the "lore" of the culture industry. As Netflix went from providing just another type of film distribution (video on demand instead of DVD rental) to championing a new "matrix era" of television they could also start producing programming without any pressures from advertisers (Burroughs, 2019: 8). Audiences became "cord cutters" who left cable networks in favour of "the perceived wireless minimalism of a streaming culture" (ibid: 13).

We should thus conceive of the culture of streamability as an extension of the culture of connectivity. As I will show in this chapter, the "stream" is an increasingly multifaceted cultural phenomenon that constitutes a tangible part of the material world, that is, actual streams of data and information that weave into and reshape our life environment, as well as an ideological trope through which society is mediated and constructed. Likewise, streamability defines geomedia as an environmental regime in a dual way. It constitutes new ways of connecting and interacting with the surrounding world *and* new ways of envisioning the environment. It constitutes a mindset *and* an entangling force through which people's lives and life environments are intertwined with the platform economy.

In the following sections, I will portray the culture of streamability based on an overview of previous research combined with first-hand data gathered in 2019.[3] In line with the general argument of this book, the discussion will eventually depict the culture of streamability as a *logistical battlefield*. Streamability is by definition a matter of controlling and organizing flows, whether we look at the front-end or back-end of media circulation, whether we speak of the automated editing of playlists or the orchestration of domestic environments. However, as I will show, the utopia of logistics, that is, managing the movement and emplacement of people, things and other matters as efficiently as possible (see, e.g., Hepworth, 2014; Rossiter, 2016; Chua et al., 2018; Hesse, 2020), which increasingly also defines the business of cultural circulation, collides with various social and material restraints. The fact that streaming platforms in comparison to older distribution technologies both *enable* and *necessitate* improved forms of flow management (for example, as we saw, adapting digital infrastructures and streams to daily rhythms, places and movements) accentuates the contrast between lived realities and imposed conventions. Likewise, from a social perspective, streamability opens up new avenues for creative work and action among those who are apt and have the appropriate resources for it, what I will call *ordinary logistical expertise*, while at the same time requiring continuous *logistical labour*. As stated in Chapter 2, logistical labour refers to mundane efforts that are basically a matter of *keeping streams alive*, and especially about maintaining the infrastructures that enable circulation and thus economic value extraction. I will start the discussion with a clarification of what streamability means, and then gradually move beyond the technological aspects of platforms and into the social realm.

CONCEPTUALIZING STREAMABILITY

Streamability is a concept that has not previously been elaborated upon for the social sciences. It has appeared, however, in two accounts of media management. First, Simone Murray used the word in an article about "media convergence's third wave" (Murray, 2003: 8) to describe how content streaming has become an increasingly important part of corporate strategies within the culture industries. Murray expands the notion of content streaming to include not just "the delivery of video or audio content via the Internet," but also "the migration of content from one platform to another" (ibid: 9). In her view, content streaming is not an entirely new thing, but it gains traction with digitization that makes content increasingly fluid, mutable and transferable. Streamability, then, is the propensity of a particular type of content, a text or a format, to migrate between platforms and thus multiply revenues. It implies that content, on the one hand, is easy for the producer to circulate and steer in new directions, yet, on the other hand, is vulnerable to "parodic appropriation and unauthorized copying" (ibid: 16). Murray concludes that the management of content streams per se is what increasingly drives the media industries: "Such a proposal provocatively insists that content no longer represents merely the filler for industry pipes but, rather, that it now constitutes the media industries' structural logic" (ibid). In other words, this signifies a logistical reorientation within the industry.

Second, in a more recent article on how to create value from the real-time flow of big data, Federico Pigni and colleagues scrutinize the characteristics of digital data streams to "offer guidelines to enable firms to profit from their untapped potential" (Pigni et al., 2016: 5). The authors provide a lucid view of how and why digital data streams matter to businesses. Digital data streams are generated through anything from credit card purchases and digital check-ins to social media posts and mobile self-tracking. They provide segmented information about who did something, when, where and for what purpose. If a corporation is able to conjoin several data streams (for example a credit card transaction *and* an Instagram post from the same evening) – so-called *splicing* – it can harvest more information about potential customers and even reconstruct entire episodes related to particular events (ibid: 9). The authors introduce the term *event streamability* to signify "the degree to which a class of events is amenable to encoding and channelling through a digital data stream" (ibid: 12). The degree of streamability is determined by the stream's *detectability* (whether any valuable elements of an event, such as time and place, can be tracked), *measurability* (whether information can be quantified and ordered) and *interpretability* (whether the data generated can be used to underpin results and ultimately decisions). To reach high degrees of streamability and thus gain more corporate knowledge about human activities there must be more devices, more platforms and more sensors producing data streams that can be harvested, spliced and computed. In effect, streamability in this context reflects the capability of corporations to *steer people* in the directions most profitable to their business and to make people comply with extended forms of interactive data collation. Again, streamability appears to be a matter of improved logistics. It serves logistical accumulation.

These accounts, due to their differences *and* similarities, give us the starting point for detailing a socially oriented understanding of streamability. Under geomediatized conditions, I argue, streamability has evolved into a *mindset* that holds a normative function not just among business strategists but among people as they go about their ordinary lives. Ultimately, life itself is seen as streamable. To clarify this development, and how the two accounts play into each other, we need to sort out two things about streamability. First, we should try to specify the ambivalent meaning of "stream." Second, we should carve out the logistical implications of streamability.

Content vs. Data

What does "stream" refer to in the context of geomedia? The aforementioned articles highlight two alternatives that are equally relevant to us: *streams of content* and *streams of data*. Both streams are constituted by some kind of *information in motion* (Berry, 2011a), but while the former type refers to carefully organized information media users encounter or seek out for the sake of entertainment, news, social updates, and so forth, the latter refers to encrypted information about digitally detected activities (whether human or non-human) that does not make any sense until the data streams have been aggregated into larger datasets and decoded through computation. While media circulation entails other streams as well (such as, electricity, electromagnetic waves and digital signals that carry what we here call content), content and data are the principal types we should engage with when developing our notion of streamability. *It is the growing prominence of these streams and the expanding efforts among various actors to manage their composition, direction and intensity that afford streamability its social and cultural impetus.*

The distinction between content and data is closely linked to what some theorists refer to as *front-end* streams and *back-end* streams (e.g., Weltevrede et al., 2014). Front-end streams are the streams we consume and interact with as users; information-as-content exposed to the public eye. Back-end streams refer to the data that are sorted and processed by corporate actors and, if we think of a media business, inform how new front-end streams are organized. While the gathering of user information to chart and sell the "audience commodity" and strategically fine-tune programming (and other cultural products) has a long history in the cultural industries, the digital automation and normalization of these circuits distinguish our era of streaming connective media from the era of broadcasting, cable networks and analogue telecommunications (e.g., McGuigan & Manzerolle, 2014). In the front end, streams come in two principal shapes. One is the transmission of audio and video content over the Internet, which replaces various types of stored or downloaded information like CDs and DVDs, as well as live broadcasting over analogue systems. The other type of front-end streams consists of so-called *real-time streams* that deliver updated packages of information at regular intervals via, for example, social networking platforms and online news channels. As mentioned by Weltevrede et al., the roots of real-time streams go back to the "push" technologies developed for the Internet in the 1990s to help users find and sort information in the expanding online environment. The "push" function meant that users were automatically delivered updates according to certain criteria and at a requested frequency. These technologies were gradually incorporated into web-browsers, for example the RSS news feed developed by Netscape, and subsequently used in many blogs, which contributed to transforming the "all-purpose static destination web" into a more "personalized and dynamic web" (Weltevrede et al., 2014: 132; see also Berry, 2011a). Today, this is how most of us encounter the web on a day-to-day basis, whether we follow a newspaper, the stock market, online auctions, people's updates on social media, or just open the default Google search page on our smartphone. We encounter what we perceive as a stream of customized messages, not least advertising, sorted according to algorithms and our personal settings.

This is where distinctions start blurring. As our platforms converge and older formats are remediated and recontextualized, the division between streaming audio/visual content and real-time streams looks more and more like a continuum with various in-between hybrid forms. Most real-time streams today include streamable video and audio content, for example a filmed news item or a video that a friend has recorded. Platforms like YouTube and TikTok are good examples of this type of combinatory streams. At the same time, streaming services like Spotify include increasingly refined forms of real-time feeds through which they promote new releases and customized playlists to their subscribers. On the interface, this is expressed by a welcoming greeting like "Good morning," which is then followed by a stream of updates such as "New episodes" of popular podcasts, "New releases for you," and music "Recommended for the day." The *Rhythm of Life* concept that I discussed at the beginning of this chapter is another example of such a real-time stream of streamed content aiming to *pull the user* into a particular rhythm of continuous, customized music delivery. Even the "radio" function on Spotify can be understood as a real-time feed as it pushes particular tracks to the users according to algorithmic processing of user data.

Similarly, the principal distinction between content and data, front-end and back-end, deserves some problematization. As Weltevrede et al. (2014) show in their analysis of different real-time streams pertaining to social media and search engines, while real-time is not to be understood as "real" in the sense of "live" or "authentic" but a curated matter, the pace and composition of different streams depend on the interplay between platform logics and the agency of users. As the authors argue, "creating a clear differentiation between real-time experience and processing becomes problematic as real-time media content is produced, processed and engaged with in real-time while at the same time the activities of users in the front-end inform the processes of processing in the back-end" (ibid: 130). These interrelations underscore how the everyday user is *woven into* the production of streams, both deliberately (through the active adjustment of settings, etc.) and less deliberately (as with automated activity tracking via cookies, sensors, etc.). Ultimately, there are no absolute boundaries between platform and user.

In certain contexts, it should be noted, people also actively engage with automated data circulation to express, negotiate, or optimize their lives and identities (whether understood as an online persona or a "real" human subject). The digital Quantified Self movement, emerging in the early 2000s, was a forerunner in this regard as its members started to deploy (and sometimes make) various self-tracking tools to generate and collate activity streams (Berry, 2012). Since then, *lifestreaming* has become a process that most people opt into more or less by default in the sense that the platforms they access automatically keep track of their (trans)actions. A core idea of the lifestream – discussed in the 1990s under the label "chronicle stream" (ibid: 389) – is that it should not just produce a time-ordered tail of enacted documents from the past, but also have a *predictive* function; containing "documents you *will* need: reminders, calendar items, to-do lists" (Freeman, 2000, quoted in Berry, 2012: 389, original emphasis). This is exactly how streams have developed. Today, most of us are used to receiving recommendations of things we should buy or people we should know. As we engage in various forms of self-surveillance and keep track of our activities, we turn our lives into a "quasi-back-end" where we harvest the data of our activities and achievements and govern our further digital interactions (including, for instance, tagged events and the circulation of online content that goes into other people's real-time streams). Of course, this is not the same thing as aggregating masses of data from larger populations, as corporations do, but it illustrates how we increasingly act as digital subjects (Goriunova, 2019) and conceive of our lives through, and in terms of, streams.

Thus, if it is true, as software theorist David M. Berry (2017: 79) holds, that "the computer sees the world as streams," perhaps this is also an outlook adopted by humans. If so, it would mean that our interaction with digital, algorithmic media systems fostered a subjectivity aligned with the premises of the system itself. Berry's ideas around the societal and phenomenological significance of activity streams lead us in that direction:

> One of the most interesting aspects to these systems is that humans in many cases become the vectors that enable data transfer, whilst also becoming the vectors that carry the data that fuel the computational economy. Our movements between systems, carrying USB sticks and logging into email accounts and distant networks creates the channels through which the data flow, or an infection is spread. (Berry, 2012: 391)

I will return shortly to the phenomenological implications of Berry's observation, that is, streamability as a mindset. Before that, it is vital to assess what it tells us about digital logistics.

Enclosure vs. Friction in Digital Circulation

Let us consider Berry's formulation, that humans are "vectors that enable data transfer." What he basically suggests is that the logic of streamability – which applies especially to social media platforms but also to the digital platform economy at large – positions human beings as *logistical devices*. As users we function as a cybernetic switch, generating streams of data in exchange for streams of content. Hence – and this is where the opening accounts of Murray (2003) and Pigni et al. (2016) intersect – to improve streamability, corporations need to control this logistical device. They need to learn as much as possible about human behaviours and how to steer those behaviours via various front-end streams (or by other means) to generate as big and valuable harvests of data as possible. These learning processes, in turn, depend on exactly the same circuits of data, which is to say that we are dealing with an enclosed system of circulation – or, at least, this is how the system is envisioned from a cybernetic, logistical point of view (Neilson, 2012: 330–331; Rossiter, 2016). The ideal situation for logistical accumulation would entail users that were fully and continuously captivated by digital information streams, moving about in an environment full of sensors, as implicitly suggested by Pigni et al. (2016). Such a situation would imply the seamless integration of the digital into our bodies and lived spaces (see, e.g., Iveson & Maalsen, 2019).

Does this mean that we are about to be absorbed into a system of data logistics, or what Andrejevic (2007) calls a "digital enclosure," where the paramount meaning of our day-to-day activities is to fuel the algorithms that predict and steer our behaviours? While this may be the logistical utopia of the platform economy, I argue for a dialectical perspective. The algorithmic exploitation of our lives does not happen without friction – which contradicts the dream of seamlessness. Rather, our lives, and especially the textures through which we dwell, are turned into a site of logistical struggle (Neilson, 2012). The techniques developed by the industry to manage streams are bound to be more or less imperfect and sometimes contested by external actors, including those intended to be captivated, or steered.

To illustrate this, let us return to the example of streamable music. Under conditions of cultural over-abundance – when there is more music available in the clouds than anyone could possibly manage – the playlist provides a technique for invoking a sense of order and control. The desire for order is not just reflected among listeners putting together their own playlists. As we saw, the logic of streamability saturates the whole platform economy and is predicated on order and predictability. Hence, as Maria Eriksson argues in a study of Spotify, algorithmically edited playlists (as well as virtual "radio stations" based on given preferences) can be seen as another type of logistical device. More specifically, Eriksson sees Spotify playlists as a *container technology*; a way of packaging and delivering content as efficiently as possible in order to grab the attention of users and monitor their streaming practices. Editorial playlists are at once "a feature that would assist users in need of musical guidance" and "an efficient means to put more power in the hands of Spotify" (Eriksson, 2020: 419), ultimately some sort of "crystal ball" (ibid: 420). This implies that playlists are sites where different interests collide.

The ability of corporations like Spotify to monitor their users' activities and absorb them into predictable patterns is circumscribed in several ways. Playlists are not just vulnerable to the bugs of machine learning. Eriksson also discusses other types of "noise," or what we could think of as *friction*, that hamper the logistical perfection of playlists. For example, playlists, like other container technologies, may be hijacked by pirates and smugglers, in this case "fake artists," who fill containers with misplaced cargo. Further, we should not overlook the fact that there is human agency involved in the back-end processes of data extraction and calculation. The industrial ambition to fully automate music editing is combatted by, for instance, representatives of the music industry who want to get their artists and tunes into circulation (Maasø & Hagen, 2020; Prey, 2020). Such pressures may influence what the interfaces of distribution platforms like Spotify look like, including suggested playlists, and thus indirectly play into the data streams and metrics that, in turn, underpin the editing of new playlists. What goes into a playlist is thus not just a matter of machine learning (in itself an ever-incomplete procedure). As Chua and colleagues (2018) suggest, it would be wrong to accept the commonplace (and industrially endorsed) view of logistics as a neutral science or skillset. Rather, we should approach logistics as an inherently *turbulent* business, haunted by internal and external threats and shaped by social, cultural and economic power-relations (see also Neilson, 2012).

Probably, the place where this condition is most obviously exposed is in the context of everyday media use and cultural circulation. This is where most logistical battles are played out and where common frustrations with logistical irrationality and over-surveillance are articulated.

STUCK IN THE STREAM – CAPTIVATION AND ENTANGLEMENT

As we have seen so far, streamability is a logic by which the governance of streams, and thus value extraction, is made more efficient and predictable. Streamability sustains *multiplied streams* (to maximize data harvests through splicing), *enclosed systems of circulation* (to minimize external noise) and *automated customization of content packages* (to maximize user captivation). These are mutually reinforcing features that describe how streamability contributes to the entangling of our lives with the digital platform economy. Ultimately, we become the "vectors of data transfer" that Berry (2012) speaks about. Now, let us consider what this means from a more phenomenological perspective and how streamability is both predicated on and challenged by human (inter)actions. The entry point here is the question of *captivation*.

"Real-time is the new crack," Geert Lovink (2012: 11) once stated, well before anyone could fully discern the social consequences of datafication and streaming media. What Lovink referred to was the captivating, even addictive force of real-time flows; their propensity to grab and suspend the user in a state of open-ended anticipation of the next sensation. Similarly, Berry (2011b: n.p.) characterizes streaming media as "messianic," that is, imposing a condition of "waiting without horizon of expectation." Engaging with real-time streams, which may entail a variety of differently paced streams, as we saw, is a future oriented activity that does not have any clearly defined goal. When using, for example, Twitter or Facebook, or even Spotify Radio, we may try to foresee what comes next or anticipate in what direction our attention might be steered, but since we can never exactly predict the updates there will still remain a sense of open-endedness. This explains how we are captivated: The information pieces of a stream are automatically customized to our previous activities while at the same time constituting ever-new sequences, including feedback-loops generated in response to things we have circulated ourselves (comments, likes, ratings, etc.). Thus, to be algorithmically guided, or steered, through the ecology of streams includes an affective dimension "as the user is expected to desire the real-time stream, both to be in it, to follow it, and to participate in it, and where the user opts out, the technical devices are being developed to manage this too through curation, filtering and notification systems" (Berry, 2011b: n.p.). The user gets into what Berry (2017) calls a *Twitter trance*.

Berry (2011b: n.p.) extrapolates this new condition of open-ended waiting as a "structure of existence." In a similar fashion, we can envision the social extension of streamability, that is, the culture of streamability, as an emergent "structure of feeling," following Raymond Williams' (1961) view of how cultural sensibilities are shaped during different periods and in relation to social, political and technological change. To the extent we are addicted to media streams (which evidently pertains more to some individuals than to others), this is basically an addiction to our own desire for "waiting in curiosity," anticipating the sensations of digital interaction. These affective mechanisms are detailed in Karppi's (2018) work on Facebook and its "affective bonds," which holds that the maintenance of connectivity platforms is largely a matter of circulating affective impulses. These impulses (manifested and measured via "likes," comments, and so forth), which are different from deeper emotions and more elaborated reasonings, provide the human energy that drives lucrative data. In a similar vein, Paasonen (2020: 10–14) shows how our ordinary, continuous interactions with devices, platforms and services, and our associated sensations before, during and after these interactions, give rise to new "affective formations" (drawing on Williams' notion of structure of feeling). Such formations, she argues, "entail both amalgamations of feeling and the persistent creation of meaning" (ibid: 14).

We may illustrate this development with the shift from analogue to digitally curated music listening. While listening to a vinyl record takes a certain degree of dedication, not least in terms of time and space, the "perfect music stream" should combine just the right amount of familiarity with just the right amount of novelty or surprise to keep its listener interested. As known from commercial radio broadcasting, this is a tricky balance to strike for those engineering the stream (or, rather, the algorithms behind it), and a balance that is regarded differently among different listeners. For example, while some people might long for the same song to reappear, others might hope to encounter something entirely new. Algorithmic curation, however, implies that if there is no positive affect among listeners they can jump to the next song, which leads to a calibration of the stream. As streamability improves and people get more captivated by streams – especially real-time streams – there is a gradual shift in our everyday affective formations and (more slowly) in the overarching structures of feeling that describe how different groups experience and go about their lives in and with media.

Then, from a social perspective, it does not matter whether streams are actually "live." Again, there is no "real" immediacy in real-time but only different paces that are established in platform specific ways through interactions between users and platforms (Weltevrede et al., 2014: 127). There is a continuous logistical tension between the user's desire to govern and intervene in streams and the externally-driven stimulation that tries to steer the user.

The important thing is that streams "are *perceived* as encapsulating users into an 'eternal now'" (ibid: 129, emphasis added). This is to say that real-time streams shape our expectations on, for example, sharing practices on social media; we expect our actions to be immediately published and that reactions will follow. The growth and diversification of such real-time feedback over the past few decades have conditioned our life environments to the extent that we now continually move in and out of various streams as part of our dwelling and adapt our lives to the paces that characterize these streams (see also McQuire, 2016). In short, while streams can be understood as "pacing devices" and their paces are platform specific as well as assembled by users "based on followings, friend connections, hashtags or News Feed settings" (Weltevrede et al., 2014: 141), this does not contradict the fact that we often experience streams as deeply captivating.

There is much empirical evidence to support this point. As Nansen and colleagues found in a study of domestic media rhythms, people "tend to drift" (Nansen et al., 2009: 193) in their engagements with platforms (see also Kennedy et al., 2020). This phenomenon can also be discerned in the following quote, taken from one of the Swedish focus group interviews conducted in 2019:

> Gabriel: I totally lose track of time. Going to Facebook can be devastating to routines. One just scrolls and clicks along all the time. Then it's like one wakes up and then like "oh, now I've been sitting here for almost an hour, I put on some tea and now it's cold." These times I feel I just hide away the phone somewhere to focus on something else.

Gabriel is a young man studying music at university. His description illuminates the captivating force of streaming media in a dual way. First, it testifies to the immanent, even redemptive, nature of dwelling in streams, the eternal now that seems to emerge as one "just scrolls and clicks along all the time." Second, and just as important, the quote illustrates a phenomenological break, or rupture, even an "awakening." Such experiences of suddenly "waking up" may have different causes, like technical failure or disconnection; strange or misplaced segments in the stream (as in my own playlist experience mentioned in the beginning of the chapter), or, as shown here, some deeply embodied signal reminding users of their daily routines, events in the surrounding world, and that time passes. Such experiences and feelings of shattered routines underscore not just how streamability reshapes the lifeworld but also how users struggle to maintain a sense of control and sometimes fail in their attempts to domesticate streaming media (Nansen et al., 2009; Matassi et al., 2019; Örnebring & Hellekant Rowe, 2022). Hence, people's sense of "being streamable," that is, to be *steered* rather than to *steer*, is not always a pleasant one. The following conversation among women in a Swedish provincial village bespeaks something other than "messianic media" (Berry, 2011b); it points to feelings of being monitored, even haunted.

> Ruth: It feels like… like Facebook, for me it used to be a way of keeping in touch with people one otherwise doesn't hear from. But now it's more advertising, targeted advertising. A lot of things that do not interest me at all, and that is most of the flow today.[…]
> Jessica: I agree with you, there is so much else in the flow now that doesn't… It's not persons one follows anymore but a lot of other crap.
> Carina: Yes, it is.
> Jessica: It's not fun and it's not interesting anymore.
> Carina: And I think it's a bit scary. If I have been to a webpage somewhere and then one or two hours later if I go to Facebook then I have advertising from that place. It's creepy.
> Evelina: Sometimes it feels like if you've just thought about something, then it comes after you.

It is interesting to compare this quote with the previous one. While both refer to how users feel that they get stuck with, or in, streams, the second quote describes what we should understand as *entanglement* rather than captivation. The difference is that while captivation refers to the human involvement in streams per se, entanglement has to do with the surrounding technological and social (infra)structures, not least commercial arrangements, that circulation depends upon and actualizes (Fast & Jansson, 2019: 131–133; Adams & Jansson, 2021). As Couldry (2017: 69) argues in a discussion around the conditions of digital circulation, "a key source of unease, whether or not it emerges in explicit normative reflection, is the sense that digital tools are necessarily entangled in distant processes, powerful processes that we cannot unpick or easily challenge." Digital captivation strengthens our entanglements with such processes, as in the case of Facebook and Google – platforms that work as nodal points in networks of global commerce and thus algorithmically steer user engagements towards such transactions. At the same time, the equation may be reversed. Our entanglements lead us into particular streams, sometimes in unexpected ways. For example, Matassi et al. found in a study of WhatsApp that the appropriation of this application did not necessarily stem from a desire to communicate with peers, or even from peer pressure to engage in social streams, but rather from work and family responsibilities that were of a more practical nature. Participants in the study compared WhatsApp to bank applications and other "stuff one feels obliged to have" (Matassi et al., 2019: 2191).

Combined, captivation and entanglement describe how streamability blurs the boundaries between self and technological environments. This, in turn, is a concrete manifestation of geomediatization, the arrival of geomedia as an environmental regime. While captivation nor entanglement are not new phenomena in media culture – debated as they were also in mass media society (under different labels and in relation to different technologies) (see, e.g., Syvertsen, 2017) – they now appear in a new light due to the industrial realization of longstanding cybernetic and logistical visions to predict and steer people's behaviour.

Still, this conclusion should not be taken too far. The notion of people, streams and environments seamlessly woven together needs to be problematized (Morris & Powers, 2015). New forms of friction and new sites of logistical struggle evolve, as we saw in the examples. Captivation may result in negative feelings of having one's attention steered or manipulated. Entanglement often brings frustration due to growing dependence on (imperfect) technologies and commercial bonds and agreements that media users enact (sometimes without understanding how it happened or what the consequences are) (see, e.g., Andrejevic, 2013; Adams, 2020; Paasonen, 2020). The common denominator is that people feel their autonomy and self-worth to be threatened. In the next section, I will elaborate this point through an account of logistical labour and the social and material frictions that characterize the culture of streamability, with a focus on music streaming.

LOGISTICAL LABOUR, OR THE TOIL AND TROUBLE OF MUSIC STREAMING

To understand how and why streamability is associated with logistical labour, we need to start out from *connective labour* as this is a prerequisite for streams to emerge. Modern society is a networked and socially disembedded society that would not function unless information was transmitted and shared efficiently (Giddens, 1991). It is a society characterized by people's ongoing efforts to keep connections stable and secure, so that social relations can flourish across longer distances. On a basic level, then, connective labour is a matter of maintaining what Paul C. Adams (2005: 34) describes as extensibility:

> The daily routines of agency, both in and out of the workplace, blend communications at various scales through various media to form a particular personal rhythm of involvement in various scales of social integration. [...] Someone asks her secretary for a report of the previous day's European sales. Someone else checks his e-mail. Someone else lifts a stack of letters and reports from throughout the United States and sorts it according to urgency. The high end of the service economy selects and promotes workers with skills in extensibility – the ability to read quickly, to use a computer, to develop and maintain hierarchies, to treat abstract and disembedded social situations as real.

While the skills needed to keep up extensibility most often pertain to rather simple procedures (scanning through e-mails), there are also more complex operations that may need professional training (using a software designed for a specific organization). What they have in common is that they describe the mundane yet fundamental nature of connective labour in modern society. Connective labour even defines the skillset saturating educational systems. Schools quite literally "make extensive individuals," as Adams (2005: 39) notes. Likewise, the remarkable expansion of streamability that we see today would be unthinkable without connective labour, as streams necessitate connections. If people did not maintain their connections – whether we speak of the routinized charging of a smartphone, the downloading of an app for electronic payments, or the keeping of a Facebook profile – there would not be any streams, of either data or content. This is especially true when it comes to social media, or what van Dijck (2013) calls connective media, as the entire business model rests on connectivity that is largely automated (and beyond the control of individuals) but nevertheless depends on users' online presence and attention.

Yet, if we consider the *handling of streams* and the preparation of the "right" social and material front-end conditions for streaming media, such matters are by definition about logistics rather than connectivity. In principle, logistical labour refers to practices conducted as a matter of maintenance and reproduction of the circulatory system, including interactions "within" the platform (e.g., liking or storing content, or updating a user profile), as well as "beyond" it (upgrading hardware and software systems, coordinating devices, or adapting other elements of the life environment to streaming). While connective and logistical forms of labour overlap and feed into one another, the theoretical distinction is important, because it helps us see how streamability contributes to the logistical bias of geomedia. Streamability evokes a certain mindset, as we saw in the previous section. It demands that people not only connect, but see the world through, and *as*, streams and to become logistical labourers to handle that world. Conversely, the spread of digital platforms that help people handle everyday logistics – from interactive maps, passports and ticketing systems to self-surveillance apps – contribute to the multiplication of streams, eventually to big data (Leszczynski & Crampton, 2016). Thus, while logistical labour was also carried out in relation to older technologies, the platform economy has turned it into its central means of accumulation. Logistical labour underpins the encapsulation of our lives into circuits of digital streams.

Moving Beyond the Platform

Let us make this more concrete. What forms of logistical labour are required to handle audio-streaming? One way of answering this question is to delineate four principal, closely interwoven areas of logistical labour: labouring with *data*; labouring with *content*; labouring with *technology*; and labouring with socio-material *environments*. The first two areas are the ones most directly related to streamability, as discussed above. Here, logistical labour boils down to "click practices" that keep the systems of value accumulation up and running and define users as "vectors of data transfer" (Berry, 2012: 391). Basically, all online activities that contribute to the circulation of data and content, or to the translation of any of these types of streams into the other, can be seen as logistical labour. Streaming, adding and liking songs, creating, sharing and following playlists, sharing songs and albums via social media, are all examples of logistical labour. It does not mean that they are *only* about logistics, of course – there are also connective and representational elements involved and from the user's point of view they are largely about self-presentation and self-expression – but they show how the magnitude and significance of logistical labour in music consumption have increased since the days of CD and LP albums, home-made mix-tapes and top-lists based on postal voting.

This is also the type of issue that research on music streaming has mostly dealt with. An overview of the field shows that there is a dominance of studies that focus on how platforms and their services work. Many of these studies are industry and market oriented and explore, for example, power relations between music streaming platforms, music producers and artists (see, e.g., Hesmondhalgh, 2020; Maasø & Hagen, 2020; Prey, 2020), but there are also critical inquiries into how these platforms, as commercial actors, monitor their users and thus reproduce cultural trends and social biases (e.g., gender) through automated curation (see, e.g., Morris & Powers, 2015; Eriksson et al., 2019; Eriksson, 2020; Maasø & Hagen, 2020; Werner, 2020). If we zoom in on user-oriented studies, we can detect an ontological undercurrent that normalizes a view of streaming as an individual matter solely oriented towards the platform and one's self-directed pursuit of diversion. There is an over-representation of avid music streamers, people with enough skills to use platforms as tools for creative and/or critical purposes, that is, as "work" or "action," according to Arendt's terminology, beyond the mandatory labour it takes to keep infrastructures, devices and platforms alive. Such users are often relatively young, well-educated and "digitally literate" (Gran et al., 2020: 13).

A number of additional studies can be mentioned to illustrate the point. Webster (2019, 2020) provides an account of how cultural intermediaries counter industrial forces through making and sharing playlists online in strategic ways. These (prod)users strive to turn music listening into a more creative activity that escapes algorithmic standardization. Along the same lines, Nag describes mobile streaming technologies in Foucauldian terms, as "technologies of the self." Based on focus group interviews with individuals with an "above average" interest in music (Nag, 2018: 33), she argues that today's easy access to streaming music generates a craving for scarcity among those who consider music an important part of their identity. They thus develop distinctive streaming practices and re-actualize older media formats. Hagen (2016), in turn, analyses how different users organize their music (especially playlists) and imagine the very nature of music streaming. She identifies variations in how people relate to streaming platforms: as a tool, as a place, as a way of being, or as a "lifeworld mediation." The latter two views resonate with the utopia of seamless integration (see also Hagen, 2015).

The degree to which users reflect on the algorithmic steering mechanisms involved in streaming varies, however, as Lüders (2021) shows in a study of which values music listeners ascribe to streaming services (see also Goldenzwaig & Åker, 2018). While most participants in Lüders' study did not see much value in algorithmic customization (compared to other features of streaming services) or did not even take notice of it, there was a small group of skilled users who interacted strategically with the system to optimize their listening experience. Similarly, Hagen and Lüders (2017) looked at the social aspects of streaming and found a continuum from users sharing frequently to users never sharing anything. In the latter group, technology was often seen as a hassle and people were worried that they might lose control over privacy. Still, Hagen and Lüders' study was limited to "music enthusiasts and users of streaming services" (2017: 658). A somewhat broader take is found in the volume *Streaming Music: Practices, Media, Culture*, where Johansson and colleagues (2018) report a research project on music streaming based mainly on focus group interviews conducted with university students in Sweden and Russia. While the researchers show how music streaming is embedded in, and embeds, the everyday lives of young people, they also stress that participants were less active in discussing, sharing and commenting on music online than expected (Johansson, 2018a, 2018b). Hence, it turned out to be an important task for the researchers to understand how the platforms (Spotify and VK) were structured in order to guide, or steer, users as efficiently as possible (Åker, 2018).

This takes us back to the question of logistical struggle. I agree with Lüders that "for critical scholarship, the elusive yet action-steering potentials of streaming services as infrastructure warrant continued efforts to understand just how these services work" (Lüders, 2021). To meet this critical challenge, however, we must also look beyond the architecture and logics of the platform to see how algorithmic power (and the potential countering of such power) is also constituted through human activities within the wider domains of day-to-day life, and how these activities feed into social power relations that also include *non-users*. Such matters have so far been little explored in research on music streaming (and streaming media at large), even though "platforms" are often treated as agglomerations of technological, commercial and political features (cf. Gillespie, 2010). One reason for this lack, it seems, is the dominant view of streaming as an individual practice expressing certain preferences and lifestyles. While some researchers have looked at social phenomena like online sharing and joint editing of playlists (e.g., Hagen, 2016; Hagen & Lüders, 2017; Johansson, 2018b), less attention has been paid to the wider social and material contexts that streaming activities (and the absence of such) are embedded in and help to weave.

A first step in that direction could be to consider to what extent the culture of streamability also affects people who are not particularly concerned with streaming services, or for various reasons not able or invited to use them. As shown in Table 3.1, whether or not people use audio-streaming services regularly depends on demographic and social factors. The results come from a nationwide Swedish survey conducted in 2019.[4] While mobile music streaming services have indeed overtaken other distribution platforms (like compact discs and vinyl records) by far, we must be aware that not everyone uses them. The most common way of listening to music in Sweden in 2019 was actually via FM radio, which 30 percent of the population did on a daily basis. The corresponding figure for using streaming services via smartphone was 26 percent. Streaming services were used more frequently among younger people, and especially those with somewhat higher education, than among older people with lower education. However, these results do not rule out the possibility that people may be exposed to the streaming activities of others. The normalization of streaming services, as we will see, also affects those who are not concerned with or able to use such services.

A similar gap can be identified if we look at people's general attitudes to music consumption (see Table 3.2). Through factor analysis, it is possible to extract three dimensions in music listening, where the first dimension seems to reflect an orientation in music listening where people are deeply engaged in music and weave music into their lives; the second dimension suggests an orientation where people are more moderately interested in music and also less independent, encountering music largely through social media; and the third dimension suggests an orientation where people would like to listen more to music but find it technically difficult and expensive to do so. Obviously, not all people would agree that audio-technologies have become "ever easier to use" (Hagen, 2016). Additional analyses (based on a procedure where the factor scores were computed into new variables; not displayed here) reveal that while the first and second dimensions correlate with younger age and higher education, the former with an aesthetic/cultural inclination, the third dimension correlates with higher age. While the first two dimensions also correlate with avid music streaming, the third exposes the opposite pattern. An interesting detail is that the inclination to state that music listening is "too expensive" does not correlate with lower income (again underlining that most avid streamers are

Table 3.1 Uses of music-streaming services via smartphone in Sweden 2019 – depending on gender, age and education level (row percentages)

	How often do you listen to music via a music-streaming service in your smartphone?			
	Daily	Between once a month and several times a week	Less often or never	Number of answers
Total	26	37	37	3904
Men	27	38	35	1949
Women	25	36	39	1953
18–29 years	53	37	10	756
30–49 years	35	46	19	1268
50–64 years	15	41	44	895
65–99 years	3	21	76	983
Low education	15	28	57	216
Mid-low education	23	39	38	1097
Mid-high education	28	34	38	948
High education	28	38	34	1643

Note: The original scale contained seven steps, which have been combined into three intervals.
Source: Online survey conducted by Kantar Sifo.

young), which indicates that this type of statement rather expresses a general sense of alienation in relation to modern music media.

As shown, social divisions pertain not just to how different users navigate in and manage digital streams, but also to how people, including non-users, relate to streaming media technology at large. Distinctions between different social groups do not only stem from the reproductive force of algorithmically imposed streams (the packaging of music) and some privileged users' efforts to stay on top of such industrial logics of enclosure. They also emerge in and through the everyday labour, the toil and trouble, it takes to enable, or disable, streams in the first place. Against this backdrop, we should assess the structuring role and growing prominence of logistical labour pertaining to the wider life environment – labour that occurs on the fringes of, and sometimes beyond, what we could reasonably understand as the "platform."

Table 3.2 Three orientations in music listening in Sweden 2019 (factor analysis)

	Orientation 1	Orientation 2	Orientation 3
Music listening is important to me.	**0.814**	0.146	-0.045
I like to listen to music in my home.	**0.766**	0.066	-0.023
I often listen to music when I'm in transit (e.g., on bus, train, bicycle or airplane).	**0.595**	0.172	-0.158
I would like to listen more to music than I do today.	**0.480**	0.083	**0.429**
I like to listen to music in headphones.	**0.495**	0.359	-0.083
I often find new music through social media.	0.218	**0.750**	-0.025
I follow one or several artists on social media.	0.206	**0.702**	-0.109
I often get help from friends or relatives to be able to listen to music.	0.007	**0.619**	0.281
I avoid listening to music because it is technically difficult.	-0.268	0.055	**0.741**
I avoid listening to music because it is expensive.	-0.213	0.127	**0.707**
I think it is difficult to find music I haven't heard before.	0.280	-0.191	**0.554**
Total explained variance 52%	*21.5%*	*15.3%*	*15.2%*

Note: Statements were graded along a five-level Likert scale ranging from "Do not agree at all" to "Fully agree." The extraction method was principal component analysis; Varimax rotation with Kaiser normalization. Rotation converged in 6 iterations.
Source: Online survey conducted by Kantar Sifo.

Textures and Texturation

Let us now turn to the remaining two areas of logistical labour. If we apply a dwelling perspective, it is clear that music streaming *takes place* not just through digital interfaces but weaves into, and depends upon, the environments of daily life at large. Music streaming and other types of sound media are particularly interesting to study, precisely *because* they amalgamate so easily with other human activities and thus expose the *textured* and *texturing* nature of dwelling (Jansson, 2007a, 2018a). We may recall here the examples discussed in Chapter 2, which showed how different members of a household felt more or less in command of streaming technology and thus more or less at home in the textures of domestic life.

The example of IKEA's *Rhythm of Life* formula underscores the complexity of these matters. On the one hand, *Rhythm of Life* is an ambitious attempt at embracing the contextuality of music listening; an attempt to customize playlists to what music is, and ought to be, to different users in different time-spaces (see also Åker, 2018). On the other hand, its failures in making music blend into everyday life expose not just the difficulties involved in user profiling but also the processual and relational nature of space and place. The kitchen is not exactly the same place at all times and a particular song does not always make the same impression or weave as easily into the "rhythm of life." As Lüders (2021) puts it, while algorithmic recommendations may "set the stage for both overt and covert tethering of people and streaming services," we should not overlook that streaming experiences are also "co-created by music listeners." What Lüders does not discuss, however, is that this co-creation involves the mundane management and adaptation of technologies, environments and social life to the demands of streamability. We may consider this type of logistical labour a form of texturation. It is a matter of making certain streams fit everyday life, and vice versa, while resisting other potential streams.

Basically, this weaving and seaming of everyday textures with and through media is not a new thing, of course. To some degree, the handling of streamability extends a well-trodden path of domestication – the moral, cultural and functional endeavour among humans to master (new) media technology (see, e.g., Silverstone & Hirsch, 1992; Berker et al., 2005; Hartmann, 2013; Bengtsson, 2018; Matassi et al., 2019). What is new, is that people's ordinary lives have become the epicentre of cybernetic value extraction based on multi-directional streams and automated surveillance (see, e.g., Zuboff, 2015; Andrejevic, 2019). Geomedia actualizes, and relies upon, networked infrastructures and devices that demand more regular adjustment, notably upgrading and synchronization, than mass media. Geomedia technologies also obey more fluid temporal and spatial logics, where streaming services, as a case in point, largely dissolve the fixed rhythms of broadcasting and absorb people (sometimes by means of intrusion) into their own, mobile streaming bubbles (see also Örnebring & Hellekant Rowe, 2022).

In an ethnographic analysis of how digital connectivity played into the domestic rhythms of Australian households, Nansen et al. (2009) describe digital platforms as a "polyphonic drone" providing the background to all sorts of activities in the home. The researchers found that the "ambient media drone" fostered expectations, even compulsions, pertaining to the open-ended flow of information, as well as frustration with sudden interruptions and a sense of growing disorder in the home (ibid: 192). This unruly, fragmented condition – reminiscent of what Paasonen (2020) calls an "affective formation" – called for active management, or *orchestration*, through everyday dwelling. It included, for example, the purposeful placing of stationary media, implementation of joint calendars and creation of technology-free zones. After all, the digitalized home was not seamless at all; rather, as Nansen and colleagues state, "this experience of 'always on' is a metric and a sense of an ambient media presence that *seams* daily life" (2009: 187, original emphasis). While their study was conducted in the early stage of streaming media it demonstrates the labour involved in orchestration *and* how different modes of orchestration evolve in different households to minimize interruptions and collisions between media and people (see also Nansen et al., 2010; Kennedy et al., 2020). In a similar way, the handling of audio-streaming is not just a media-oriented and individual activity; it is a form of logistical labour that interweaves with the social and material contexts of households and other settings.

To conclude, streaming media seems to make our everyday environments more and more similar to what Ingold (2008) calls a *meshwork* with diffuse boundaries between humans, technologies and other things in and of the environment (see Chapter 2). Our labouring with such media cannot be separated from our labouring with other things and people, and their workings upon us. Dwelling in and of itself constitutes logistical labour through which enduring textures can emerge in our lives, in our domestic home spaces or elsewhere. These textures enable and contradict – in one word, co-constitute – the force of streamability and are thus at the core of the logistical struggles we see arising today. Still, to maintain a sense of security and control, we must continuously *adjust* our modes of dwelling. This point problematizes Ingold's ecological perspective of the environment. It underscores that logistical labour is oftentimes more than a pre-reflexive form of activity. Even when it comes to such an ordinary activity as music listening, social relations are at stake. They are sometimes complex and tense. Likewise, technologies are not unproblematic, as we have seen. They are disruptive, confusing, sometimes out of order, and continually calling for our attention (especially when they are new, or old). Such reflexive attention – the orientation towards *things as objects* (which is obviously something other than the attention measured in the platform economy) – is an inescapable aspect of modern-day dwelling and lays the ground for deeper skills that gradually reshape labour (whether logistical or other) and define *how we should dwell* in order to belong among our fellow human beings. This is also how logistical expertise is produced and legitimized under the regime of geomedia, and how socio-cultural differences and gaps emerge among groups and individuals, as we will see next.

THE SYMBOLIC VIOLENCE OF ORDINARY LOGISTICAL EXPERTS

As we saw, streamability is more than an industrial logic; it translates into a *mindset* and an *entangling force* that underpin geomediatization. It demands social and material adaptation and normalizes certain skills. As this development evokes distinctions between those who are able to control everyday infrastructures and those who are not, between people who feel thoroughly at home in their life environments and those who do not, we can also speak about a segregating culture of streamability. In this section, I will advance two points. First, I argue that the type of everyday expertise that counts in relation to streaming media, and thus gives such media a deeper social meaning, is largely about logistics. What I call *ordinary logistical experts* are key to our understanding of the culture of streamability. Second, I argue, logistical expertise constitutes a form of symbolic power (Bourdieu, 1979/1984) and as such manifests and reproduces social dominance.

Let us start with an illustration. Tables 3.1 and 3.2 prompted us to consider how streamability affects those who want to listen to music but are a bit older, perhaps with lower education. It is not just the concrete issue of making networks, devices and platforms work that may cause frustration, however. There are also deeper feelings of being marginalized in a society where one's skills no longer count and where new opportunities for autonomy and integration through media seem unattainable. In a Danish study on mediatization, Cecilie Givskov could identify a sense of *urgency* among the older citizens she interviewed. Her respondents described a double pressure, since "the imperative to adapt to media change" was combined with a cultural imperative "to remain in control, autonomous and active, as part of the cultural mainstream" (Givskov, 2017: 62). Thus, while new media could provide solutions to certain limitations that come with older age, notably related to the ageing body, lack of media skills led to halted extensibility which in turn reinforced the feeling of losing control over one's life (see also Givskov & Deuze, 2018). As a consequence, other forms of dependence were likely to increase, for example on family and close friends who could assist in various practical matters, including media. Such everyday "support persons," sometimes called *warm experts* (Bakardjieva, 2005; Klausen & Møller, 2018; Hänninen et al., 2021), are individuals willing to help without expecting anything in return. Theoretically, their existence can be seen as a manifestation of geomediatization; the inevitability of adapting to new media and acquiring certain skills, not least related to streamability. Age, or generation, is in this regard just one of many social parameters that intersect and together shape how different individuals come to experience and handle streamability and, in a wider respect, geomeditization. Ordinary logistical experts are not always young, and their expertise is not always unanimously warm, as we will see.

There are two sides to the amalgamation of streamability and logistical expertise. On the one hand, media technologies are *constitutive* of logistical expertise. Many of our new media platforms are about managing movements and processes in time and space (see Chapter 5). Increasingly sophisticated platforms, especially mobile apps, are introduced to manage anything from family logistics, sports activities and travel planning to the fluctuations of the stock market. Those who learn how to manage these platforms are also better equipped to manage logistics in various realms of day-to-day life. To somebody interested in stock trading, for example, there are today numerous apps giving the user access to tools for continuous supervision and analysis as well as to advanced trading techniques. While some of these apps are commissioned by banks and other financial institutes that offer advanced services for trade, others are funded through advertising and designed solely for monitoring and information exchange. Some are even closely affiliated with social media and entail elements of gamification. In either case, they indicate how the culture of streamability epitomizes logistical skills and fosters a cadre of ordinary experts whose practices are formative to wider population.[5] The term "ordinary" is used here to underscore that we are dealing with lay, informal expertise grounded in everyday practice rather than in professional activities. It is also to stress the ordinary, quotidian nature of the culture of streamability, and of geomediatization processes at large, following Raymond Williams' (1980) classical view of culture (see Jansson, 2018a).

On the other hand, those who want to make good use of streaming media, and especially those interested in realizing the dominant vision of "seamless integration" of information and data into everyday environments, are implicitly requested to *acquire* logistical expertise. This is exactly what we saw in the previous section on streaming music services. Again, such skills are not necessarily based on formalized knowledge or education. It is certainly true, as Peters (2015: 21) argues, that "each new medium breeds a cadre of specialists who figure out how to manipulate and program its special carrying capacities and standards," and that "brokers and intermediaries – those who control the files, stand at the switch, or speak two languages – are the ones who earn the fortunes and make or break empires." But there are also ordinary skills that do not translate into entrepreneurial success or professional careers but into symbolic resources that rather define the power geometries of everyday life.

Let us turn to the Swedish focus groups once again to see how the two sides of logistical expertise are articulated and sometimes blend to the extent that they are practically inseparable. The following is from a conversation between younger music listeners who live in a small town. They are very interested in music and one of them, Gabriel, is also studying music.

> Gabriel: There's always some music with me and if it's not through media it's in my head. Often, there's music at work and often it's in the kitchen and then I have speakers. Then I have separate speakers by the TV set and then I'm casting music from Spotify to that system if I want to sit by the desk or read. Otherwise, I sit by the

piano and listen to music and play at the same time in my earphones. There I listen to music a lot. When I'm out walking too, but it varies. So, these are the places, I guess.
Interviewer: And you?
Karl: I listen when I'm in motion you could say. If I'm working or walking or moving about. Quite a lot when I'm at home too. I turn on Google Home and it goes on and plays in the background most of the time.
Interviewer: Google Home, is that the one you can talk to?
Karl: Yes, speakers. It's linked to Spotify. So, I can tell it "I want to hear this song" and it plays it.

Here, streaming technologies underpin the vision of being able not just to access music at all times and all places but also to create an environment that is adaptable to various individual needs and circumstances. The way in which Gabriel has planned and uses the domestic environment, and the way in which Karl has integrated different platforms to make the soundscape more interactive (via voice command), bear witness to deeper technological *and* logistical skills. At the same time, their weaving of music into dwelling has strong logistical implications, since almost anything they do, or plan to do, is adapted to their handling of audio-streaming services and technologies. Their relationship to new audio-technology follows an established gendered (male) pattern (Keightley, 2003) and is akin to what Nansen and colleagues call *rational idealism*, where users actively manage, even customize, how new technology should work in relation to the demands of a household. This can be distinguished from what the same scholars call *naturalization*, where "dwelling evolves over time based on the inheritance of cultural norms" (Nansen et al., 2011: 694), and new waves of "media stuff" are accepted more or less casually. The fact that Gabriel and Karl both live alone further explains why their visions of logistical control, a fully connected, streamable home and life, can be realized without much friction.

This leads us to the issue of symbolic power. As we saw in Chapter 2, the exercising of technological expertise is often embedded in domestic power relations (see also Morley, 1986), where some members of a household may typically agree to obey the technological and infrastructural preferences of others and become dependent on their skills; sometimes as a matter of convenience, sometimes in resignation. What is important to note here, however, is that such skills are not just practical in nature. They are also symbolic and as such translatable across a variety of social realms where they take on normative meanings. While ordinary experts show through their media use which technologies are currently to be regarded as indispensable and which skills count as valuable for mastering volatile media ecologies, they also *communicate* about media. They normalize a material culture *and* (re)produce discourses that legitimize their own expertise while exposing the lack of expertise among others. Typically, they represent a type of "smartness" that mirrors and endorses the "smartness" encoded into new technology, which means that they not only place themselves at the forefront of the "development" but also channel corporate visions of streamable geomedia technologies as culturally indispensable (Fast, 2018). Such normalizing *interaction with* and *communication about* contemporary media environments reveal how the logistical bias of geomedia is socially shaped, and socially shaping, even segregating (see also Fast et al., 2019).

This problematizes Ingold's (2008) view of "open environments" with permeable surfaces between humans and things. While dwelling is closely entangled with, even inseparable from, many material things – as shown in the above conversation about streamable music – this does not pertain to all things and to all people (or, at all times) in the same way. Sometimes, dwelling entails moments of symbolic struggle, in language and in practice, through which an objectifying distance is created between people and their things, between people and people. The following conversation about audio-streaming technologies, taken from a focus group interview with senior citizens in a mid-size city in Sweden, reveals how such struggles may unfold.

> Birgitta: I've been thinking about buying an Internet radio for the last two years, but I just haven't gotten to it. I know all that about Spotify and blah blah blah… But I know someone who has an Internet radio and it's so amazingly easy to access all kinds of foreign stations and tune into one's favourites and carry it with you and put it in the bathroom if you are there. So, an Internet radio, that's actually something I might buy.
> Olof: You don't have one of these [pointing to a smartphone]?
> Birgitta: Well, yes…
> Interviewer: I'm thinking, how do you mean, because you're using your smartphone and there you have all the channels.
> Birgitta: I know, but then I need a loudspeaker.
> Interviewer: With Wi-Fi?
> Birgitta: Yes, exactly, and they run out of battery all the time.
> Olof: You could use Bluetooth – then you don't need to…
> Birgitta: Yes, but still the same, the battery in this [the phone] would run out. I can plug it in too of course, but I recall that the Internet radio…
> Olof: That needs electricity too [laughter]?!
> Birgitta: Yes, absolutely, but what the heck… it was…
> Lennart: I just have an ordinary table radio.
> Bengt: And if you say you'll take the Internet radio with you into the bathroom then it won't be connected to the network but has better sound in it.
> Birgitta: I have such a small apartment so I'll place it in the doorway, but well, well…
> […]
> Olof: But I just want to tell you that there are a lot of good apps precisely for world radio.
> Birgitta: Yes, I have them all, or most of them [laughter], thank you!
> Lennart: I have a kitchen radio with all digital, international channels. You can buy those.

In this conversation, Olof takes the role of a warm expert (although a stranger) who tries to guide Birgitta to the most convenient way of streaming international radio channels. There are, however, several passages in the conversation that widen the gap between the two persons and gradually undermine the self-confidence of Birgitta. Instead of trying to understand why Birgitta thinks an internet radio would be a good solution, Olof insists (through what seems like a helpful gesture) on a solution that implicitly disqualifies the perspective of Birgitta. There is even a humorous way of suggesting that Birgitta lacks the most common knowledge, that a radio "needs electricity too." The social significance of ordinary logistical expertise – whose actual scope and depth is of course difficult to specify based on this type of interview – becomes obvious as the ability to reflexively and with self-confidence assess and articulate which forms of streaming work where and under which premises. It is exercised as a form of *symbolic violence*.

Pierre Bourdieu developed the notions of symbolic struggle and symbolic violence in relation to his theory of how cultural taste plays into social reproduction (Bourdieu, 1979/1984, 1980/1990). Bourdieu's point is that the ideas, preferences and forms of knowledge that are associated with the dominant classes in society – defined in terms of either economic and/or cultural and educational assets – hold a normative function that saturates how other groups judge "good" or "bad" taste, "valid" or "invalid" knowledge. Those who have acquired the appropriate forms of capital are in a position where their worldviews are legitimized, and accepted by others, through symbolic practices that annihilate or marginalize other views. The interesting thing about symbolic violence, then, is that it is often implicit; it is a "gentle, invisible violence, unrecognized as such" (Bourdieu, 1980/1990: 127). The person who is in a dominant position does not have to attack or specify illegitimate knowledge but can effectively (re)produce subordination through ignoring certain utterances, or, as above, through warm expertise and what Bourdieu (1979/1984: 255) calls "linguistic ease." In other words, the illusion of "natural distinction" is "based on the power of the dominant to impose, by their very existence, a definition of excellence which, being nothing other than their own way of existing, is bound to appear simultaneously as distinctive and different, and therefore both arbitrary (since it is one among others) and perfectly necessary, absolute and natural" (ibid).

In a society spearheaded by elite figures like Mark Zuckerberg, Jeff Bezos and Elon Musk it is not surprising that skills pertaining to the logistics of digital media streams are difficult to ignore or put into question. They point out in what direction society is going and where the power lies. Those who completely lack such skills are not just hindered from managing and/or claiming autonomy in relation to streamability per se; they are also increasingly disqualified from *speaking about* their own everyday environments, and how to navigate in them, in an authoritative way. As Hannah Arendt (1958/1998) argues in *The Human Condition*, speech is the key to human life, as well as a precondition for political action (see also Topper, 2001). Hence, the inability to even characterize the lifeworld leads to a sense of uncertainty, alienation, even resignation in the face of incomprehensible *and* inevitable social facts (cf. Draper & Turow, 2019).

In the aforementioned interview, this tendency is further exposed as the conversation continues. A particularly interesting passage concerns Swish, a mobile platform for electronic payments:

> Ingela: Try to go shopping without Swish at some places.
> Birgitta: Soon we'll not be able to see a doctor anymore.
> Lennart: It's really hard, and it means more and more. Companies and stores, everything relies on payment systems that must work.
> Birgitta: And won't accept cash payments. There is nobody on the entire earth that is as extreme as we are in Sweden.
> Lennart: Sweden is bad.
> Birgitta: Not even the tourists can come here and pay.
> Olof: I was in Stockholm last week and, and it's very much like they don't accept cash anymore.
> Birgitta: Yes, it's terrible.
> Ingela: But they take Swish.
> Olof: Or you'll put it on your card. But Swish they don't accept very often.
> Birgitta: And they don't accept certain foreign cards, only some, really stupid...
> Jerry: Isn't it quite often Swish?
> Birgitta: ... I've had relatives coming here from abroad and not being able to ride the local city bus. They can't use it, end of story. There was a kind driver who let them travel for free. What is this? Very modern!
> Interviewer: What did you, Jerry, say about Swish?
> Jerry: No, I just asked, don't they have Swish in Stockholm?
> Olof: Yes, but they don't use it very often. It's more between small organizations and so forth.
> Interviewer: But you mean that there are many cash-free stores?
> Olof: Yes, exactly.
> Ingela: But shopping at the market square, then you should have Swish right?
> Olof: Then it's Swish but in an ordinary store nobody wants Swish.
> Birgitta: No, not there.
> Jerry: No, no.
> Solveig: Swish has probably bypassed my consciousness; it doesn't exist to me.
> Olof: Because it's like this, if you have Swish linked to a certain bank account then every Swish costs three bucks, not for the person sending, no, but for the one receiving!

The discussion about Swish is not only replete with misunderstandings concerning technological matters. It also contains misunderstandings between the participants that expose the difficulties in communicating about things that are beyond one's everyday horizons, especially with people one has not met before. As such, the focus group format proves an efficient way of exposing the confusions surrounding new media technologies and infrastructures today – confusions that the geomedia regime both produces and denies. There *must be* a certain level of confusion and disorientation (in dominated groups) for symbolic power to prevail; at the same time, there must not be any doubt as to which forms of expertise are to be taken as socially valid and "normal." The only person in the focus group that exposes some degree of logistical expertise, again, is Olof. He holds a central yet somehow detached position in the discussion. While the general experience in the group seems to be that society – especially Sweden and Stockholm – has become increasingly fragmented and hard to overview, Olof tries to counter some of the obvious misunderstandings that flourish in the group with facts and explanations. Paradoxically, though, the efficiency of symbolic power is quite weak here, since most of the other participants are even too estranged from the issues at stake to have anything to lose (or win) in the discussion. Ordinary logistical expertise remains a vaguely recognized symbolic asset.

We might link this condition to Bourdieu's understanding of gifts as a potential means of symbolic violence. Even immaterial gifts like the kind of help offered by warm experts can be seen as a way to dominate, or possess the other person. A warm gesture puts the receiver in a subordinated position since the inability to offer a similar gift in return, or return a favour, implies a "lasting obligation" (Bourdieu, 1980/1990: 126). However, the situation in the interview indicates that if the gap between giver and receiver is too wide a gift in the shape of "good advice" may go unnoticed. It means that it remains unrecognized as a gift, and thus fails to do much harm other than manifesting the incommensurability of cultural horizons. In other words, to fully work as symbolic power logistical expertise has to be recognized as culturally valid knowledge, aligned with the dominant interests in a society (whether aligned with cultural or economic capital), rather than just an utterance among others.

To conclude this discussion, and the chapter, let us try to summarize what it means to live in a culture of streamability. One thing that is clear from the interview with seniors is that even if people lack the skill to contribute in an adequate way to conversations around a particular streaming technology, like Swish, such platforms, and especially social media, have become so ordinary and well-known among people that they feel obliged to at least express some vague understanding of how they work. Streams have become a commonplace phenomenon to dwell with, and *imagine*, regardless of whether or not they are literally understood as streams, and regardless of whether they are actively or passively enacted, or managed. They are part of *lived space*, to speak with Lefebvre (1974/1991). Against this background, logistical expertise has emerged as an increasingly important asset for *getting around* and *feeling at home* in the world. Logistical expertise, as we saw, concerns a wide spectrum of skills and practices, ranging from the ability to install and upgrade various devices and applications and knowing how to regulate or modify digital content and/or data streams to the wider concerns related to how life environments, and *life as such*, should or should not be adapted to the pressures of logistical accumulation. Logistical expertise has also turned into a valid asset for expressing opinions about what our geomediatized society *is* and perhaps *should be* in the future. This is how logistical expertise, via speech, becomes a form of symbolic capital and a way of maintaining a sense of control beyond the ordinary toil and trouble of logistical labour.

It should be noted, finally, that logistical expertise probably works differently in different social settings and across social space. For example, certain cultural class fractions are disposed to maintain a sense of independence from technology and may take pride in being partially disconnected from digital media (see, e.g., Fast et al., 2021). There is even a new business sector emerging to help people (those who can afford it) disentangle from streams (see, e.g., Karppi et al., 2021). Still, such variations notwithstanding, ordinary logistical expertise unfolds as a way of transforming, or developing, logistical labour into *work* (with durable outcomes) and *action* (with political implications). Of course, there are other ways of countering geomedia, but mastering the codes that define the core of a regime is most often a first step towards human emancipation. I will return to these important issues in the final chapter of the book.

NOTES

1. Quoted in *DiDigital*, 14 September 2020 (author's translation from Swedish), https://digital.di.se/artikel/ikea-och-spotify-i-unikt-samarbete-for-kundernas-livsrytm.
2. See also *DiDigital*, 15 March 2020, https://digital.di.se/artikel/ikea-och-amazon-i-samarbete-sa-blev-tech-lika-viktigt-som-kok-och-sovrum.
3. The interview material was gathered through six focus group interviews conducted in 2019 within the research project *Music Ecosystems Inner Scandinavia*, funded by EU Interreg (see Chapter 1 for additional details).
4. The survey was part of the research project *Music Ecosystems Inner Scandinavia*, funded by EU Interreg, in collaboration with the research project *Measuring Mediatization*, funded by the Ander Foundation (see Chapter 1 for additional details).
5. A good example of the role of ordinary logistical expertise and the close interplay between different realms of streamability was the distortive investing into particular stocks, especially Game Stop, in early 2021. A number of influential commentators on Reddit, a news sharing and discussion site, managed to influence masses of minor investors to buy shares in devalued companies and thus multiply their value in a short time, partly as a protest against the domi-

nant financial system, especially hedge funds practising banking (speculation in value decline). This highlights the more general symbiosis of information streams (on social media platforms and elsewhere) and streams of economic transactions.

4. Transmedia travel

It has happened quite a few times recently that I, alone or with my family or friends, have made plans for trips that were never realized. While this may be a truly annoying experience caused by unexpected and unwanted events (the COVID-19 pandemic being the most obvious and consequential example) there have also been many less significant cancellations caused by the fact that not all plans were intended to be realized in the first place. In these times, when booking apps and various rating systems are constantly available on our mobile devices, when a hotel reservation can be made by a click just to be cancelled a few moments later (or whenever necessary), and payments are often due much later, it is easy to "keep all options open" in order not to miss out on particularly good deals or certain destinations or dates. Simply put, as prospective tourists we dwell in several parallel travel worlds at the same time and can gradually decide which ones to dismiss and which ones to engage with further (if we have the resources to do so). At the same time, new plans take shape and new potential travel companions may be dragged into (or drag us into) the circulation of tourism prospects. This is all very different from the days, not that long ago, when we visited a travel agency and talked to a sales representative who gave us a few options, maybe showed us some pictures in a catalogue, and then helped us with the booking.

The interesting thing about this shift is that while it points to increased lightness, flexibility and fluidity, it also extends labour processes. As we circulate hotel options, restaurant recommendations, or even travel documents, or start a private group chat on social media to communicate and share photos with our friends during and after a trip, we feed the platform economy and as such pursue a form of labour whose extended purpose is to reproduce the basic conditions of our lives. This labour of circulation brings tourism into our lives long before and long after any actual trip has taken place. Likewise, our attempts to seal-off tourism spaces from other social realms while travelling have become increasingly problematic as platforms and devices are not just indispensable to us but also interconnected. What we see is how *transmedia*, as a mode of cultural circulation, intensifies processes of social and spatial *de-differentiation*.

I say "intensifies" because de-differentiation is not a new diagnosis of post-industrial society. A similar idea framed the *post-tourism debate* of the 1980s and 1990s. Theorists like Feifer (1985), Munt (1994) and Lash and Urry (1994) argued that tourism in (post)modern, post-Fordist societies was becoming less spectacular. It was spread out across ever more time-spaces of everyday life and for a growing share of the population it was a standard way of encountering the world. The coming of post-tourism was associated with improved standards of living and more efficient and diversified forms of travel. It was also linked to new media and the aestheticization of everyday life (Featherstone, 1991). Due to new forms and genres of communication, notably television, lifestyle magazines and later on the Internet, people were turned into "armchair travellers" whose journeys started at home, in the form of fantasies and plans that were sometimes realized, sometimes not. In this way, the everyday saturation of tourist images – emanating from producers both within and beyond the tourism industry proper – led to the popularization of the so-called tourist gaze and blurred boundaries between home and away, between reality and image, and between tourism and social life at large (Urry, 1995; Tomlinson, 1999; Haldrup & Larsen, 2009). As Lash and Urry put it in their book *Economies of Signs and Space* (1994: 272), "what is consumed in tourism are visual signs and sometimes simulacrum; and this is what is consumed when we are supposedly not acting as tourists at all."

Since the turn of the millennium, however, the post-tourism thesis has been relatively absent from the theoretical debate. The term "post-tourism" figures occasionally in the tourism literature (see, e.g., Mason, 2004; Powrie, 2005; Wijngaarden, 2016), but is mostly taken as a particular, self-reflexive attitude among tourists rather than as a social condition bound-up with the broader transformations of society (but see Campbell, 2005; Haldrup & Larsen, 2009; Jansson, 2018a, 2018b). Current uses of the term rarely live up to the grander claims of the original post-tourism protagonists, who saw the post-tourist as a key figure of the de-differentiated, postmodern "semiotic society" (Lash, 1990). Yet, rapid changes in media and communications since the turn of the millennium, especially the shift from mass media to transmedia, have reinforced precisely those forms of de-differentiation that were intimated by post-tourism.

The aim of this chapter is to explicate how the normalization of transmedia in society contributes to further de-differentiation along the lines of the post-tourism thesis. The case of tourism is particularly relevant to discuss in the context of geomedia since it is a business that has from the very start been preoccupied with the circulation of representations as a form of "spatial phantasmagoria" (Jansson, 2002). In tourism, we can get a particularly clear view of how transmedia reshapes representational media affordances and what this means to the human condition. Notably, most research on digitalization and tourism suggests that the practices and spaces of tourism are increasingly open-ended and hard to delimit. There is also a qualitative difference as to what drives de-differentiation today compared to in the 1980s and 1990s. The difference has to do with the fact that the semiotic society is gradually transformed into a logistical society (see Chapter 1). Today, the force of de-differentiation is not only, and perhaps not mainly, tied to the circulation of (tourism) imageries but to logistical accumulation and the prominence of logistical labour as an integral part of dwelling. As such, under geomedia, it is not just tourism expanding into other realms of social life but also, and increasingly, the other way around. If the original post-tourism thesis stated that people were turned into tourists most of the time, we might say today that people (also as tourists) are turned into (logistical) labourers most of the time, constantly partaking in the circulation of information and data to keep the wheels of the platform economy turning.

Along these lines, what I intend to explore here is a series of overlaps, or intersections, where tourism and labour come together as equally normalized parts of dwelling. It may sound strange to see tourism as part of dwelling, as the fundamental idea of tourism is to escape the ordinary; however, it is precisely this (largely mediated) ordinariness of tourism, and, conversely, the spectacularization of the ordinary, that makes it relevant to talk about de-differentiation. Together, the intersections I present compose a broader picture of what I call *transmedia travel*. The term "travel" fits my purposes, since it is etymologically related to the Old French noun *travail*, and the verb *travailler*, which means to work or toil. The same etymological root can be found in Danish, for example, where the word *travlt* describes a situation where somebody is busy or preoccupied with something. Indeed, before the arrival of modern communications infrastructure, moving geographically from one place to another was quite troublesome, requiring a lot of manual effort. Today, the labour of mobility may not be related as much to the act of moving per se as to other activities, like handling various documents, gathering information, and communicating with people about the trip, all of which are absorbed into transmedia systems of circulation. While such logistical labour may seem "light" in comparison, its economic and cultural impetus on society is huge. As we will see, transmedia travel is spread out across social realms where logistics and phantasmagoria, orchestrations and imageries are woven together in hitherto unseen ways. The exposé begins with a clarification of transmedia as a mode of circulation and how it reinforces the basic tropes of tourism.

TRANSMEDIA AND THE LURE OF TOURISM

As discussed in Chapter 1, transmedia indicates how representational media affordances are reshaped under geomedia, enabled by digitalization. Simply put, the texts, images and sounds that appear in media are no longer bound to particular devices or technologies but continuously move across different platforms – implying users' ongoing logistical labour – whereby they are also (potentially) altered and recontextualized by users. Today, transmedia affects the way people (are expected to) live, work and make sense of the world. It also affects tourism. Transmedia extends the interweaving, or de-differentiation, of tourism and other realms of social life. This no longer happens mainly through touristic simulations and sign-play, as argued by proponents of the original post-tourism thesis, but through the over-expansion of logistical labour.

The post-tourism thesis was formulated at the threshold of digitalization when satellite television and mobile phones were multiplying, but still before the general breakthrough of the Internet, smartphones and social media. It was formulated during a period when it was possible to anticipate what digitalization would imply for tourism and other sectors of society, for example, in terms of growing flexibilization of production; differentiation and specialization of the market; and de-differentiation of cultural, social and geographical realms (Lash, 1990; Lash & Urry, 1994). As to the latter, Lash and Urry (1994) argued that new telecommunications infrastructures, notably fibre-optic cable networks, sustained time-space convergence on a global scale (1994: 25), and led to the "de-territorialization" of everyday culture (ibid: 307). Similarly, they argued that the "post-tourist does not have to leave his or her house in order to see many of the typical objects of the tourist gaze" (ibid: 275). Yet, mass media was still the dominant mode of cultural circulation, relying on freestanding analogue and/or digital technologies of production and distribution. Audiences were relatively easy to envision – albeit not easy to measure or understand (Ang, 1991) – as located in front of TV sets and VCRs hopping from channel to channel whereby a "collage of disconnected stories intrude and shape everyday life" (Lash & Urry, 1994: 244), constituting a perpetual "flow" (Williams, 1974).

Digital media technologies brought along the possibility to record, transfer and store greater volumes of information at greater speed, which had a significant impact on the efficiency of mass media channels like television and radio. More significantly, however, digital media sparked a development towards greater interactivity and thus blurred lines between producers, mediated content and consumers. This was more than a technological shift. Digitalization – referring to "the way many domains of social life are restructured around digital communication and media infrastructures" (Brennen & Kreiss, 2016: 1) – entailed a gradual shift from mass media to transmedia as the dominant mode of cultural circulation in society (Fast & Jansson, 2019).

The notion of transmedia dates back to analyses of cross-promotion and narrative "world-building" in popular culture franchises like *Teenage Mutant Ninja Turtles* (Kinder, 1991; see also Freeman, 2015; Fast & Örnebring, 2017) and has, since the 1990s, been used mostly to describe the proliferation of fan cultures and digital storytelling across different media (see, e.g., Jenkins, 2006; Scolari, 2009). Along with digitalization and datafication, however, similar industrial logics and modes of user engagement have spread into a plethora of social realms, including social activism (Costanza-Chock, 2014; Soriano, 2016), education (Tárcia, 2019) and work (Fast & Jansson, 2019). The main breakthrough of what is here understood as transmedia – a mode of cultural circulation – came with the introduction and expansion of smart mobile devices (iPhone 3 released in 2007) and social media platforms like Facebook (founded in 2004) and Instagram (launched in 2010, since 2012 owned by Facebook), which also gave rise to new business models across the media landscape. Today, in deeply digitalized societies, the printed newspaper is seen as a secondary product to the digital multi-platform circulation of news; the shares of the audience consuming broadcast radio and television are continuously shrinking compared to the audiences of streaming services, and people are expected to constantly interact with and re-circulate content they encounter through social media.

There are three key characteristics of transmedia that set it apart from mass media (Fast & Jansson, 2019). The first characteristic is closely related to what we discussed in Chapter 3. As professed by Murray (2003) in her account of the digital economy, neither cultural content nor users and their practices are maintained within one technology and modality but *stream across* platforms and devices, whereby the modes of representing and consuming the information may also change. Today, as users encounter real-time streams with news-flashes, advertising, and so forth, on their smartphones, they are also redirected to additional online content that may entail a variety of modalities, like video clips and user-generated comments or ratings, as well as to other platforms and formats delivered through other devices.

Second, as Jenkins (2006) argued in his work on transmedia storytelling, users are increasingly invited to take part in the processes of circulation, which means that information is continually *re-moulded* and *re-contextualized*. This happens through various forms of online sharing, commenting, tagging, liking, rating, remixing, etc., whereby mediated content may also take on new meanings as it moves between users and platforms (especially on social media).

Third, transmedia circulation leads to the *generation and industrial accumulation of digital data*, including geodata, which means that users are automatically entangled in processes of surveillance and consumer profiling, materialized in the shape of location-based advertising, personalized recommendations, and so forth, across platforms (see, e.g., van Dijck, 2013; Striphas, 2015; Karppi, 2018; Wilken, 2018; Bernard, 2019). With transmedia circulation, there is no longer the same need for external surveys to map the audience; what is important from the industry's point of view is that users stay connected and remain active as *digital subjects* (Goriunova, 2019), that is, willing to give away and stream data.

The digital subject is not a "real" subject, it must be stressed, but a strategically designed and implied "mode of address," whose real-life counterparts are expected to manifest themselves as data producers. The digital subject, following Goriunova (2019: 2), is "distinct from the living self," entangled with the industrial logics and performances of transmedia:

> This concept includes a subject of a data profile or of a Facebook stream, a history of browsing or search engine queries, mobile phone positioning records, bank transactions, sensor data, facial recognition data, biometric movement recognition data, or e-mail inboxes, among other things. The digital subject thus *moves between* captured, unique, and persistent biological characteristics and premediated forms of symbolic expression, judicially inferred subjects of actions and performed identities. (Emphasis added)

The key term here is *movement*. The digital subject is an in-between, intermediary position – neither subject nor data – defined by its particular mode of generating data streams. In the context of tourism this happens, for instance, when sharing images on a social media platform, searching for affordable accommodation or checking in at a restaurant in a foreign city. The commercial imperative in transmedia environments to continuously produce such in-between, continuously mobile, quasi-subjects represents the most recent extension of post-tourist simulacra. At the same time, it represents *a logistical business as much as a semiotic one*, signifying the general shift to logistical accumulation in capitalist society. The deployment of tourism phantasmagoria in transmedia marketing becomes a rational way for the connectivity industry and other commercial actors that benefit from big data analytics to turn liminal desires into profitable digital data streams.

As such, transmedia circulation obeys the logic of streamability pertaining to both cultural content (Murray, 2003) and digital user data (Pigni et al., 2016). This implies that the generation of profit among commercial actors online stems from the production of "audience engagement" rather than from the production and circulation of content per se (cf. Murray, 2003). As Karppi (2018) notes, "engagement" can refer to any kind of user activity that generates data that can be aggregated, computed and turned into new, targeted offerings or improved logistical efficiency of the system. This highlights the role of users as a "cybernetic switch" within logistical accumulation (see Chapter 3). From the commercial point of view, the more data stream across platforms, and the more detectable, measurable and interpretable these digital data streams are, the better (Pigni et al., 2016: 12–13). This, in turn, invokes a condition where streams of data and information are managed in an increasingly dynamic, open-ended manner (Jenkins et al., 2013), while at the same time kept within an enclosed, commercially governed system that automatically monitors and commoditizes ever expanding areas of social life (Andrejevic, 2007, 2019).

Before we turn to the significance of transmedia in relation to "actual," corporeal tourism, it should be noted that tourism imageries and spatial phantasmagoria play an important role as a driver of streams. The lure of such representational registers is by no means new. Liminal spaces and events, often with eroticizing and exoticizing undertones, have a longstanding history as means of evoking consumer attraction, and the desire for tourism is supposed to harbour energies that may also spill over into other consumption practices (see, e.g., Sturken & Cartwright, 2001; Strain, 2003; Salazar, 2012). What is new, however, is that such imaginaries are now deployed not merely to spark an interest in various products and services (including tourism), but to stream users, or more precisely their data, between platforms that may have nothing or little to do with tourism. This means that media users are often addressed as digital subjects with (assumed) liminal, tourism-related desires and as such expected to stay more attentive and engaged.

There is still no systematic overview of where, in which business sectors and under which cultural conditions, tourism phantasmagoria is mainly deployed as a driver of transmedia streams. The very principle, however, was illustrated in a case study of online casino advertising (Jansson, 2020). Having analysed the start pages of virtually all online casinos operating in Sweden, altogether 149 casinos in November 2018, about one-third of them were found to deploy tourism-related depictions of the game-world as a liminal space. While the principal end of online casinos is to make users spend money on gambling, the aim of using tourism imageries is to make users shift their attention and activity from one place online to another, that is, to *move* and eventually *enter* the encapsulated virtual world of the casino (cf. Gale, 2009). These logistical efforts are part of a broader field of online transactions that involve more stakeholders than the casino enterprises – notably social media, news media and various entertainment media that also serve as platforms for casino advertising. All of these stakeholders benefit from the generation of digital data streams to fine-tune their businesses.

Again, this exposes the epicentre, as well as the ambiguities, of logistical society. It is a society where symbolism and phantasmagoria are the fuels injected into the machineries of digital circulation. Dreams of liminal experiences, adventure and exoticism – what we may also think of as projections of human affect (cf. Karppi, 2018; Paasonen, 2020) – still saturate capitalism in the midst of technological progress and increasingly abstract modes of logistical accumulation. The argument I want to pursue in this chapter, however, takes a slightly different route. My concern is not liminal fantasies, whose deeper meanings would call for a more psycho-analytical approach, but rather how transmedia reproduces precisely these touristic desires by sustaining a logistical invasion of tourism. My point is that transmedia as a mode of circulation leads to a new form of social and spatial de-differentiation – one where *tourism blends with logistical labour*. This form of de-differentiation has not yet rendered any systematic treatment among tourism researchers or other scholars. While transmedia has been given some attention in the literature on media and tourism (Månsson et al., 2020), most research follows the "Jenkins legacy" focusing either on the usage of transmedia storytelling for the promotion of tourism destinations and place brands (see, e.g., Parmett, 2016) or on tourism concepts and practices formed around popular transmedia products (see, e.g., Hills, 2016; Norris, 2016). Likewise, while the de-differentiating role of media in relation to tourism has been studied and discussed occasionally (see, e.g., Jansson, 2007b, 2018a; White & White, 2007; Haldrup & Larsen, 2009; Mostafanezhad & Norum, 2018) the specific conditions of transmedia have not been teased out. As we will see in the following sections, transmedia not only coincides with pre-existing de-differentiation processes but intensifies them up to the point where divisions between dwelling, labour and tourism collapse. I call this intersectional area *transmedia travel*.

VARIANTS OF THE VIRTUAL TOURIST

According to the de-differentiation thesis, people in postmodern societies are continuously mobile via various means of communication and thus, potentially, "tourists most of the time" (see, e.g., Lash & Urry, 1994: 259). During the mass media era, an emblematic incarnation of the post-tourist was the "armchair traveller" who could indulge in the phantasmagoria of tourism adverts, travel programmes on TV, and glossy magazines with feature articles from around the world. Similar themes were encountered when walking out the door and into the built environment (Feifer, 1985; Eco, 1986; Ritzer & Liska, 1997). The post-tourism argument is thus one concerned with the *ubiquity of tourism* as an attitude and a source of imaginative enjoyment in everyday life. Ubiquity also brings along more fine-grained distinctions (Munt, 1994), which are present in the realm of virtual travel just as they are in corporeal travel. People tend to seek out the types of media contents and formats that resonate with the types of travel with which they mainly identify (Jansson, 2002).

Since the 1990s, the notion of the "virtual tourist" has become all the more relevant and has taken on more concrete articulations, ranging from urban beaches and "indoorization" (Fredman & Tyrväinen, 2010; Ferrero Camoletto & Marcelli, 2020) to "virtual worlds" (Gale, 2009) and "networked travel" (Larsen et al., 2007). Virtual tourism has turned into an everyday pastime, regardless of time and place. Carving out a personal "tourism diet" has become a more time-consuming issue. Transmedia accentuates this development along two main trajectories: *continuous travel planning* and *multi-sited dwelling*. As we will see, both trajectories are sustained by logistical labour, albeit in quite different ways.

Continuous Travel Planning

With transmedia, armchair travelling becomes less confined to the realm of spatial phantasmagoria and more closely linked to concrete travel plans. The step from a mediated travel impulse or fantasy provided through, for example, a tourism advert to actual planning has become much shorter since one does not have to visit a travel agency or pick up the phone and order a tourism catalogue. Even before the breakthrough of smartphones and social media, searching for travel-related information and customer reviews, especially about accommodation, was one of the most common things people used the Internet for (Gretzel & Yoo, 2008; Lee & Gretzel, 2010). With "smart tourism technologies," notably mobile apps and online systems for booking, rating, reviewing and comparing destinations, itineraries and modes of travel, the practice of online tourism planning has become even more important and interwoven with everyday life (Xiang et al., 2015; Huang et al., 2017). Attractive destinations, hotels, tours, hosts, and so forth, may be bookmarked for future purposes and shared with prospective travel companions regardless of place and time, which means that one person may entertain several different travel plans at the same time, among which only a few, if any, might get realized. This is just as much about adding some extra flavour to day-to-day life as it is about finding the "right destination" and the "right experience" to the "right price." Since much travel planning now occurs across different platforms, including social media, the boundaries between information seeking and enjoyment, and between logistics and phantasmagoria, continue to blur (see, e.g., Chung & Koo, 2015).

At the same time, however, the boundaries are not allowed to fully collapse. From a social-semiotic perspective, the differences between "tourism" and "labour" must be identifiable to the everyday consumer. As we saw above, in order for data streams to flourish there must not be an end to the lure of tourism and the positive feelings projected onto this temporary getaway. Likewise, there must still exist something that is *not* tourism; a taken-for-granted *homeworld* sustained through continual labour, from which the travelling subject's outlook originates (alluding here to Husserl's distinction between the "alienworld" and the "homeworld"; see, e.g., Steinbock, 1995). What happens in transmediatized travel planning is that the logistical acts of navigating, finding, circulating, measuring, and so forth, nurture and elaborate tourism phantasmagoria. As such, there is no obvious end-point to it (even though the prospects of realization are certainly important to drive the processes forward). Rather, tourism planning becomes an extended stage of *suspension*, where logistics and phantasmagoria intermingle *and* reinforce one another.

While transmedia contributes to the normalization of tourism planning in dwelling (which does not mean that this "pastime" is equally attractive or attainable to everyone), it should be stressed that this trajectory of de-differentiation is not opposed to, but rather reinforced by, traditional mass media logics (cf. van Dijck & Poell, 2013; Chadwick, 2013). The importance of broadcasting and film as information sources in tourism planning has also grown during recent decades, at least according to studies from the American context (Xiang et al., 2015: 522). This is reflected in transmedia advertising for hotel booking sites, airlines, tour operators and other tourism-related businesses, integrating social media and mass media channels (e.g., television and public screens). By extension, tourism planning turns into a more complex arena of socio-cultural differentiation and distinction. Research suggests, for instance, that the online tourism domain entails a "bifurcation" between "traditional online travellers" (ibid: 523) searching for standard products, and travellers whose online practices lead in more alternative and diversified directions in search for unique experiences.

Multi-sited Dwelling

In his book *What is Globalization?*, Ulrich Beck (2000) advances the notion of "place polygamy" as a description of how people in late modern societies often feel attached to and involved in many places and cultural contexts at the same time. Extended mobility, not least due to migration and international working conditions, implies that people's life biographies are globalized. Mediated interactions both foster and respond to such conditions (e.g., following the news and staying in touch with people in one's home country or region). Place polygamy may eventually result in cosmopolitan modes of sensing the world. Based on multiple experiences from other places, near and afar, people are better equipped to reflect on their own life conditions "from the outside," that is, from viewpoints beyond the local (see also Beck, 2006). However, there is no direct connection between place polygamy and cosmopolitanism as most people largely engage in settings that are not "too different" from what they are used to and as the logics of the market tend to reinforce the same tendency. As we can learn from research on tourism, lifestyle migration and expatriate dwelling, the social and cultural consequences of place polygamy include encapsulating as well as cosmopolitan tendencies (see, e.g., Jansson, 2011, 2016a, 2016b; Molz, 2012, 2013; Christensen & Jansson, 2015; Benson, 2016; Polson, 2016a). Even trips to culturally and geographically remote places may well occur among likeminded people and be saturated with discourses that reproduce worldviews and languages that are familiar to the travellers. The same thing goes for most kinds of tourism-related media, whether we speak of tourism brochures, TV programmes or alternative tourism apps.

While Beck's understanding of place polygamy could be discussed at length, my aim here is to show how the basic thought figure might be elaborated in light of transmediatization. Since Beck wrote about place polygamy, the media landscape and people's daily media diets have changed drastically. Now, people no longer seek out exotic places in the media or engage in commercially manufactured tourism phantasmagoria in a sporadic fashion. Rather, via social media they are *continuously involved in the tourist activities of others*, including family, friends, acquaintances and various media personalities. While other people's journeys used to be experienced through occasional postcards, phone calls and photo albums, typically consumed *after* the trip, transmedia enhances people's ability, and propensity, to take part in tourist activities more or less as they happen and in much greater detail, including various interactions between travellers and "armchair travellers." Touristic impulses – from selfies and sunsets to more elaborated travel blogs – saturate the lifeworld via real-time streams engineered by the connectivity industry to spark maximum data traffic through further user engagement (Karppi, 2018). Research shows that most tourists nowadays stay in touch with friends and family while travelling, using a variety of online channels. Tourists not only *take* photos but, to an increasing extent, also *share* them and *comment* on them online (see, e.g., Lo et al., 2011; Munar & Jacobsen, 2014; Schwarz, 2021), contributing to a continuously expanding attention economy that has Instagram as its locus (see, e.g., Marwick, 2015). As pieces of information circulate across platforms and devices, people get increasingly aware of, and virtually drawn into, tourist activities when they are not travelling themselves.

I thus argue that there is a qualitative difference between place polygamy and what I call *multi-sited dwelling*. The former describes life-biographies defined by attachment to multiple places. The latter, by contrast, describes how people through mediation not only move their minds to a different place, what Scannell (1996) in his phenomenology of modern broadcasting calls the "doubling of place," but also take part of, and sometimes take part in, other people's activities, that is, selected parts of dwelling. This is not to say that people are always attached to the things other people share online. Most things that circulate may even go unnoticed. Yet, my point is that life-biographies are in this way *opened up* to other, *potential* forms of dwelling via a wide range of digital streams. In contrast to television viewing, for example, interactions via platforms like Facebook, Instagram and Snapchat occur anywhere, anytime, often on the move, and comprise anything from para-social interaction with celebrities to two-way communication with close friends. As such, they normalize the type of combinatory, virtual *and* corporeal mobility that Hjorth and Pink (2014) call "digital wayfaring," and which Urry (2007: 171) earlier described as "mobile communicative travel." Similar approaches are also found in the emerging research area on "mobile socialities" (Hill et al., 2021). An interesting aspect to such mobile media practices is that they often *appear* the same regardless of whether people travel across the globe or visit the local restaurant – and their representations eventually intermingle via the interfaces of real-time streams (pictures of and comments on meals, smiling faces, gatherings, landscapes, and so forth).

Media theorist Shaun Moores (2012) makes a similar point in his discussion of mobile phone use, which sometimes takes place in not-so-private settings. Moores borrows an example from conversation analyst Schegloff (2002), who describes a situation where a person engages in a private telephone conversation among strangers in a train carriage. This person, then, is clearly not just in two places (or spaces) at the same time but in two different *situations* – the private situation defined in and through the conversation, including things described by the distant interlocutor, *and* the situation on the train (which the person also affects through pursuing an intimate conversation that nearby people are able to hear, but are pretending not to). What unfolds here is a condition characterized by the pluralization of social situations as they unfold and intersect in real-time. It is thus something more, ultimately *something else*, than a doubling of place. It is better understood as an instance of multi-sited dwelling, which may, but does not have to, be part of place polygamy as conceptualized by Beck.

I agree with Moores (2012: 21) when he argues that "analyses of social interactions and experiences need to be sensitive to such doublings and intersections" (as the one referred to in the example). Moores is also the media scholar who has most persistently advocated a dwelling perspective in media studies, with a particular eye for the everyday movements, or "little mobilities" (ibid: 87), within which people's media engagements are embedded, whether we see media as just material stuff or as "means of transport" (ibid: 89). However, Moores does not unite this perspective with any elaborated account of the current media regime, geomedia, or the specific affordances tied to mobile platforms. While this may have something to do with his overall endeavour to avoid media-centrism (Moores, 2018), I believe that the implications of the dwelling perspective (which Moores adopts from Ingold) could be further advanced if combined with a concern with geomedia as an environmental regime.

Digitalization has not just improved the human possibilities for extensibility (Adams, 2005) and made technologies more portable, or "miniaturized" (Elliot & Urry, 2010). An even more pervasive transformation under geomedia, and what Zuboff (2015) calls "surveillance capitalism," concerns the logics by which our interactions with/in media environments are steered, that is, how we, as media users, are required to pursue *monitorable logistical labour* in relation to digital streams. Even if we shift our analytical focus away from people's uses of particular media products to issues of dwelling and infrastructure – an ambition that in Moores' case aligns with a deliberate move towards non-representational theory (see, e.g., Thrift, 2008) – we should not, and cannot, overlook how transmedia circulation and the underlying industrial logic of streamability alter the relations between dwelling and environment. Today, transmedia streams are the environment, and our dwelling with and in these streams is more than ever constitutive of who we are. One might then say that the realization of cybernetically steered value chains, upon which this latest revolution of the media environment rests, accentuates Adams' (2005) point that the human self is at the same time *grounded* and *extensible*, and that communication operates in both directions. Similarly, our lives with transmedia manifest Ingold's (2000: 169) basic understanding of dwelling as a site where "self and world merge [...] so that one cannot say where one ends and the other begins." As activities and events stemming from the *dwelling of others* form the raw material for digital streams that criss-cross and *constitute* our media platforms (Richardson, 2020b), as evidenced not least in relation to tourism, they also co-constitute our life environment and intersect with our own dwelling.

This leads us back to the notion of multi-sited dwelling and its relation to transmedia travel. While it should be noted that human beings have always *dwelled together* with others and shared their personal experiences and plans as part of dwelling – during the last centuries also at-a-distance via letters, postcards and telephone – there are elements that set transmedia circulation apart from earlier modes of dwelling together. I will present them as three inter-connected points and explain how they play into the collapsing boundaries of tourism.

First, if the standard way of encountering tourism as part of day-to-day dwelling used to be the more or less deliberate consumption of tourism imageries through, for example, television and magazines, such encounters now largely occur *involuntarily* through real-time streams where a variety of tourist spaces and activities, as well as tourists themselves, appear in a seemingly random way. While some subjects, places and events may be familiar and expected, others give glimpses of ongoing activities that would otherwise have remained unknown, unexplored or even avoided. Most of the time, real-time streams deliver at the same time more *and* less information than the user wants – drawing the user's attention to certain things (including algorithmically selected celebrity posts, commercials and so forth) while keeping other things off the radar. This also means that glimpses of tourism activities and engagements with those travelling may occupy the lifeworld in practically any kind of situation, as a form of "presence bleed" (Gregg, 2011; see also Fast & Jansson, 2019).

Second, since real-time streams are more or less *undifferentiated*, obeying an automated and intensified version of the commercial logic of uninterrupted flow (Williams, 1974), the same thing goes for everyday encounters with tourist representations. In real-time streams, some people's mundane activities coalesce with the more fateful moments of others; some people's work-related activities coalesce with the more remote tourism adventures of others. Furthermore, as research shows that tourism-related sharing practices are marked by thematic and aesthetic diversity, such streams may entail phantasmagorical representations of typical tourism sights and events alongside backstage oriented glimpses of, for instance, the inescapable logistical labour of travelling (see, e.g., Munar & Jacobsen, 2014; Jansson, 2019; Cassinger & Thelander, 2021; Schwarz, 2021).

The third point has to do with *immediacy*, the fact that things posted online go into streams instantly (in principle). Thus, the tourist activities of others are often encountered, consumed and interacted with *on-the-go* and blend with one's own ordinary undertakings. While this may not have any other consequence than a slight shift in how dwelling is framed – some things sticking to one's mind while others float by – it may also cause people who are not travelling to be "dragged into" the activities of those who do. At the most basic level, this is a matter of social responsiveness expressed through mundane acts of online logistical labour, that is, "liking," commenting, "retweeting," rating, forwarding, and so forth. But there are also wider logistical implications akin to the type of "fluid meeting cultures" discussed by Urry (2007), meaning that parts of travel planning and co-ordination are handled while away rather than before a trip. Transmedia extends this tendency, making it much easier for travellers to keep up instant communication with an indefinite number of persons and engage them in anything from airport logistics to bar recommendations.

In all, multi-sited dwelling is a phenomenon of much wider purchase than just tourism. We deal with different modalities of digital wayfaring, rather than with any sharp distinction between tourists and non-tourists. We deal with a social condition where life is played out on multiple arenas, and along multiple paths, at the same time, and where human subjects are mutually following each other's undertakings, sometimes without any clear intention or commitment. Andersson (2021: 205) describes this as "ambient communication," a condition where communication "moves between and conflates the background and foreground of attention." This is not to say that all people are engaged in transmedia streams to the same extent, or in the same way, or that streamed information reflects the deeper layers of human dwelling. My point is to show how multi-sited dwelling constitutes an intersectional space where things that used to be more or less separated from one another come together in kaleidoscopic, sometimes unpredictable ways. Due to transmedia, the nature of dwelling has become more complex than indicated by notions like "place polygamy," "doubling of place" and "extensibility." Now, place polygamy extends beyond place into the fleeting moments of human existence; places and situations are not doubled but manifold; human subjects are not just extended in space but also captured, entangled into cybernetic, logistical systems that mould their subjectivities (cf. Neilson, 2012).

Accordingly, we have also seen how transmedia blurs the lines between home and away, between logistics and phantasmagoria, between dwelling and tourism. As we now turn to corporeal transmedia travel, and the second intersection of tourism and labour, we get the chance to consider the same phenomena from the opposite viewpoint; the ordinary "homeworld" collapsing into the "tourism-world."

DECAPSULATION THROUGH ENTANGLEMENT

As transmedia circulation entails the ubiquitous crisscrossing of different social contexts and continuously steers our attention in new directions there is an obvious risk that our ordinary media use (to the extent we use mobile transmedia platforms) does not just support us in tourism planning and feed us with glimpses of ongoing journeys but also leads to *decapsulation* once we are actually away. Decapsulation should be understood in relation to its opposite – the mutual practices through which travellers and tourism stakeholders *encapsulate* tourism experiences as a closed-off "tourism-world" of extraordinary forms of recreation, diversion and/or potential self-growth (see, e.g., Li, 2000). From a phenomenological viewpoint, encapsulation can be seen as the symbolic-material production of tourism as a "temporary getaway" from the centre of ordinary life (Cohen, 1979: 181). According to the encapsulation/decapsulation dialectic, media are key ingredients in establishing a sense of tourism when people are away on their journeys (Jansson, 2007b). Emblematic media rituals like photography, sending postcards and collecting various media-related souvenirs (anything from stamps to vinyl records) have long reinforced the sense of being away and enabled tourists to bring memories of the tourism-world back to their homeworld. Lately, travel blogs have been found to play an encapsulating role in relation to longer tourism journeys (Bosangit et al., 2015). However, media may also interrupt tourists in their striving for encapsulation, whether we speak of recreational holiday trips or distinctive forms of experimental and existential travel (cf. Cohen, 1979). Magic may be broken through sudden media intrusions, such as the unwanted work-related phone call or e-mail (see, e.g., Dickinson et al., 2016; Kirillova & Wang, 2016), the main reason being that digital media in general and transmedia in particular keep people entangled with the overarching structures of modern life (whether technological, commercial or social in nature) (Adams & Jansson, 2021).

While the threat of decapsulation also existed during the mass media era, transmedia accentuates this trajectory of de-differentiation. The accentuation has occurred largely since the encapsulation/decapsulation dialectic was first formulated (Jansson, 2007b). Individuals who want to avoid decapsulation must maintain a strong discipline as to how they use social media and other transmedia platforms in order not to get virtually transported out of the tourism-world and back to their homeworlds. Anyone who has ever posted something on Facebook or Instagram knows that the real-time stream of updates can hardly be avoided (often triggering extended scrolling) and that social responsiveness is often taken as mandatory (see, e.g., Karppi, 2018). Similarly, to most people, just picking up the smartphone means that a stream of push notices, e-mail messages and system-related reminders risk bringing one's attention away from the here-and-now of tourism and into the phenomenological homeworld where the user needs to discriminate between different kinds of information. The simple act of sharing a tourist image on social media, a common ritual that has largely replaced postcard writing, opens up a series of possible exit routes and decapsulation threats, further accentuated as most users are keen also to see how such messages are perceived (liked, commented upon, etc.) by others. In short, transmedia implies greater ambiguity. Touristic media rituals are difficult to disentangle from everything else going on online; and more serious attempts at avoiding this type of "context collapse" (Marwick & Boyd, 2011) would generate further logistical labour. Disentangling, and convincing others that one intends to be unavailable for some time, for example, may be more complicated than actually pursuing the sort of symbolic exchange, and thus logistical labour, that is expected from people on the move. The same condition pertains to various forms of work-related travel (business trips, conferences, etc.), as shown in previous studies (e.g., Fast & Lindell, 2016; Jansson, 2018a).

Again, it should be stressed that patterns of media use vary a lot between tourists in terms of purposes and attitudes to digital (dis)connection (Wang et al., 2014; Dickinson et al., 2016; Kirillova & Wang, 2016; Magasic & Gretzel, 2017). Not all tourists strive for encapsulation, and certainly not in the same way. A study by Fan et al. (2019) is instructive in this regard. Having interviewed 47 Chinese tourists concerning their modes of online interaction and patterns of direct social contact during their journeys, the researchers arrived at six ideal types maintaining greater contact with the "original zone" or the "liminal zone." Most in touch with the liminal zone (basically the local textures of the tourist destination) was the so-called "digital detox traveller," followed by the "disconnected immersive traveller." Both types were marked by significant degrees of digital disconnection. At the other extreme were the "daily life controller" and the "social media addict," that is, people who stayed in touch with the homeworld either through monitoring practical issues via media or engaging intensely in both tourism-related and other exchanges on social media. In-between these extremes were the "dual zone traveller" and the "diversionary traveller." While the former maintained mediated contacts with the homeworld as well as social contacts with the foreign place, the latter showed little commitment to either of the zones and forms of contact.

The findings underscore the need to look deeper into how different groups of tourists maintain the boundaries of home and away, between the ordinary and the liminal, and how they handle the opportunities, but also threats, of further de-differentiation. The findings also, more implicitly, point to the *absence* of any type of tourist that uses media intensely to get immersed into, and close off, the foreign place. The most immersive travellers are obviously those who prefer disconnected modes of travelling. Whereas engagements on social media and other platforms may enhance tourist experiences through sharing practices and self-reflection (Bosangit et al., 2015), they also *open up* the tourism-world to more mundane communicative circuits. Sometimes, this leads to experiences of not fully enjoying the here and now (Stumpf et al., 2020).

Accordingly, the risk of decapsulation, and de-differentiation in tourism more generally, raise further demands on individuals to develop reflexive strategies, and turn them into routines, for handling complex media environments and the consequences of transmedia streams while travelling. A good example can be drawn from one of the Swedish focus group interviews referred to earlier in the book:

> Peter: When I'm on vacation I don't want to bring my computer or have my mobile phone turned on… I bring an older spare telephone, which is not a smartphone and only contains the numbers of those I'm travelling with. So, they can reach me but nobody else. Of course, it's difficult. That addiction that I have to check Facebook is still there, but no, that's not possible. Still, by the end of that week one already feels that it's been pretty nice.

While this person, a middle-aged man, may not be representative of the "common tourist" (at least not in any statistical manner), the attitude signals an underlying dilemma that most people travelling for leisure purposes must handle. Keeping an extra, "dumb," phone is a type of travel routine that is probably more advanced and takes more preparation than most people are willing to devote. However, the interesting thing is the *purpose* of the procedure, namely to get rid of certain digital entanglements and thus the very cause of decapsulation already before the actual journey. Otherwise, concerns like "whether to connect or not to connect," "whether to share or not to share," and so forth, would linger also while travelling and thus ruin the traveller's desire to escape precisely such considerations while away (Jansson, 2018b; Schwarz, 2021). In a study among tourists who had just returned from their journeys, Stumpf et al. (2020) found many examples of cognitive dissonance pertaining to how the tourists had used their smartphones. While regularly used as a tool for getting around and for gathering and sharing information about certain sights, travellers also described their mobile devices as a source of intrusion that they wanted to avoid as much as possible while on vacation.

The enigma of digital reflexivity and potential distress caused by failed online interactions can also be found beyond mainstream tourism. Studies among "voluntourists," that is, tourists engaged in volunteer work, show that the "use of social media platforms today complicates the ethics of photographic practices, as the ease of sharing photographs accentuates and stirs up the unequal relations between the photographer and the photographed" (Sin & He, 2019: 215). Similarly, research on urban explorers, a type of alternative tourist striving to find, explore and document abandoned and derelict buildings and off-grid places, has identified different registers of "reflexive hesitation" related to the difficulties involved in assessing the social consequences (for oneself and others) of picture taking and online circulation (Jansson, 2018b). It is not surprising that "digital detox tourism" has also emerged as a new form of experimental tourism, promoted as an emancipatory way of dissolving the problem of media-related reflexivity altogether – at least for some time (see, e.g., Li et al., 2018; Syvertsen & Enli, 2020). I will return to such post-digital tendencies in the final chapter of the book.

SELFIE LOGISTICS, OR THE PERFORMATIVE LABOUR OF EMPLACEMENT

The third, and final, aspect of transmedia travel concerns how logistical accumulation turns tourism itself into a realm of logistical labour, and as such is woven into social life at large. I will start out from an example that from the outset may not seem to have anything to do with tourism.

During the COVID-19 pandemic we have seen a renaissance of what might be called "ground communication," that is, the use of signage on the ground to mark out where we are supposed to stand (or not) in order to keep a distance from other people. Lines, circular dots and written instructions prevent us from taking that extra step without first considering whether there is a risk of coming too close to others. This type of ground signage can be seen as a categorical example of logistical media, as defined by Peters (2015). Its purpose is to steer the movement and emplacement of people (and other mobile things) in time and space. In the same way that white or yellow lines and arrows painted on the ground are deployed to guide traffic, ground-based logistical media are now found in most kinds of public spaces, whether we visit a café, a library or a department store (to the extent that such places are accessible under pandemic conditions).

While this most recent expansion of ground signage was not expected, even less desired, it extends a trend that has been observable in many urban and/or tourism-related settings since the 2010s. In particular, the breakthrough of image-based social media like Instagram has made *selfie spots* a common ingredient in the tourism and platform economy. Selfie spots are stamped onto the ground, or indicated by a sticker (most often a circular "spot"), at places where municipalities, tourist sites and other public or private actors have an "attraction" they want to expose to the wider public. The selfie spot often includes a preferred hashtag denoting the particular place, establishment or event. Hence, people's ordinary image-sharing practices contribute to free place marketing while at the same time generating profitable data streams. As a logistical device, the selfie spot holds a three-fold function: steering people's movements and emplacements; steering data traffic; and steering future tourists and others to certain sights.[1]

We may think of the selfie spot as the tip of an iceberg; the public manifestation of a thriving new economy based on logistical accumulation, and, thus, logistical labour, rather than on semiotic/representational processes. The selfie spot exposes how streamability (evoking predictable, detectable and extensive data streams) and transmedia circulation (evoking streams that crisscross platforms and devices) interact and saturate, even override, the tourism business as we used to know it. This does not mean that representations have become economically insignificant – far from it. From a tourism and place branding perspective, there is a lasting concern that the *right* images of a place or an event get into circulation. And even though the platform economy is basically indifferent to the semiotic content of streams (and thus to the visual features of places) as long as there are extensive volumes of predictable and computable meta-data to splice and harvest, the same economy has much to gain from the representational competition, or "place wars," that characterize tourism. The selfie spot defines a win-win situation whereby people are steered to places whose representations are likely to accelerate computable data traffic that supports further place promotional efforts.

This is obvious not least in cities and regions that have to struggle with a reputation of socio-economic stagnation, crime and other negative values. For example, the city of Detroit has managed to turn some of its abandoned industrial plants (as well as other derelict buildings), formerly part of the world's most thriving economy, into destinations for more adventurous tourists. Among the Top-11 "Most Instagrammable Spots in Detroit" listed by Visit Detroit, places like the Michigan Central Station (now renovated by Ford Motor Company after many years of decay and non-use) and formerly abandoned houses and vacant lots (now turned into art projects) are mixed with more classical tourist spots like monuments and skylines – all accompanied by explicit geotags and hashtags and instructions on how the motif might contribute to the visitor's Instagram feed. As a case in point, the so-called Heidelberg Project, which is No. 4 on the list, is presented as an "outdoor art environment that's been a part of Detroit since 1986," where "art is created from vacant lots, abandoned houses and more," and "definitely something for your Instagram followers."[2]

Still, this emphasis on appearance and aesthetics does not contradict the overall logistical shift. We can see it clearly if we consider the historical trajectory of tourism and how representational and logistical processes were once related to one another. While representational practices were part of defining the nature of modern tourism from the very beginning (not least tourism photography and the mandatory postcard sent to family and friends), signage, guidebooks, maps and tour guides aided foreign visitors to reach the "best sights" to consume (see, e.g., MacCannell, 1973, 1976; Urry, 1990/2002, 1995; Larsen, 2006). As tourist destinations competed to have their sights exposed via postcards and souvenirs, a variety of entrepreneurs could make money on producing and selling postcards or helping people to get from one place to another. However, there were hardly any commercial incentives or forces that pushed people to circulate information just for the sake of extended circulation. Logistical infrastructures like the post or the telegraph were run as public services operating *in the background* of other human activities, in tourism as well as in other social realms. Against this historical backdrop, the expansion of the platform economy and logistical accumulation might be compared to a hypothetical development whereby the postal system had become the key driving force of the economy, continuously nudging people to visit as many places as possible and sending as many postcards and letters as possible – messages that were also scanned, analysed and archived in order to decide where to set up more mailboxes, advertisements and sales offices for stamps, envelopes, pens and other circulatory utensils. With transmedia platforms, infrastructures are no longer only in the background. Platforms like Facebook and Instagram are *more than infrastructures*. They have become the epicentres of an expansive attention economy that moulds people's movements and subjectivities, in tourism as in daily life.

As such, the selfie spot is an embedded (and quite microscopic) part of the overall orchestration of people's *performative* and *logistical* activities. A great variety of establishments like bars, restaurants and museums, as well as entire neighbourhoods and cities, try to adapt to the force of transmedia in order to gain positive recognition, and ultimately visitors. Polson (forthcoming), for example, reveals how the circulation of images depicting graffiti and street art, notably selfies taken by visitors in front of murals, feeds into the strategic *recoding* of formerly industrial districts, in Polson's case the so-called RiNo (River North Art District) in Denver, Colorado. Since the launch of an annual street art festival in 2010, RiNo has attracted a growing number of creative businesses and a steady stream of visitors drawn to the artistic vibrancy of the area. The economic revitalization has spilled over onto adjacent neighbourhoods, whose under-privileged populations are gradually being displaced due to the inflow of capital. Gentrification processes like this illustrate how social media play a key role in altering the meaning of cultural expressions, such as the "grittiness" of graffiti that is now often deployed to generate a "postindustrial spirit" and sense of urban adventurousness, hence making run-down areas attractive to new clienteles and amenable to new types of investments (see also Zukin, 2010). Similarly, Andron (2018) demonstrates in a study of organized street art tours in London how the aesthetic construction of "streetness" is an intrinsic component of broader urban strategies through which the gazes of the artistically inclined early gentrifiers are steered towards novel urban attractions (see also Ley, 1996, 2003). The social media practices of these groups, in turn, contribute to the acceleration of spatial recoding processes.

What unfolds, I argue, is a platformed version of "destination culture" (Zukin, 2010), driven by the *performative labour of emplacement*. This development affects what it is to be a tourist. As mentioned before, neither logistical nor representational activities are new to tourism. The desire to capture, document and share extraordinary sights and liminal experiences (as well as other things) during and after a trip has always been accompanied by various efforts to manage mobility. What is new, however, is how they *come together* as a form of ongoing labour spurred by the industrially and socially invoked norm to share, or spread, images and other representations to others (see, e.g., Jenkins et al., 2013; van Dijck, 2013; Özkul & Humphreys, 2015). This tendency can in itself be understood as a form of de-differentiation – *a situation in which the labour of moving and emplacing the body at particular sites is guided by the incentives for immediate social recognition, which in turn demands further logistical labour in the form of digital circulation*. Tourism, as a form of "digital wayfaring" (Hjorth & Pink, 2014), is thus increasingly turned into self-performance, or "recognition work" (Fast & Jansson, 2019), where journeys are curated and consumed in transmediated form by travellers themselves.

The consequences of this development take us even further along the trajectories of de-differentiation. On the one hand, the simplicity of using a platform like Instagram to share snapshots opens up for the inclusion of a broader spectrum of motifs than traditionally featured in tourism, especially among travellers who feel uncomfortable with replicating the "tourist gaze." As Cassinger and Thelander (2021: 171) argue, the "Instagram gaze" is often oriented towards "ordinary" people and moments rather than the typical tourist sights. On the other hand, what I call the performative labour of emplacement is not limited to the circulation of images figuring sights, events and moments related to tourism. It is a practice that also penetrates into ordinary lifeworlds and contributes to the internalization of certain modes of gazing *across* social domains. For example, as Dinhopl and Gretzel (2016) argue, the "tourist selfie" is difficult to disentangle from other modes of self-representation that make up people's social media repertoires. Similarly, events and practices that cannot be defined as tourism are often framed and circulated along similar visual registers, bringing about an "aestheticization" (Featherstone, 1991) and "exoticization" (Szerszynski & Urry, 2006) of everyday life. Younger individuals, in particular, develop expertise when it comes to managing their Instagram feeds – what Manovich (2017) calls "Instagramism" – sometimes as a means to acquire some degree of microcelebrity or "Instafame" (Marwick, 2015). Such curation processes also include logistical elements, such as the geo-tagging of images and "checking in" at places, as well as the reflective awareness as to which sides of one's online persona(s) should be *placed where* and *posted to whom* (that is, using different, more or less public, accounts), which reinforce the significance of emplacement and feed into the mutual classification of people, places and practices (Lindell et al., 2021). In all, these tendencies point to how a growing awareness of the "audience" (Lo & McKercher, 2015) shapes people's considerations of which types of images, places and "selves" are worthy of circulation. Transmedia extends the relevance of Lash and Urry's (1994) post-tourist argument that the tourist gaze is more and more entwined with everyday life, and by the same process altered (see also Haldrup & Larsen, 2009). The boundaries between the ordinary and the extra-ordinary continue to blur.

Let us return here to the selfie spot. While the phenomenon shows how logistical accumulation reinforces de-differentiation through conditioning spatial practices and moulding places of attraction (notably as "destinations"), it is also a site of struggle. In the above discussion, we have touched upon issues that may be socially or politically controversial. For example, if the tourism industry implements selfie spots, Instagram guidance, and other forms of logistical nudging devices to steer the flows of visitors and their transmedia practices, there will also be groups that feel their autonomy and distinctiveness threatened. The reflexive middle-class tourist might have to look for new destinations to gain a more valuable form of recognition than what "Instagrammable" murals in post-industrial Denver or Detroit can offer. Likewise, spatial transformations that entail not just aesthetic but also socio-economic alteration and exclusion, that is, gentrification, will meet resistance. Under-privileged groups may feel a rising sense of alienation in their own neighbourhoods due to aestheticization processes channelled through social media (see, e.g., Walters & Smith, forthcoming). In all, logistical accumulation constitutes a lingering threat, directly and indirectly, to different groups of people and for different reasons.

Tellingly, walking the streets of RiNo, Denver, on a hot day in August 2019,[3] I could observe how such struggles and their logistical undercurrents had also left their marks on the ground. Among other ground media, there were activist messages stamped onto the concrete sidewalk (Figure 4.1). As a pedestrian – half tourist, half professional observer, and indeed a digital wayfarer – I was steered online to various transmedia networks, including most of the dominant

Source: Photo by the author.

Figure 4.1   Activist ground media, River North Art District (RiNo), Denver, Colorado, 2019

connectivity platforms, to be part of movements fighting climate change and global and local injustices. The situation was emblematic to the ambiguities of transmedia as well as to the de-differentiation processes of logistical society. Under the regime of geomedia, we are continuously steered *elsewhere*, towards further logistical labour, while still not crossing the confines of digital extraction. Not even counter-hegemonic actions escape the tenets of logistical accumulation. Pedestrians, tourists, activists, workers – geomedia and the expanding platform economy turn everyone without distinction into logistical labourers. As Zuboff argues in her raging critique of "surveillance capitalism," it is precisely this type of "radical indifference" – the abolishment of any "organic reciprocities between surveillance capitalist firms and their population" (Zuboff, 2019: 21) and the normalization of technological dependencies pertaining to "processes that are intentionally designed to bypass individual awareness and on which we must depend for effective daily life" (ibid: 25) – that makes collective action one of the biggest challenges facing our contemporary, digital civilization. What are the possibilities of challenging a logic of accumulation – whether we call it logistical accumulation or surveillance capitalism – that converts life in its entirety into labour? This is the type of critical issue we will address in the final chapter of the book.

NOTES

1. It should be noted here that selfie spots, along with other types of guidance, are sometimes implemented for security reasons. Research shows that selfie-taking practices may be harmful not just to photographers who run the risk of falling from heights or being hit by vehicles but also to surrounding people. For example, as Flaherty and Choi (2016: 2) note in a research overview in *Journal of Travel Medicine*, "enthusiastic selfie-takers at major sporting events have been responsible for knocking cyclists off their bikes at the Tour de France." One of the authors advises that "tour operators and their guides should warn their clients of these risks, and public signage at popular 'selfie spots' should reinforce this advice" (ibid: 3).
2. Information retrieved from the Visit Detroit website, https://visitdetroit.com/instagrammable-spots-detroit, in February 2021.
3. I want to thank Erica Polson for excellent guidance during my visit to Denver.

5. Guidance landscapes

> Unlike the mass media of the twentieth century, digital media traffic less in content, programs, and opinions than in organization, power, and calculation. Digital media serve more as logistical devices of tracking and orientation than in providing unifying stories to the society at large. Digital media revive ancient navigational functions: they point us in time and space, index our data, and keep us on the grid.
> (Peters, 2015: 7)

We have in the two preceding chapters considered how digitalization and datafication reshape connective media affordances and give rise to a culture of streamability (Chapter 3) and, likewise, foster a new mode of cultural circulation – transmedia – which represents the alteration of representational media affordances (Chapter 4). We have also discussed how these transformations entail a logistical bias. It means that our engagements with media, whether we want to connect with others or use media technology to depict or document the world we live in, are increasingly a matter of handling transmedia streams, that is, a form of logistical labour. It also means that many of our most ordinary undertakings, understood as elements of dwelling, are intertwined with the expanding platform economy, providing the raw material for logistical accumulation within data-driven industries. In this chapter, we turn to the final register of media affordances: *logistical affordances*. We will look into a realm of media society that has for long remained relatively invisible to media studies, and also, due to its infrastructural nature, to many people, but now seems to define the dominant imprint of geomediatization. While most forms of mediated communication have come to entail logistical affordances, as John Durham Peters argues in the opening quote, the basic category of logistical media has also changed, especially since the rise of *locative media*. By locative media I mean, simply put, technologies whose operations are place-contingent and thus traceable in time and space.

The aim of this chapter is to chart what this latest transformation of logistical media means to the human condition. While this may sound like an overly grand ambition, I will at least try to reach a basic understanding of how locative media affect people's *doings with space* (Lussault & Stock, 2010). What happens to people's capacities for ordering, orientation and sense of belonging in increasingly transitory (media) landscapes? And, vice versa, how do people's ordinary relations with space, their habitus of dwelling, condition what they do, and are invited to do, with increasingly advanced logistical media? As always when we deal with the prospects and promises of new technology, what may seem like avenues of empowerment to some may foster a sense of imprisonment or alienation among others. Further, as I will argue, such tensions are not just linked to technology per se but also pertain to the formation of *political landscapes* that normalize and put technological regimes into place. One such landscape that will figure in this chapter is related to the geomediatized city and what is commonly called *platform urbanism*. I am interested in how geomedia as an environmental regime translates into a particular kind of urban landscape that functionally and discursively responds to the demands of the new platform economy and logistical accumulation. What does this landscape look like? Who belongs to it, and to whom does it belong?

I will explore these questions through four steps. First, I will clarify what it is that logistical media "do," that is, how such media can assist people in their "doings with space" (Lussault & Stock, 2010). Following Peters' (2015) understanding of logistical media and Lussault's (2009) notion of "elementary spatial competences," I crystallize three principal levels of logistical mediation. These are related to people's everyday endeavours to *orient* themselves in space and time and to *coordinate* and *orchestrate* their spatial practices in relation to the movements and placements of other people and things. Second, I assess the transitional force of locative media. The key term here is *guidance*. Under the regime of geomedia, I argue, the automated provision of customized guidance, tailored to *who* and *where* platform users are (going), revolutionizes everyday logistics. The advent of *locative guidance technology* implies that logistical affordances become not only adaptive to the user but also coalesce with certain forms of spatial representation. Of key importance is what I call the *hospitality discourse*, that is, publicity related to destination culture (Zukin, 2010), meant to promote attractive places and thus contribute to the steering of lucrative human mobilities to certain locations in the city (or elsewhere). This development, which we identified also in the discussion of selfie spots (Chapter 4), is essential to platform urbanism and leads to the production of a particular kind of landscape.

Hence, in the third section of the chapter, following especially Cosgrove (1984), Olwig (2003, 2005) and Zukin (1991), I consider the significance of logistical accumulation as an ideologically driven *landscaping* process that normalizes a certain *social formation* (Cosgrove, 1984). The discussion culminates in two concrete case studies presented in the final section of the chapter. They look at two particular areas of the platform economy: *alternative tourism platforms* and *mobility as a service*. Based on analyses of mobile applications and promotional material, I discuss the social and political implications of emerging *guidance landscapes*. As these landscapes legitimize the authority of a new cadre of logistical experts and digital landlords (Sadowski, 2020a) they also necessitate a logistical underside, that is, a largely concealed substratum of material labour through which the professed landscapes of frictionless urban logistics are supposed to become a lived reality (to some).

FROM ORIENTATION TO ORCHESTRATION

Logistical media, as Peters (2015: 37) asserts, are tools and techniques whose job it is "to organize and orient, to arrange people and property, often into grids." If we pull the two basic terms apart, *logistics* and *media*, we can reach a clearer view of what this means. Logistics refers to the business, or science, of managing the movement and emplacement of people, things and other matters in time and space as efficiently as possible. Efficiency can be measured in different ways, of course. Most often, as in the classical contexts of warfare and trade, it means that the "things that move" should move fast, cross or eliminate borders without friction or delay, and reach their intended destinations in a predictable way, with maximum precision, to as low a cost as possible in terms of energy, time, money and other scarce resources (see, e.g., Hepworth, 2014; Rossiter, 2014; Chua et al., 2018). The clarity of this formula reveals why logistics has historically been depicted as a neutral science, whose utopia of orderly and frictionless circulation supposedly has little to do with ideology or the exercise of power. As shown in more recent accounts, however, logistics deserves more critical scrutiny since logistical operations are in some sense always imbued with ideology and thus also subject to various forms of resistance (see, e.g., Neilson, 2012; Hepworth, 2014; Chua et al., 2018; Hesse, 2020). Likewise, as Peters (2015: 38) holds, while "logistical media pretend to be neutral and abstract," they often "encode a subtle and deep political or religious partisanship." While Peters conceives of media in the widest, "elemental" sense of the term, basically as all things that somehow overcome or dissolve the boundaries or distances between entities (see Chapter 2), the most pertinent way to think about media and their affordances, I argue, is to situate them within human civilization. Affordances are only actualized inasmuch as they are recognized by humans as an environmental resource or deliberately produced through techniques by which humans can more easily interact with, or master, their social and material environments (Gibson, 1979/2014).

Logistical media, then, should be understood as tools, ranging from rudimentary materials to advanced technological infrastructures, whose affordances enable humans to organize communicative activities in time and space. What logistical media *do* may not look very much like communication in the first place, if by communication we mean "the reconciliation of self and other" (Peters, 1999). But their capacity to orient people and assist them in matters of ordering and steering (of information, things, people, and so forth) is fundamental for any deeper form of communication to occur, ultimately to the persistence of civilization per se.

As such, the perceived "neutrality" of logistical media is not an objective fact. It is a function of their status as a normalized *cultural form* (Williams, 1974) whose role in society is not to convince or entertain people, but to make (certain forms of) communication possible. This understanding of logistical media resonates with Rossiter's (2015, 2016) outline of a logistical media theory, where one of the key dimensions is to study "*the materiality of practices that condition the possibility of communication*" (2015: 219, original emphasis). It has also much in common with the notion of *cultural techniques*, as theorized by thinkers like Friedrich Kittler (1985/1990) and Bernhard Siegert (2013), who see "media as the material substrate of culture" (Siegert, 2013: 51). This means that logistical media include a variety of "inconspicuous technologies" and infrastructures of knowledge and discourse that are not directly concerned with representation but with the "exterior and material conditions that constitute semantics" (ibid: 50; see also Peters, 2015: 25–30).

As I develop these ideas into a theory of so-called guidance landscapes, I will approach logistical media from an anthropocentric perspective. This is not to rule out the "more-than-human" implications of logistical media. It means that I am concerned with the role of logistical media and their digital extensions *in the context of human dwelling* and ultimately as a formative part of the *human condition* in the early 21st century. The notion of "guidance landscape" highlights and extends an important point made in Chapter 4: that logistical media are *more than* taken-for-granted infrastructure. They are increasingly part of the cultural imaginary that shapes our view of the world. Arriving in a new city, for example, we are not just embedded into logistical structures for automobility, money transactions, electric supply, and so forth, but also nudged to contribute as much as possible to logistical accumulation. Besides the information we receive via our digital devices, helping us to navigate and giving us advice about where to go and when, the city is full of signs that promote things like platformed mobility services and food deliveries (including the branded appearance of these services per se), and encourage us to circulate our images, experiences and ratings of the places and venues that we visit. As I will show in the final part of this chapter, the guidance landscape becomes a way of organizing logistical labour into a social formation (Cosgrove, 1984). But we should not get ahead of ourselves.

One way of sorting out what logistical media mean to people in their day-to-day lives is to begin with the spatial pragmatics developed by French geographer Michel Lussault (2007, 2009). Compared to Ingold's anthropological, largely Heideggerian, understanding of dwelling, which focuses especially on pre-reflexive, embodied skills (see Chapter 2), Lussault is more interested in the active and intentional human subject. He moves beyond the basic Heideggerian notion of "being-in-space" and conceptualizes dwelling as practice or "doing *with* space," which is to suggest a more active relationship with space "for example in the question of geographical referents of identity, values of landscape etc." (Lussault & Stock, 2010: 14). Lussault's ideas can help us assess what kinds of skills are required for people to manage different spatial tasks or "tests" in different situations, and to assess how the development of new tools condition the capacities of different individuals and groups. As I will discuss below, Lussault's pragmatic approach is different from, but does not necessarily contradict, Ingold's (2011) arguments concerning the permeable surfaces of people, tools and other materials of the environment. Nor does it deny the socially structured and structuring function of bodily *hexis* in relation to people's movements *in space* and *along paths*, as discussed by Bourdieu (1997/2000).

One of Lussault's key contributions to spatial theory is his list of six "elementary spatial competences" (Lussault, 2009). These are: the competence of *metrics* (to assess distances); the competence of *scale* (to assess geographical sizes and proportions); the competence of *emplacement* (to find a place for oneself, others and objects); the competence of *delimitation* (to divide space into relevant units and establish boundaries); the competence of *crossing* (to overcome borders, gates and other limits); and the competence of *itinerary* (to compose and pursue a certain spatial trajectory). These categories should be seen as analytical tools for assessing how particular situations raise unique spatial challenges and how human beings hold varying capacities to pursue different spatial tasks, alone or together with others. For example, as Lucas (2019a) shows in a Lussault-inspired study of how tourists manage to get around in Los Angeles, whether or not people are successful in accomplishing certain spatial tasks depends on a combination of factors that go beyond their motives, tastes, physical abilities and economic means. He found that it was particularly important that they had chosen a suitable place to stay (to be in proximity to certain sites, means of transport, etc.) and that they were able, and felt confident, to master transit systems and various rules and conventions pertaining to the foreign environment (traffic signs, road networks, etc.). As a consequence, some tourists navigated flexibly, independently and over great areas during their stays, while others moved very little and, in some cases, felt frustrated at not being able to reach places of interest. While these observations point especially to Lussault's competences of metrics, emplacement and itinerary, other situations and tasks may require other competences and skills. Likewise, some of the tourists who were less capable of getting around in Los Angeles might be more capable in another city (depending, for example, on language and other cultural similarities).

It is not my intention here to go deeper into each of Lussault's categories. Following Lucas' (2019b) elaboration of Lussault's work, I find it more useful to synthesize three major *stakes* that to varying degrees characterize each particular situation and each spatial configuration that an individual may encounter. These spatial stakes are, according to Lucas (2019b: 5), related to *placements*, *distances* and *limits*. The first stake concerns the fact that individuals must continuously make judgements as to which places are most appropriate for certain practices and learn which skills are needed to dwell in a particular place. The second stake concerns the need to manage the movement from one place to another in an efficient way and sometimes also to make up (realistic) plans for the itinerary. The third stake concerns not just spatial limits and the challenges associated with crossing borders and boundaries but also other factors (individual, social, environmental, etc.) that set limits to what a person can do with space. Combined, the three spatial stakes determine to what extent certain spatial practices are manageable among different individuals. For example, while Person A may be highly skilled in using urban transit systems and have expertise in the organizational aspects of long-distance travelling, Person B may be better equipped to access certain enclosed places and understand the cultural codes that pertain to these places. If A and B travelled to the same destination, their ways of coping with spatial stakes (before and during the trip) would be different and lead to diverging experiences.

Spatial pragmatics may seem like an instrumentalist, even simplistic, way of analysing spatial practices. There is obviously a risk that human beings are depicted as altogether rational subjects that in more or less skilful ways pursue their intentions in relation to clearly identifiable stakes. However, if we think of spatial stakes as a set of ordinary, largely taken-for-granted registers through which human subjects encounter and experience the world, also while going about their daily routines, we can see that there is a possibility of applying spatial pragmatics as a meaningful *elaboration* of Ingold's dwelling perspective. As we discussed in Chapter 2, Ingold (1993: 158) conceives of tasks as "the constitutive acts of dwelling" and introduces the notion of *taskscape* to capture how dwelling is interlaced with human life environments and gradually transforms them into more tangible and thinkable *landscapes*. In Ingold's view, taskscapes describe the sedimented paths along which people orient themselves in dwelling and thus (re)produce certain social and material textures. Spatial pragmatics, I argue, enable us to pursue a more systematic treatment of taskscapes and at the same time get at their logistical aspects, whether these pertain to routine activities or to more specific, intentional projects.

As we can see, there are clear similarities between Lucas' (2019b) "spatial stakes" and our basic understanding of logistics; the handling of distances (including speed, direction, itinerary, etc.), placements (points of departure, destinations, exchange points, etc.) and limits (borders, regulations, scarce resources, etc.) is also at the core of logistical operations. What sets logistics apart from other spatial practices, however, is that it is limited to the management of flows, or streams. All spatial practices (and stakes) are thus not logistical in nature. At the same time, if we consider which kinds of human activities *are* logistical in nature, we can see that they extend beyond those issues of individual orientation that primarily figure in the works of Lussault and Lucas. Logistics is not only, and not even most prominently, about handling one's own movements but also a matter of *coordinating* and *orchestrating* different types of movements in relation to one another. Thus, as we move on to discuss how locative media revolutionize logistical tools it is important to distinguish three principal levels on which human beings are engaged in the mastery of flows.

The first level is *orientation* and coincides with the above examples of how people move their own bodies in space. It is a matter of finding one's way and finding a place or location, often at (or within) a particular time. This capacity is not only about navigation, that is, the ability to realize a particular geographical trajectory. It also includes the capacity to make relevant judgements (according to varying parameters) as to which places are worth going to in the first place. While such decisions are often a matter of taste and everyday habit, for example when people decide where to go for a drink or a meal after work, and thus not a function of logistical competence alone, there are also situations and contexts in which the ability to orient oneself among different spatial options (sometimes within a time limit) is important. It is quite a different thing to assess which is the "right" restaurant for one's taste (serving a particular type of food to a reasonable price) in a foreign city with a foreign language and unfamiliar customs than it is back home. Without the appropriate skills, and tools, it may even be a rather stressful experience.

The second level concerns the *coordination* of multiple paths of activity, or taskscapes, in time and space, that is, how individuals direct their movements in relation to the movements of others, or synchronize flows to accomplish a certain task. We can refer here to Ingold's (2011) example of sawing a plank to grasp the essential meaning of coordination. The person who skilfully saws a plank must *know* and also be *able* to master a body technique that involves several coordinated movements carried out with the right pressure and the right angle (of the saw) and where the movements of both hands must be synchronized to begin and finish the process as smoothly as possible. If we extend this motorial example to concern social life, we find a great variety of instances where coordinated action is crucial to achieve a desired outcome, not least in terms of *timing*. Such instances include different types of meetings, where people come together at (or depart from) a particular time and place (at least virtually), as well as cooperative tasks that involve some kind of sequential activity, meaning that somebody "takes over" a task or prolongs a given trajectory from where another person left it. We may recall, for instance, the classical case of the Olympic torch relay, which provides a rudimentary illustration of the importance of logistics in all kinds of exchanges, including the coordination of human mobilities and flows of material objects, money and information.

The third level is *orchestration*. It is about managing complex assemblages of flows in time and space. There is no absolute division between acts of coordination and acts of orchestration, as so conceived. As a theoretical figure, however, we may think of the former as the constitutive parts of the latter, which is to say that while coordination pertains to single, relatively clearly defined tasks or events, orchestration concerns how to manage more complex arrangements, incorporating many different tasks, that also produce a more enduring structural outcome. For example, we may think about the military and how an army operates logistically. At the level of orchestration, a military organization must be able to make a number of specialized units work together in a synchronized and predictable manner, for example, in terms of units equipped for certain types of movement in certain types of terrain, material deliveries arriving at the right places at the right time and information provided to the right actors at the right time. This necessitates an overall structure that is strategically *durable*, and thus can be practised under different conditions, yet *flexible* enough to make the whole army adaptable to specific situations and circumstances. As such, orchestration provides a framework for single tasks – such as the delivery of a message or the relocation of a specific unit – whose realization, in turn, depends on coordination. In light of this example, it is no coincidence that Nansen and colleagues (2010, 2011) speak about "domestic orchestration" rather than "coordination" when they discuss how households strive to manage their media flows (see Chapter 3), ranging from the furnishing of a digital "home office" to rules guiding dwellers to where and when certain types of media consumption may (or may not) occur.

At all three levels, there are spatial stakes to handle, in terms of distances, placements and limits. Also, at all three levels *and* in relation to the spatial stakes (alone or combined) there are tools to help people manoeuvre (and thereby engender) logistical taskscapes. We can thus combine logistical levels and spatial stakes into a two-dimensional matrix for classifying different types of logistical media (or, rather, the prominence of different variants of logistical affordances in different media). This is not to say that any particular tool is good for only one logistical purpose – say, that a map would be useful only to handle stakes of distance at the level of orientation – but we are better equipped to think through, schematically, the historical legacies of logistical media (such as, why they were invented and for whom) and to identify how they operate in different realms of society today, sometimes in places where one would not expect them to be.

To illustrate the point, let us consider which media characterize the different levels. At the level of orientation, we find tools that help people find their way and find a particular place without getting stuck or delayed in the process.

Traditionally, there are maps and sextants to estimate distances and itineraries; compasses and binoculars to find the right direction; various types of listings or catalogues to help make decisions about where to go and where to stay; as well as tickets, passports and other means for crossing boundaries, and fuel gauges and other meters to manage limits. Processes of coordination are by their nature more time-biased and thus accompanied by logistical media like calendars, clocks, church bells, factory whistles, time-tables, staple clocks, speedometers, and so forth. However, this does not mean that the aforementioned tools are not important to coordination as well, and vice versa. At the level of orchestration, finally, we find logistical media that are intended to overview and handle more complex constellations and infrastructures of flow, such as towers, radar systems and other means of aerial observation; flow-charts, signage systems, algorithms and other means of predictive steering (of people, objects and information); as well as archives, registers and inventories to keep track of where people, things and resources are (going). This is the type of flow management that predominantly figures in the social scientific literature on logistics, dealing especially with global trade infrastructures and various transit systems (see, e.g., Kanngieser, 2013; Hepworth, 2014; Gregson et al., 2017; Danyluk, 2018). Due to digitalization, similar ideas are now applicable also to ordinary life, whether viewed from the perspective of human subjects or organizational entities.

Against this schematic backdrop, we can scrutinize how digitalization revises the *modus operandi* of logistical media, especially through the normalization of *locative guidance* as a cultural form that pertains to all three logistical levels. While locative media, as we will see, improve the logistical capacities of human beings in general, who are aided to cooperate across time and space and to "reach their destination," whether in life or in the local neighbourhood, it is also obvious that geomedia – taken as a complex environmental regime (see Chapter 2) – invokes further logistical challenges that people need to cope with on a day-to-day basis (see Chapters 3–4). Consequently, there are now also logistical media invented to handle the consequences of escalating transmedia streams.

FROM LIGHTHOUSES TO LOCATIVE GUIDANCE

Much of the literature on logistical media focuses on orientation, and especially navigation. In his work on the (pre)history of radar systems, one of the pioneers of the field, Judd A. Case (2013: 379), defines logistical media as "media of orientation" that "order and arrange people and objects." While logistical media should be understood also as "media of coordination" and "media of orchestration," as argued above (and also implicated in Case's work; see also Rossiter, 2015, 2016), it is fruitful to the current analysis to start out from orientation to build an understanding of the various consequences of contemporary, place-contingent technologies. Let us begin with a historical preamble and think about the lighthouse, one of the most exemplary types of logistical media. As Peters (2015: 105) notes, "[l]ife at sea is a logistical art" where all kinds of signalling systems, ranging from passive elements in the environment (lights, flags, bells, horns, etc.) to more active technologies like radar and sonar systems have been invented to enable seafarers to avoid dangerous coastlines and underwater obstacles. The main function of the lighthouse is to convey its own position, which people at sea may then relate to its position in the nautical chart and estimate a safe passage. Except for every lighthouse having its unique sequence of flashes to enable identification, sometimes in relation to other visual signage (as in the case of line beacons), there is neither a message to decode nor any fluctuation as to what the lighthouse stands for. The purpose of beacons and lighthouses is to steer (away) ships and as such organize the flows of traffic at sea.

In combination with other navigational instruments like the compass, sextant and nautical chart, visual signage makes up a logistical ensemble whose historical development has gradually improved the capability of seafarers to handle spatial stakes; to assess their position in space and decide how and when to reach their ports of call. A crucial part of this development is famously described by Bruno Latour (1987) in his theory of "immutable mobiles," which is basically a logistical theory of how Western societies through explorations at sea expanded their cultural and economic horizons and gained deeper knowledge of what the rest of the world looked like. This process occurred through cycles of accumulation, where each new expedition provided further details about foreign territories through the collection of objects and logging of observations (the log book being yet another logistically biased medium). Here, cartography became the means to master, and dominate, places at a distance. Maps were the key logistical tool for "bringing home" an accurate view of foreign terrains and, in consequence, making it easier to access these far-away places again and again. Maps are thus (in their original form) an example of what Latour calls immutable mobiles, characterized by their mobility, stability and combinability. Since maps can be easily brought back and forth, providing a miniaturized view of the world that is gradually refined and combined with additional information, they provide not just a resource for safe navigation *through* space, but also a way of mastering and controlling space *at a distance* through the establishment of more predictable flows. A map's basic function as a medium of orientation (again, in combination with other logistical tools) is thus lifted to the levels of coordination and orchestration.

The important thing here is not the genealogy or cultural history of lighthouses, nautical charts and other logistical media. The important thing to consider is what they do, how they affect the human condition. While the examples from seafaring and early modern explorations may seem remote in relation to the purpose of this book, we should acknowledge two principal points. First, beyond their obvious function as wayfinding tools, logistical media make travelling more predictable and thus less adventurous. As common routes are established, marked out (in the landscape as well as in maps) and communicated among people, travelling becomes a more ordinary business. Individual expectations on what a journey might bring and "how things work" at the foreign destination get more fixed and reliable, also among those travelling a route for the first time. As such, logistical media contribute to *spatial ease*, which means that those who hold the appropriate resources can extend their scope of dwelling – that is, phenomenologically speaking, "shrink the world." While such familiarization-at-a-distance also has much to do with representational processes, not least popular premediations of space (Jansson, 2013) that foster various types of place attachments (see Chapter 4), the ability to reach a certain place and get around there smoothly contributes to a sense of spatial mastery and ease that further accelerates the process of familiarization.

This leads us to the second point, which I will also return to in Chapter 6: the fact that spatial mastery largely depends on access to and mastery of certain tools. As argued in spatial pragmatism, the ability to "do with space," that is, to manage spatial stakes in order to inhabit and thus co-construct space (Lussault & Stock, 2010: 15), is intrinsically bound up with the ability to master various *techniques*. These techniques are related not just to the body (as in the act of walking, riding a bus or setting the table) and to the environment and its various rules (walking in the right place in the street, taking the right bus, and setting the table for a dinner party rather than for breakfast) but also to the mastery of tools (see also Lucas, 2019b). This is to say that while logistical media in general contribute to a growing sense of spatial ease among people, they also turn logistical expertise into a matter of handling, and *adapting to*, various tools – which implies that one must also know which tools are relevant for handling certain spatial stakes. Logistical media, as we will see, thus cannot be uncoupled from questions of spatial dominance, even colonization. This means, in turn, that media theory provides a valid entry-point to get at the social tensions and struggles lurking under the surface of seemingly smooth logistics (whether in global trade, urban governance or cultural circulation).

Now, let us fast-forward from the era of analogue nautical navigation to our current world of locative media. In light of the historical examples, we can see how locative media advance logistical affordances. We may even think of them, as Rossiter (2015: 210) suggests, as "media of logistics" that operate *across* the levels of orientation, coordination and orchestration. The fact that locative media are "place-contingent" means that the operations they carry out, such as the type of information they circulate, depend on where the device is located *and*, as a consequence, that devices (and other networked objects) are traceable in space and time (Wilken & Goggin, 2015). These technological features are enabled by the combination of global positioning systems (GPS), digital communications networks and, in most cases, the Internet. While the applications of locative media vary, as do their cultural and ideological framings (Zeffiro, 2012) – ranging from place-contingent real-time streams of information; various mapping and coordination tools integrated in social networking platforms; and locative games such as Pokémon Go, where users interact with(in) a geographically adaptable game-world, to subversive art projects and digital software for global supply-chain management – there are certain common denominators to acknowledge in relation to the current analysis. Most essentially, we should consider that locative media are both *active* and *prescriptive*.

First, if we consider the "activeness" of locative media, it means that technology enacts some kind of relationship with the surrounding world. As Case argues in his analysis of radar systems, earlier navigational systems like war horns (a system for collecting sounds) and compasses were often "passively logistical" (Case, 2013: 386), meaning that they only *collected* information from the environment in order to enable decisions on orientation. By contrast, radar (which stands for Radio Detection and Ranging) is a system that actively *sends out* electromagnetic waves that bounce back from objects in the environment and thus enables the navigator not just to assess directions but also to visualize the distance to specific objects and thus to order and arrange them in space. Something similar can be said about locative media, even though they operate through digital networks and associated infrastructures. Due to the fact that connected devices both transmit and receive digital signals they enable flexible forms of mapping. In a conventional digital map service, such as Google Maps, smartphone users can immediately see where they are located in the geographical terrain, and monitor where they are going.

In an overview of how such locative mapping *and* navigation technologies evolved via earlier means of navigation, based for instance on radar and so-called dead reckoning (the continuous calculation of position based on speed, direction and elapsed time in relation to a spatial fix), Abend and Harvey (2017) speak of a shift from logocentric to *egocentric* navigation, referring to the fact that the individual, vehicle or vessel carrying the locative device is always automatically located *in the middle* of the cartographic representation, typically indicated as a blue dot. This also means that the frame of the map adjusts along with the movement (see also Abend, 2018). Under such conditions, as Thielmann (2007) argues, the intersection of territorial experience (e.g., following one's movement through the car window) and the reading of interactive maps (e.g., via a car-navigation system) produces what can be understood as a hybrid, "third" space through which human subjects envision their journey (see also de Souza e Silva, 2006). This mode of mediated orientation becomes even more salient as people are also invited to gather additional information about the environments they travel through, including anything from traffic situations to commercial services, based on geo-tagged data projected onto the cartographic representation of the terrain.

The digital activeness of locative media also provides the underpinning for new forms of prescription. Whereas the traditional lighthouse was prescriptive in the sense that seafarers were guided to take a certain course, it did not differentiate among its recipients. It did not matter who were on board which kinds of ships, or where they were heading. The signal was always the same. If we instead consider early car navigation systems, as discussed by Thielmann (2007), we encounter a form of prescription that did adapt to the destination as well as to where the driver was located in the terrain. However, their mode of guidance was still quite limited and awkward as they could only present rudimentary, standardized information about the road network, and as the journey continued the driver had to load new maps that were stored on cassette tapes. Contemporary locative media, by contrast, are based on GPS tracking and insert the detectable subject into a representational space where geographical positions are linked to a variety of Internet-based sources of information. Zooming in on a digital map, the user can access further information about nearby locations and instantly obtain a customized route to a particular place. In less than two decades, such interactive functions have moved from the experimental realm of tech-laboratories and art projects to become rudimentary affordances of our media environment (see, e.g., Zeffiro, 2012). What is particularly important to consider is that the combination of location-awareness and datafication sustains prescriptive processes that are customized not just to location but also to the individual's digital *profile* (Bernard, 2019), based on past activities (browsing history, online transactions, geo-tagging, and so forth). As Pablo Abend (2018: 104) argues, "the egocentricity that prescribes the experience for the end user is used for commercial interests here and geomedia becomes part of much broader efforts to control and steer the 'dwelling in the web' (Thielmann et al., 2012)." As such, contemporary locative media sustain modes of prescription that reach beyond the strictly geographical aspects of navigation (the map and the terrain). They also provide continuous geo-social guidance regarding *emplacement*, that is, *where (and when) to go* in the first place.

Under the regime of geomedia, I argue, logistical media have not just evolved technologically due to locative media; they have also taken on a cultural form that I will call *locative guidance*. The term indicates that guidance has become locative and that locative media are *at the same time place-contingent and place-prescriptive*, obeying the connective logics of the platform economy (as discussed in previous chapters). This is also where we get to the core of the logistical struggles saturating geomediatized societies.

On the one hand, locative guidance implies that a sense of spatial ease is closer at hand than ever before. Anyone with a connected smartphone and relevant skills can search for and decide on suitable places to go, also in foreign terrains, and eventually get there in the most suitable way, and even grow a sense of local familiarity (Jansson, 2019). It has also become easier to pursue certain forms of social coordination since appointments do not necessarily have to be scheduled in advance but can be managed "on the fly," as a form of ongoing "micro-coordination," for example via location-exposing social networking platforms (Saker & Frith, 2018). As Judy Wajcman (2019a, 2019b) shows in her analyses of the design of digital calendars and scheduling applications, the vision behind such logistical tools – linked to what she calls the *organizational gaze* – prescribes perfected guidance that eliminates the very act of scheduling and instead automatically *steers* people to the right places at the right time.

Then, on the other hand, this means that the logistical *and* commercial logics behind locative guidance push the very meaning of guidance to its limits. As a case in point, Calvignac and Smolinski (2020) found in an experimental study of sightseeing walking-tours that tourists equipped with a locative guidance application kept their movements closer to the recommended itinerary and were less keen on following impulses based on things that caught their attention along the way than those using an analogue guide only. Thus, in this study, people's gaining of spatial ease also implied more conformist ways of appropriating space. In society at large, this tendency is often reinforced by commercial imperatives. In order to provide automated guidance (regardless of which realm of activity we look at), people's activities must be tracked (via digital data streams), amalgamated, computed and eventually *engineered* to benefit the stakeholders investing in the systems (especially through advertising). From this perspective, locative guidance is a *means* as much as *symptom* of logistical accumulation. It enables techno-capitalist industries to improve their capacity to orchestrate and "control the mobility of labour, data, and commodities as they traverse urban, rural, atmospheric, and oceanic spaces and traffic through the circuits of databases, mobile devices, and algorithmic architectures" (Rossiter, 2015: 211). It feeds the burgeoning platform economy and brings it closer to the logistical utopia of frictionless, enclosed flows of people, goods and information. With logistical accumulation, the distinction between guiding and steering dissolves.

Locative guidance provides an archetypal illustration of the Janus face of geomedia. As stated previously in this book, I would refrain from stipulating any unitary social consequences of this new regime. There is rather a need to look closer, empirically as well as theoretically, at how logistical tensions and struggles unfold and are experienced by human beings under *different* conditions and in *particular* contexts. As I will discuss in the following two sections, there are reasons to assess both how locative guidance is part of building more flexible, or lively, urban landscapes where the sense of spatial ease – pertaining to orientation, coordination and orchestration – grows stronger by the day among those holding the right skills, tools and other resources, *and* how there is also a logistical underside to this development, such as invisible forms of exploitation where continuously growing amounts of labour go into the maintenance and lubrication of those (primarily urban) infrastructures that enable locative guidance. Roughly formulated, any platform or system that provides empowering guidance to some groups will have a detaining impact on the lives of others. As I will return to in Chapter 6, such forms of domination may well bear the seeds of more active forms of political resistance among those who feel that their lives are steered rather than guided and that they are excluded from the geomediatized landscapes that now emerge.

LOGISTICAL ACCUMULATION AS LANDSCAPING

I have thus far argued that locative guidance emerges as the dominant articulation of logistical media, that is, the *cultural form* such affordances take today. This points to a development that is not just technological. The normalization of locative guidance does not only mean that there are now more advanced functions available to those who want to further their skills, or expertise, when it comes to handling various mobilities and streams. It also means that there are certain normalized *expectations* in society as to what such technologies are good for and to whom, that is, what moral and ideological meanings they carry in relation to culture at large (cf. Nagy & Neff, 2015; Bengtsson, 2012). If television emerged as a medium that accelerated and normalized what Raymond Williams (1974) famously termed "mobile privatization," then what are the corresponding social and spatial transformations characterizing our era of locative guidance? If television (just to reiterate Williams' example) was part of a social formation that prescribed a new way of viewing and engaging with the public world at-a-distance, notably from one's private (suburban middle-class) living room, then in what sort of social formation is locative guidance embedded? To get at these critical questions, in this section, I will advance the notion of *guidance landscape* as a way of illuminating how logistical media are increasingly lifted out of their traditional position as "invisible" infrastructure to become part of the explicit and expansive spatial (urban) vision of the platform economy and thus imbued with *ideological meanings that legitimate the logic of logistical accumulation*. To concretize the argument, I will consider concrete examples pertaining to the realms of alternative tourism and urban mobility services.

Let us first clarify the important distinction between environment and landscape. Thus far, the discussions of this book have mainly concerned the former concept. I have argued that geomedia is to be understood as an environmental regime that sets new standards as to how human beings relate to the surrounding world. Geomedia implies that media technologies are increasingly enmeshed with the environment, as well as with the human body, which leads to a situation where experiences of dwelling *in* and dwelling *with* media collapse into one another. The logistical bias of geomedia, the fact that digitalization accentuates the infrastructural nature of all media, further contributes to this condition (Peters, 2015). As outlined above, locative guidance turns dwelling into a mode of "doing with space" (Lussault & Stock, 2010) where even foreign environments are increasingly manageable (albeit not equally among all people), yet potentially alienating as individuals are also *steered* through space and *entangled* with the very systems that underpin guidance. If the environment is a structure of directly perceived functions and affordances, something that humans experience "on foot" as the context of dwelling, then the landscape is how the environment *appears* when viewed at a distance, as the meaningful articulation of a *social formation* (Cosgrove, 1984). If we want to understand how geomedia shapes spatial inclusion and exclusion, why certain groups feel attracted and invited to the emergent terrains of the platform economy, and others do not, we should shift our perspective from the world of spatial pragmatics (environment) to the world of cultural meaning (landscape).

Much has been written about landscapes and yet there is no fixed definition of the term. One reason to this, it seems, is that the concept holds more of a sensitizing function (cf. Blumer, 1954) than fulfils the criteria for explanatory research. The geographical discourse around landscape that emerged out of Carl Sauer's classical work, especially *The Morphology of Landscape* from 1925 (see Sauer, 1963), and became known as the Berkeley School of American cultural geography, has always been controversial, even rejected by geographers advancing more positivistic approaches to the study of spatial constructs. Sauer and his followers, notably David Lowenthal, refrained from seeing the landscape merely as a material matter to be measured and categorized and instead actualized how meanings and conceptions of space were contextually shaped and thus varied between historical periods and different groups (including geographers). As such, their concern with morphology was a concern with form and *shape*, as in the German word land*schaft*, and how such spatial forms evolve in relation to human understanding and cultural expressions. As Kenneth Olwig (2003: 872) states in an overview of the Lowenthal legacy, their work on landscape advocates a phenomenological, explicitly anthropocentric epistemology that transcends the boundaries between geography and social anthropology, ultimately advocating a "larger science" of the human condition. In one of his essays, Lowenthal (1961: 260) emphasizes that we are all, as human beings, engaged in geographical thought and as such continuously involved in the shaping of our world as place: "The surface of the earth is shaped for each person by refraction through cultural and personal lenses of custom and fancy. We are all artists and landscape architects, creating order and organizing space, time, and causality in accordance with our appreciations and predilections." Here, landscape attains an intermediary, cultural function as a spatial structure that consolidates "the relation between the world outside and the pictures in our heads" (ibid: 241) – a formulation that Lowenthal borrowed from Walter Lippmann's (1922/1961) famous book *Public Opinion*.

The notion of landscape that guides our current analysis owes much to this tradition of thought. However, in contrast to the original humanistic perspective, we should pay more attention to the material and ideological forces at play in society, in our case related to logistical accumulation and the platform economy, which invoke certain dominant ways of constructing and seeing the landscape. As such, while the landscape is culturally volatile and contextual it is also biased. As individuals, we are not as free to make up our own view of the world as the writings of Lowenthal might lead us to think, but are socialized into certain *ways of seeing* the landscape (cf. Berger, 1972) as well as certain *ways of feeling* about what we see. This is why the landscape is not just "pictures in our heads" but also a social formation shaped by the dominant mode of production in society, as Denis Cosgrove (1984: 39–65) argues. As so conceived, landscap*ing* is an ongoing process of cultural production, determined not mainly by those who dwell in and labour upon the land, but more decisively (especially under capitalism) by those who are able to appropriate, control and exploit the land (and those who labour upon it) for the sake of economic gain (ibid: 64). These dominant class fractions also have a normative influence, mediated through aesthetic devices like taste and style, on how landscapes are envisioned and represented in society – as something to admire, long for, or escape into (or from). In this sense, the landscape is a means of possessing and exercising control over space and how it should evolve. For researchers, it is an entry point to analysing not just aesthetic ideals but also how social power is exercised.

To be theoretically precise, I conceive of landscape as mediating along two dimensions. First, landscapes stand in-between representations (including "the pictures in our heads") and the "real" material landscape. This means that landscapes should neither be reduced to cultural images, texts and sign systems, as theorized especially by post-structural thinkers (see, e.g., Duncan, 1990: 11–25), nor understood merely as the outcome of dwelling, something that humans continuously produce and become part of, as argued by Ingold (1993). In the words of Kenneth Olwig (2008: 81), while the first version "constructs a feeling of possession and staged performance in a hierarchical social space," the second "engenders a sense of belonging" and a "place of dwelling and doing in the body politic of a community." While it is indeed possible to use the word "landscape" to describe both pictorial sceneries and the actually evolving shape of the land, I agree with Olwig that it is more useful to locate landscape in the middle, and as *the outcome of some kind of communication*. The material formation that evolves through dwelling and labour (see also Szerszynski, 2003) is not a landscape until it has been interpreted, reified and viewed at a distance. Conversely, the landscape-as-representation, such as a painting or a postcard, is not just a representation of space but just as much the exposure of certain shared ideals, values and gazes (Olwig, 2005). As such, the landscape is a way of both *staging* and *concealing* (typically, forms of oppression and labour). The landscape is a *political* landscape, as Olwig (2005: 36) suggests; "an objectification of human thoughts and feelings" and thus a realm of negotiation and struggle, of alienation as well as empowerment.

This brings us to the second axis of mediation, which concerns the political nature of landscapes under capitalist conditions. Here, as Sharon Zukin (1991) argues in her work on urban transformations in post-industrial societies, we should conceive of landscape as mediating between *market* and *place*. This is to highlight the tensions between dominant spatial forms imposed by market forces to sustain extended circulation and extraction of economic capital and more vernacular (less panoramic) views of society, originating from labouring life forms. Zukin's perspective, which traces the main 20th-century transformations of urban form and imagery to the shift from a Fordist industrial society (Detroit) to a post-Fordist society of themed consumption (Disney World), is thus akin to Cosgrove's (1984) notion of the landscape as a social formation. In maintaining that landscapes entail the "architecture of social class, gender, and race relations" (Zukin, 1991: 16) and thus exaggerate certain phenomena while concealing others (echoing dominant interests), it can best be described as a version of cultural materialism (see Williams, 1980). As Zukin (1991: 17) depicts the evocative landscape of post-industrial places like Vancouver and Silicon Valley: "Its image of ecology, leisure, and 'liveability' feeds off the consumption preferences of professionals in a service economy, even though those preferences conceal an underbelly of business and personal strain, female minority workers jammed into assembly jobs, and mounting suburban blight." A key point here is that landscapes by means of their cultural, communicative nature attain a moral significance in that they not only reflect or articulate the interests of dominant groups but also *prescribe* certain forms of desire, notably in terms of consumerism, and thus tend to forecast and contribute to major shifts in social formations. In this way, Zukin (1991: 260) argues, landscapes operate as cultural capital that can also be exchanged into real economic value, as seen for example in processes of gentrification and the reconfiguration of formerly industrial settings.

This is where we should consider the meaning of "guidance landscape." I take this term to signify two interconnected aspects of the emerging landscape(s) of the platform economy. First, it refers to a landscape that articulates the social formation and main direction of a society where locative guidance has become the norm, that is, materialized as cultural form. Second, "guidance landscape" highlights the theoretical understanding of landscape per se as a structure of moral and aesthetic orientation, that is, guidance. The fact that landscapes evolve through objectifying communication implies that they incorporate and convey the dominant ideas, thoughts and feelings that circulate in a culture and as such become socially prescriptive; enticing to some, alienating to others (Olwig, 2005). This means that it is possible for us, as scholars, to grasp contemporary guidance landscapes as social formations *through* their representations (while these representations per se are not to be understood as landscapes). In effect, following the cultural materialist approach, we shall conceive of logistical accumulation not just as a logic of the economy, but also as a logic of culture that sets the scaffolding as to which types of landscapes are desirable, even thinkable, today. One of the key functions of contemporary guidance landscapes is *to steer people towards those skills, norms and modes of spatial and technological appropriation that legitimize and prolong logistical accumulation.*

If Detroit signified the industrial landscape and Disney World epitomized the coming of a post-industrial, semiotic landscape, then, in the current analysis, we want to concretize the appearance of the guidance landscape. In the following section, I will study a couple of symptomatic representations taken from the businesses of *alternative tourism platforms* and *mobility as a service*. My ambition is to demonstrate how the landscapes envisioned in these branches of the platform economy normalize certain ways of appropriating space and managing different forms of logistics. My argument is that guidance landscapes legitimize the apparatuses of logistical accumulation through promoting platform urbanism as a distinctive and desirable form of dwelling. Platform urbanism, in turn, is made up of a triadic relationship between *logistical guidance*, *spatial ease* and *hospitable spaces* (Figure 5.1).

Here, the discursive accentuation of hospitality stands out as a key to the intermediary, cultural *and* economic significance of guidance landscapes. The fact that locative guidance not only supports people in their endeavours to get around and coordinate their activities in the geographical terrain but also systematically prescribes certain routes into the social realm, as discussed earlier, means that it necessitates (and benefits from) environments that stand for openness, warmth and other hospitality-related values. If people are to be guided, or steered, in their day-to-day activities there must be places around them that have something attractive on offer. This, in turn, means that locative guidance adds to the competition between different hospitable spaces – what could be seen as yet another form of logistical struggle – and normalizes certain forms of hospitality. As we will see, there are social biases as to *whose*

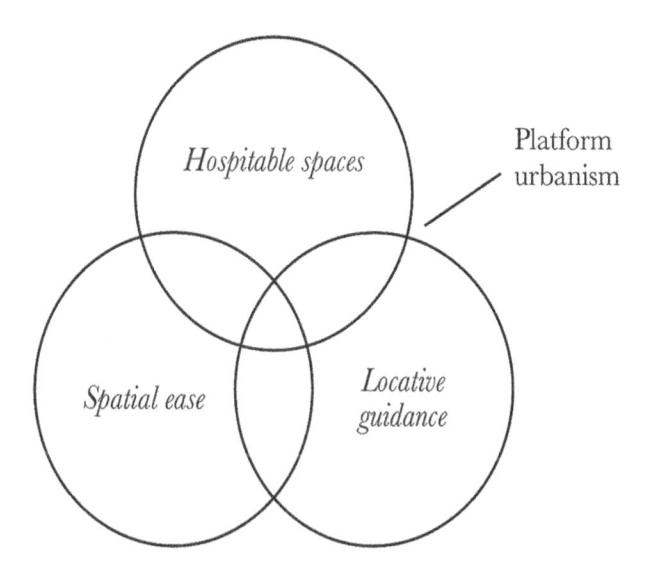

Guidance landscape

Figure 5.1 The relationship between guidance landscape and logistical accumulation

[Venn diagram with three overlapping circles labeled "Hospitable spaces", "Spatial ease", and "Locative guidance". An arrow points to the overlap labeled "Platform urbanism". Below the diagram: "Logistical accumulation"]

interests and desires these hospitable spaces actualize and who benefits from locative guidance in building a sense of spatial ease.

ENTER THE GUIDANCE LANDSCAPE

Landscape's intermediary nature provides it with a dual analytical potential. When we study landscape (understood in the above sense), we are concerned with the relationship between developments in the "real" material world and how certain formative groups in society *see* the world, that is, a particular kind of *gaze*. There is thus a chance that our current analysis of "guidance landscapes" can tell us something about the socio-material consequences of logistical accumulation *and* the dominant perceptions of urban life that flourish among those with the highest stakes in the platform economy. Therefore, in this final section of the chapter, I will discuss two specific articulations of the guidance landscape to illuminate the cultural and economic forces that shape the human condition under geomedia. Both cases are related to the platform economy. The first case is linked to our discussions on transmedia travel (see Chapter 4) and concerns the appearance of *alternative tourism platforms*, that is, platforms aimed at tourists who prefer to see themselves as different from "ordinary tourists" and search for places and activities off the beaten track. Here, I look at a particular mobile application called *Spotted by Locals*, which provides interactive guides to "hidden" spots in major cities around the world. The second case concerns *mobility as a service*, where I unpack the promotional videos of Voi e-scooter networks and Lynk & Co cars and car sharing platform to reconstruct the landscape envisioned and produced by these actors.

What the cases share, besides their anchoring in the platform economy, is that they depict a particular type of city and a particular type of urbanism. They depict a landscape where new platforms disable most logistical hassles and produce ways of dwelling in the city that are marked by hospitality and spatial ease – thus adding to a positive and welcoming image of the city. While the businesses of *Spotted by Locals* and Voi are concretely linked to urban spaces and infrastructures, Lynk & Co would not necessarily be so – it is a solution for connected automobility regardless of place. Yet, as we will see, the promotional discourse of Lynk & Co is decisively urban in nature. While I have deliberately chosen examples that can tell us something about urban transformations, this is not a coincidental bias. As Sadowski (2020b: 450) points out, the platform economy is an urban phenomenon due to the benefits such an economy gains from "the population density and spatial proximity of users/workers in cities." Thus, the distinction between "platform economy" and "platform urbanism" is open-ended; just like the platform economy is dependent on and drawn to the creative dynamics and resources (notably labour and consumption) of larger cities, that is, "urbanism," cities are responding to and reshaped by the platform economy (in particular what I term logistical accumulation). As Sadowski continues, "as platforms become fixed in place, so too, do citizens and governments begin to rely on them as fixes for the deficiencies and inefficiencies of cities," which ultimately means that platforms are "remaking cities in their own image" (ibid: 450). As suggested by Figure 5.1, this is exactly where the analysis of landscape comes into the picture.

Before turning to the cases, it should also be noted that the platform economy and platform urbanism are not to be mixed up with the "smart city." The notion of "smart city" is typically used as a descriptor, sometimes an imaginary (Sadowski & Bendor, 2019), of technological development programmes initiated by governments to provide more efficient services and secure public spaces to citizens and to manage infrastructures related to, for example, telecommunications, traffic, and the supply of energy and water. When a system is "smart" it means that it is based on the incorporation of sensors and other means of data collation into the urban fabric that can help public institutions and corporations to calibrate and optimize their operations, not least in terms of logistics. While platform urbanism also revolves around "smart" technologies, the core issue here is not urban governance but the extraction of value from various consumer services linked to urban life (see, e.g., Barns, 2020; Richardson, 2020a, 2020b; Sadowski, 2020b; Rose et al., 2021). This includes mundane things like working, commuting, exercising, dating, eating, drinking, in short, urban practices of dwelling. What the platform economy does, especially, is to turn unused resources – like a spare bedroom, a half-empty car, a toolbox or non-used office space – into productive assets, things that consumers can get access to via rent or subscription (see, e.g., Richardson, 2015; Sadowski, 2020a). It also creates entirely new infrastructures for daily interactions – ranging from casual dating services and social media to food delivery, co-working spaces and e-scooter services – and turns some people into urban micro-entrepreneurs, for example, as they start making extra profit on keeping rooms or apartments for rent via Airbnb or sharing their car via an app (for an overview, see Barns, 2020). As such, the platform economy adds to the *density* of urban life forms, filling out empty pockets and adding new layers of on- as well as offline interaction.

Furthermore, as Stabrowski shows in a study of Airbnb hosts in New York City, platform urbanism tends to spur and legitimize logistical accumulation – here, the production of "calculable individuals (hosts and guests), users with traceable and verifiable track records – or 'reputations'" (Stabrowski, 2017: 332) – by means of discursive regimes that emphasize things like community, empowerment and sustainability, or, more generally, *hospitality*. These efforts are formulated *in opposition* to long-established urban institutions as well as alienating forces of large-scale capitalism. The logistical labour of Airbnb hosts, "to remain continuously engaged in turning over their units as frequently (and as frictionlessly) as possible" (ibid: 333), goes hand in hand with promotional efforts that bespeaks flexible entrepreneurship and a certain kind of civic community akin to pre-industrial *Gemeinschaft* (ibid: 339) (see also Richardson, 2015).

As the guidance landscape now enters the stage (or, rather, as we enter into it), we can take notice of a similar condition: *platform urbanism in general, and locative guidance in particular, are promoted as saviours from the drawbacks of industrial society*, whether we speak of over-tourism, traffic jams or a general sense of cultural and social conformism. This image of progressiveness that guidance landscapes evoke (true or not) communicates with certain class fractions rather than others, just like platforms and technologies provide affordances that are meaningful, or even discernible, just to some people – preferably those with the same worldview as tech-designers themselves (Wajcman, 2019a). Similarly, guidance landscapes tend to *conceal* the logistical underside of platform urbanism, notably certain forms of paid and unpaid labour, as well as certain bodies and identities (cf. Rose et al., 2021). A good example is the riders delivering meals ordered via platforms like Deliveroo. As Lizzie Richardson shows in an analysis of the "flexible arrangement of the delivered meal," the convenience experienced by the customers of this service is predicated on the "coercive flexibility" (Richardson, 2020a: 628) of riders. These individuals have to "make themselves available to work" (ibid: 629), that is, freeing up time and a suitable means of transportation. However, when available, they cannot be certain that there will actually be any work, or what they will earn. This emphasizes how the guidance landscape, in its capacity of mediator, operates as a logistical, even biopolitical machinery that steers (attracts or repels) different forms of capital and different bodies in different directions.

Alternative Tourism Platforms

As we saw in Chapter 4, geomedia accentuates processes of geo-social de-differentiation. This stems especially from the open-ended mode of cultural circulation sustained by transmedia platforms. The boundaries of tourism and non-tourism activities are blurred and the managing of tourism-related information streams (broadly conceived) turns into everyday logistical labour. At the same time, and largely as a *response* to de-differentiation, many new, "alternative" tourism platforms are introduced – platforms targeting travellers interested in places beyond the radar of mainstream tourism. There are today numerous mobile applications and online communities providing guidance combined with services like accommodation and guided tours for those craving "other" forms of leisure travel; "discovering hidden wonders around the world" (*atlasobscura.com*), or "rediscovering your city" (*untappedcities.com*). They share a certain motto: "Don't be a tourist" (*messynessychic.com*).

The "alternativeness" of these media stems from their self-proclaimed ambition to deliver something else than mainstream tourism experiences. In functional terms, they provide locative guidance related to three areas of activity: (1) getting in touch with locals and other travellers; (2) finding accommodation, transportation, guided tours and other services; (3) sharing experiences and recommendations of places and events to visit (including photos and images). However, as we will see, the significance of alternative tourism platforms reaches beyond tourism practices per se. As they respond to the interests of reflexive middle-class travellers and reinforce a sense of spatial ease, they also play into the (trans)formation of urban landscapes. When self-reflexive tourists start exploring, documenting and sharing information about "alternative" places online, as shown for example in studies of urban explorers and ruin tourists (Klausen, 2017; Jansson & Klausen, 2018), they also reinforce the process whereby these places are turned into sites of aestheticization, exploitation and, ultimately, gentrification. As such, the de-differentiating tendencies we discussed in Chapter 4 do not pertain to more structural issues related to socio-economic stratification.

The underlying social mechanisms are not new. As long as tourism has been considered a mass phenomenon in affluent societies, upper- and middle-class consumers have been spurred to seek out more specialized, or "alternative," forms of travel in order to uphold distinctions in relation to the "golden hordes" (see, e.g., Feifer, 1985; Lash & Urry, 1994; Munt, 1994). Visiting "genuine" neighbourhoods and places off the beaten track, ranging from local food markets to abandoned industries, is a way for such travellers to escape the "tourism bubble" and keep up a sense of autonomy (see, e.g., Molz, 2012, 2013; Jansson, 2018a, 2018b). Similarly, as previous research shows, "alternative" or "transformational" forms of tourism accompany early stages of urban renewal as they play into the general imperatives of urban destination culture (see, e.g., Zukin, 2010; Tegtmeyer, 2016; Polson, forthcoming). Locative guidance, I argue, is an increasingly important ingredient in this development as it steers travellers to, and through, certain physical and social environments rather than others (see, e.g., Boy & Uitermark, 2017; Frith, 2017; Zukin et al., 2017). It thus also normalizes a particular type of landscape.

To concretize this, we shall look closer at an alternative tourism app called *Spotted by Locals*, which invites its users (on the welcoming screen) to "Experience 70+ cities like a local."[1] Those who buy the full version of the app get access to numerous travel guides and recommendations pertaining to "no tourist highlights" presented "by handpicked locals only" in capitals and other big cities around the world. At the same time, users (locals or not) are encouraged to participate through sharing their own spots. The guides and recommendations can be accessed through virtual entrances to each city, symbolized by "Instagramified" images (quadratic shape and a filter that accentuates contrasts and colours). These images normalize a particular, aestheticized way of looking at urban places. The fact that guides are made available offline (which is one of the selling points) suggests an adventurous mode of travelling and implicates that some users might go off the beaten track to places where Wi-Fi connections are scarce and mobile coverage is unstable. Practically, however, this seems to be relatively unlikely given the type of urban places put on display. They are mostly tied to urban lifestyles with an inclination towards cultural consumption and the sharing economy. Typical highlights include restaurants with "great vegetarian and vegan options," sometimes located in transformed buildings like old hospitals and factories; bars characterized by a "bohemian atmosphere," frequented by "artists and philosophers;" cultural venues like "street art urban galleries" saturated with "creative anarchy;" micro-breweries, pop-up stores and various places of "urban farming" and "vertical farming." There is also an accent on multi-culturalism and a strong focus on "pure" cosmopolitan encounters in local settings, such as "real Asian and Vietnamese stuff and food," as well as a mythologization of certain historical periods. For instance, certain venues in Berlin are presented as "survivors of early post-Wall years, reflecting the spirit of that time period."

This example exposes a very particular urban landscape. Its nature becomes clearer if we study how the app constructs the linkages between locative guidance, on the one hand, and hospitable spaces and spatial ease, on the other. Beginning with hospitable spaces, the question that should be asked is; who are invited to appropriate which kinds of places, in what ways – and who are excluded? The anticipated users of the app, and thus the "preferred tourists," are obviously looking for previously non-exploited sites and distinctive activities that are still not too expensive. Such travellers are likely to be younger and positioned in the cultural rather than the economic parts of social space (Bourdieu, 1979/1984). It is a group of travellers drawn to the *local*, understood as something genuine and close to the everyday life of "ordinary people," rather than to spectacular or exclusive environments. At the same time, "the local," as represented in *Spotted by Locals*, seems to be already moving away from vernacular culture and the more or less "vulgar" tastes of the working classes. While elements of "grittiness" are typical to early gentrification processes (Polson, forthcoming), they must be semiotically "sanitized" to fit the hospitality discourse of platform urbanism. The promoted taste pattern thus resonates with the kind of "adventurous" dwellers, especially artists, cultural workers, students and certain academics, that persistently and over several decades have pioneered gentrification processes before real estate prices have escalated (Clay, 1979; Zukin, 1991, 2010; Caulfield, 1994; Ley, 1996). Part and parcel of early gentrification is an *aestheticization* of urban places resonating with the norms and values of the cultural fractions of the middle classes (Ley, 2003). Paradoxically, however, the emancipatory and egalitarian ideals of these groups translate into ways of consuming the city – vegan and vegetarian food, pop-up stores and "creative anarchy," as stressed by the current example – that turn into means of exclusion vis-à-vis the more rooted population (Zukin, 2008). As such, alternative tourism apps are a good example of how media and tourism contribute to what MacCannell (1973) famously described as "staged authenticity," and what Relph (1976) around the same time called "other-directed places," where places are shaped to fit certain types of external gazes.

Turning to spatial ease, two questions should be asked. How does locative guidance affect the mastery of cultural and material geographies among different groups in the city? Which groups have access to particular technologies and platforms and can make use of them in a beneficial way? Again, it is obvious that locative guidance (and geomediatization at large) leads to a division between advantaged and disadvantaged groups. The acquisition of new locative media turns some travellers into logistical experts and spatial connoisseurs, and contributes to their sense of belonging in foreign places. While this is not to say that visitors to a city are actually able to grasp the deeper layers of social life, the increased spatial and cultural ease with which they can find their way to "hidden" places and coordinate events "in their taste" adds to already privileged forms of mobility (Polson, 2016a). Similar to what Latour (1987) argued in his work on immutable mobiles, locative guidance becomes a way of *dominating space* at a distance, which in turn provokes the classical question of who has "the right to the city" (Lefebvre, 1968/1993). While alternative tourism apps underpin local platform economies as well as cosmopolitan encounters, for instance through guided tours, accommodation services and private dinner arrangements, they also play into the power balance between "locals" and "cosmopolitans" (Hannerz, 1990). Urban landscapes are gradually adapted to, and shaped by, the latter group and their desires, including the provision and promotion of digital infrastructures that reinforce mobile lifestyles. While Internet access is an increasingly normalized public service there are still occasional needs among tourists, especially in technologically less advanced regions, to find "Wi-Fi hotspots," "Internet cafés" and other amenities to make full use of mobile applications. As Polson (2016a, 2016b) shows in a study of international female travellers to Bangalore, India, the functionality of mobile technology is indispensable not only for geographical mastery but also for achieving a sense of safety when moving outside the comfort zones of mainstream tourism.

Spotted by Locals is just one of numerous apps that speak to a crowd of tourists that refuse to see themselves as tourists; whose journeys are envisioned as independent from the tourism industry and whose destinations should be (at least seemingly) untouched by staging efforts (cf. MacCannell, 1973, 1976). Other examples include *NuFlit*, *WithLocals* and *Vayable*, as well as apps dedicated to particular cities, for example *GoingLocal Berlin*. These apps represent an expansive entrepreneurial sector at the intersection of platform tourism and platform urbanism and can be described as distinctive media accessories for reflexive middle-class travellers. They allow these groups to handle spatial stakes more conveniently and sometimes at a distance, especially related to *emplacement*, and thus reduce the logistical frictions of travelling. At the same time, as these groups reach the "right" types of places, people and experiences in predictable ways, they also produce a new type of "tourism bubble" (Molz, 2013).

Therefore, what are the social implications of the landscape engendered by alternative tourism apps? How do these platforms affect what people expect from the city and how they manage their "doings" with urban space? This question remains largely out of reach as long as we do not consider the inside experiences of city dwellers, tourists and various service providers and workers. Yet, given the above points regarding the aesthetic and material adaptation of cities to the platform economy (e.g., Sadowski, 2020b), we can conclude that platforms like the one discussed here normalize the habitus and gaze of culturally oriented middle-class fractions. As alternative tourists look for the "authentic" and the "hidden," they are also part of (re)producing certain middle-class/elite scripts for urban transformation (see, e.g., Centner, 2008; Elwood, 2021). We can also see this in the commercial mythologization of the media-driven sharing economy and upgraded versions of the "creative city" (see, e.g., Pratt, 2011; Richardson, 2015). Cultural capital plays into the recoding of urban places and neighbourhoods that, in turn, become increasingly attractive to investors. Locative guidance contributes to this process in bringing together people with similar interests and complementary spatial demands, including tourists *and* local hosts and service providers. Similar mechanisms for social and spatial clustering have been identified in analyses of how platforms like Instagram and various customer rating apps (related to restaurants, accommodation, etc.) contribute to the stratification and segmentation of city spaces based on cultural preferences (Boy & Uitermark, 2017; Zukin et al., 2017; Polson, forthcoming). In this way, what I call guidance landscapes articulate and reproduce the interests of reflexive middle-class travellers, gentrifiers and various spatial entrepreneurs, including those who buy apartments for speculative purposes and for setting up Airbnb businesses as a way of appropriating authentic sites for enriching their habitus (cf. Bosma & van Doorn, forthcoming). While guidance landscapes promote a certain kind of *de*-differentiation – the amalgamation of subject positions and "gazes" among various stakeholders – they also instigate *re*-differentiation in terms of spatial and socio-economic ordering. Behind all this, as we will discuss next, operate the hidden landlords of the platform economy.

Mobility as a Service

In an article about the most recent extensions of the platform economy, Sadowski argues that platforms can be compared to landlords. What platforms have in common with landlords is that they function as a form of *rentiers* and thus "possess similar positions of mediation, powers of access, purposes of extraction" (Sadowski, 2020a: 565). For most types of platforms, the key element of their business model is that they gather some kind of fee, or rent, for providing their users with *frictionless, digital access* to a particular service, such as streaming content, social networks, accommodation, transportation, and cloud-based storage solutions. The underlying logic, which is also applicable to landed property, is to turn things (including places and activities) that are not in themselves a source of value creation into a financial asset. This is what Uber has done in the realm of mobility, Airbnb in the realm of accommodation, and WeWork in the realm of work space – just to mention a few well-known examples. As these platform companies offer "X-as-a-service" premised on the appropriation of a particular mobile app (as well as added services like mobile payment solutions, etc.), rather than selling the customer a product through a single transaction, they tie people closer to the platform economy and can accentuate their trading in digital data (see, e.g., Couldry & Mejias, 2019b). As such, these increasingly ubiquitous, interconnected but largely hidden landlords of the platform economy orchestrate and extract capital from a steadily growing area of human activities-as-data:

> Don't think of the platform as the landlord who owns a rental home. Think of it as the owner of a shopping mall who invests in property in order to facilitate productive activity. For every good and service exchanged in the shops. For every social interaction between people meeting at the mall. For every person who just browses and walks around. The mall's owner takes their cut of the value generated. (Sadowski, 2020a: 568–569)

A much-debated and mythologized part of this overall development is the transformation of mobility into a service. Instead of owning bikes and cars, people should rent or subscribe to them via mobile apps – what is more generally described as "sharing." It is a business that bespeaks sustainability and more hospitable cities, and explicitly strives to decrease the volumes of car traffic and the number of non-used vehicles. In effect, the argument goes, this will lubricate mobility and logistics for the individual city dweller. The question of whether these services actually improve environmental sustainability, and if so, on what terms, has been widely discussed and it is not my purpose here to assess the validity of such statements. The purpose is to unveil what kind of urban landscape is envisioned from the business perspective. Therefore, I have chosen to analyse commercial videos from two influential actors within this expanding sector, both of them based in Sweden: the e-scooter network Voi, and the car manufacturer and sharing platform Lynk & Co.

Voi are a Stockholm-based company that have received large amounts of venture capital to set up e-scooter networks around Europe. While Voi began their services in Stockholm in 2018 their e-scooters are now, as of September 2021, available in 68 European cities. As a user, you download an app that enables you to search for an available e-scooter, which you may then use within the limits of the Voi zone by scanning a barcode. On their webpage, Voi states that they are "Helping cities reach their climate target" and that their service has been climate neutral since January 2020. The company addresses *both* individual users and cities, trying to attract the latter to *collaborate* in partnerships to create "Cities made for living":

> We are passionate about shaping cities for people, reducing pollution and breaking traffic gridlock across Europe. Our mission is to provide sustainable and inclusive last-mile mobility solutions, enabling people to move freely while at the same time helping cities reach their 2030 climate goals.[2]

Turning to Lynk & Co, we encounter a slightly different take on mobility as a service. This is a Chinese-Swedish company, owned by the Chinese Geely Holding Corporation, which also produces Geely and Volvo cars. The first Lynk & Co car model, sharing a platform with Volvo, was introduced in 2016 in China. Today, there are several models, international distribution, and, most significantly, a new type of sharing platform targeting "young professionals." It means that you can either subscribe to the car for a monthly fee and share it with other members via a mobile app, thus regaining some of your fee, or download the app and become a member who can rent a car from those who have a private subscription and are willing to share their car. As the company states on their webpage: "This is the streaming platform of mobility: a month-to-month membership that gives you a car and which you can cancel any time."[3] In addition to these options, it is also possible to order and buy a car via the Internet. Emanating from the car industry, the sector most often pinpointed as *the* problem when it comes to building sustainable cities, Lynk & Co still maintain that "We're on a mission to change mobility forever." The company states that they want to compensate for the fact that cars are used only 4 percent of the time. They see themselves as part of "a movement" and offer their members access to specially designed clubs at central locations (so far only in Amsterdam and Gothenburg).

Let us now look at the films, which are automatically screened as loops when visiting the companies' websites.[4] The Voi film, a 27-second loop with 17 short clips, addresses cities. It follows a young, black woman dressed in street fashion (jeans jacket, black skirt and white sneakers), as she navigates the city using a signal red Voi e-scooter. Throughout the film, Voi's central message is stated across the screen: "Dear city, Let us introduce you to a world made for people – with less pollution and traffic jams." As viewers, we follow the woman during a sunny autumn afternoon, from the peaceful moment when she is eating an ice-cream (as red as the e-scooter) in front of a grey concrete wall to the time at dusk when she is doing yoga and playing with her dog in a park. In-between these moments, she is in transit. She passes over a bridge using the bicycle lanes. The camera shifts from her smiling face to a panoramic view of her moving silhouette passing over the bridge with a huge railway depot in the background. In this scene, it is possible to identify the city as Berlin with key landmarks like the TV tower on Alexanderplatz looming in the periphery. The advert communicates a period of tranquility and inner harmony, perhaps symbolizing the time *after work*. The red e-scooter is present in most sequences, sometimes in motion, including close-ups of the wheels spinning on the asphalt, sometimes placed beside the woman as an accessory or a companion. The same thing goes for the black helmet with the company's logo printed on it. Mobility seems effortless, light and fun. Very little road traffic is visible; just a few cars can be glimpsed in the background in two of the scenes. Likewise, besides the connected vehicle, there is no sight of digital technology. The film depicts time-spaces of *disconnection* and presence in the "here and now." The fact that the central character is a young woman, and a woman of colour, who occupies urban space in this seemingly effortless way also mobilizes a sense of safety, security and capability attainable to all inhabitants of the city.

The promotional video for Lynk & Co is intended to present the car, which is (further down on the same page) described as "A smartphone on wheels" that offers "Hassle-free mobility." The film is 100 seconds long and composed of 63 scenes. As such, it is more than three times as long as the Voi video, but has *exactly the same rhythm*, showing each scene for one-and-a-half seconds (1.58) on average. The film begins with a bright, vertical shot of a black car parked in an urban concrete landscape, followed by a quick zooming-in of the front of the car. After this first encounter with the car, we can follow it, as well as a similar car, but dark blue, in different stages of mobility through the city until the final scene where one of the cars is again parked in a parking lot, now in half darkness and with the urban silhouette and late sunset in the background. The cars are shown moving through a variety of urban spaces, especially those signalling inner-city life and small-scale services as told by discrete, even minimalistic signposts stating things like "Coffee–Breakfast–Lunch," "Bastard Burgers," "Lush, Fresh, Handmade Cosmetics," and "Eklund–Göteborg–New York" (a real estate agency) that flash by, as well as night-time neon lights, notably a red sign with the word "Open." The film is obviously shot in Gothenburg, where the company's Swedish headquarters is located. As viewers, we get aerial views as well as close-ups of the cars passing in front of modern waterfront buildings in the former harbour and shipyard area and making quick turns around stone paved street corners in the older parts of town. A number of short clips show other activities in the city, all caried out by young people: we see the bare legs of a man bicycling in street traffic; a woman with sunglasses dancing at a night club; a man in bathing gear (trunks, swimming goggles and snorkel) on a river boat; a girl in shorts and baseball cap running up an escalator; two men crossing the street carrying skateboards; a man playing with his dog in a park. While the look of these urban bodies signifies plurality in terms of ethnic background, they are all slim and flexible. A few panoramic views are also included – one displaying the river and skyline of Gothenburg in the sunset, two others showing the car passing over a bridge with the urban skyline in the background (daytime and night-time). Connective media are more visible in this film than in the Voi commercial. In one of the opening scenes, there is a close-up of a smartphone in somebody's hand, showing the Lynk & Co app through which the user searches for an available car. In another scene, the car stops for a red light; there is a zooming-in of the navigation system in the car and a hand touching the screen whereafter the car makes a quick turn, suggesting that it is being rerouted. In all, the video depicts mobility as perpetual, effortless, liberating, and tightly woven into the urban texture, day and night.

How can we understand the guidance landscape based on these short films? Of course, they do not tell us much about people's actual experiences of dwelling with mobility platforms or even how they relate to this type of spatial representations. What the films do, however, is to reveal a formative gaze, a certain way of seeing the city. There are four inter-connected features, or biases, I want to highlight.

First, the guidance landscape is a landscape of effortless mobility and urban life without frictions. We may call this a *kinetic bias*. Mobility as a service means that transport solutions are seamlessly woven into the urban texture, either as smart, colourful accessories that you can easily bring with you when they do not transport you (Voi), or as a fully connected logistics system, "a smartphone on wheels" (Lynk & Co), that guides you to your destination and assists you in finding available parking space. Mobility is *always a possibility*, regardless of where in the city you are, or when. While it is predictable, of course, that there is a kinetic bias in the promotion of mobility services, the films point to a tendency identified in studies of other apps, namely that the mobility of bodies and objects are taken as key to the movement of data. Notably, in a study of eight non-profit apps in Milton Keynes, UK, Rose and colleagues found that even these apps, which actually did not have to capitalize on digital data (providing guidance, for instance, on cycle and walking pathways, heritage sites, age-friendly urban access and places for breastfeeding) were designed with a particular type of engaged, (cap)able and mobile user in mind. The apps, and their designers, anticipated making their users more mobile: "Just like data, the app user had to be on the move – or if already mobile, more so. […] Just as data are assumed to travel ever faster and more seamlessly, so interactions with it are assumed to be immediate and on the move" (Rose et al., 2021: 66–67). As such, the kinetic bias seems to cut across such "smart city" initiatives and commercial versions of platform urbanism like the ones foregrounded here. It is significative that the two films try to depict mobility services, as well as the entire urban formation, as inclusive in terms of gender and skin colour while at the same time only showing young and (cap)able bodies in motion.

It should also be stressed, second, that the "freedom of mobility" depicted in both films (and explicitly claimed on the websites) also implies *control* – control over one's movements and orientations, which is in turn predicated on the service providers' control over data. Locative guidance, as discussed before, is a matter of controlled, even steered, mobilities. The films present a version of the guidance landscape that resonates with what Cuppini (2017: 502) describes as an ongoing "logisticalization of the entire urban field." They underscore that logistics is not exterior to the urban condition, as sometimes implied in works on the so-called logistics city with its sprawling areas of container ports, cargo terminals and warehouses (see, e.g., Rossiter, 2016), but increasingly penetrates into the most mundane spaces of urban life: "What emerges is the image of an urban fabric constituted through interconnected urban agglomeration and 'operational landscapes'" (Cuppini, 2017: 502). Guidance landscapes, I argue, are precisely about such agglomerations; they normalize a view of the city where flexible yet controlled mobilities and streams (that is, logistical accumulation) by and large come to replace the modern factory as well as the spectacles of "semiotic society" (Lash, 1990; Zukin, 1991; see also Chapter 1). At the same time, and in tune with the mythology of logistics as a neutral "science," this view is de-politicized; it effectively hides the exploitative and segregating logics of extraction that characterize digital urbanism (see, e.g., Elwood, 2021).

There is more than mobility to these films, however. The third bias of the guidance landscape, I argue, concerns the "horizontal" integration, the mutual embodiment, of humans, material infrastructures and nature into a harmoniously evolving urban ecosystem. This *ecological bias* unfolds through the emphasis on activities linked to leisure and play taking place on "street level," woven into the urban fabric, and in contact with nature, especially what looks like municipal parks. The two films are very similar in this regard, even though Lynk & Co do not present any main human character but a number of individuals appearing in different clips suggesting a close relationship between "hassle-free mobility" and the good things in life. The city appears as a landscape of human-scale and environmentally sound places that mobility services can *take you into*. Both films include episodes with humans playing with their dogs in a park – a theme connoting deep-seated values of companionship, embodied presence and nature-culture integration. Likewise, they depict small-scale establishments offering "that little extra" that makes life more exciting and provides "time-off" from the toil and trouble of everyday labour. To the extent the vehicles are *not* moving in local neighbourhoods or around parks and waterfront settings, they *pass over bridges* where the city is placed in the background as a signifier of metropolitanism and infrastructures in need of evolution. The guidance landscape is a landscape where everyone is assumed to find their way, to bypass or pass over the frictions of the city, and become one with the urban organism, as well as with nature.

This leads us to the final bias, which concerns digital technology, or, rather, the *withdrawal* of such technology. We may here speak of a *post-digital bias*, referring to the fact that even though media are depicted as a precondition for "smart," liberating mobility, the focus is rather on *life made simple*. As urban dwellers no longer have to worry about the hassles associated with owning and driving a private car (or an e-scooter for that matter) they can realize other values and fulfil other goals in life, notably those that fit the overall discourse of sustainability. Of course, we should not overlook the fact that the Lynk & Co film presents the convenience of their digital platform as well as the benefits of locative navigation systems. Still, digital interfaces are not centre-stage and require no more interaction (it seems) than the swipe of a finger. As Deuze (2011) argues in his account of *media life* (see Chapter 2), digital media have largely withdrawn from our direct attention and are here to be understood rather as platforms for *reconciling humans with place* (Jansson & Adams, 2021a). This is particularly obvious in certain scenes – like the final scene in the Voi film where the main character stands in a yoga position in the midst of the greenery – which seem to advocate a *re*-connection with the "here and now"; a life disentangled from the mundane pressures associated with digital networks (Hesselberth, 2018; Adams & Jansson, 2021; Enli & Syvertsen, 2021). While this bias may seem paradoxical given that digital media are the very precondition for the services promoted in the films, it points to a tendency that has also been identified in relation to other areas of platform urbanism, notably co-working spaces (see, e.g., Fast & Jansson, 2019; Merkel, 2018) and the aforementioned case of alternative tourism.

In all, I maintain that these films tell us something important about guidance landscapes, and thus about the direction in which logistical society is heading. The films can be read as a celebration of *logistical freedom and control*; projections of a dream of spatial ease, the suspension of all spatial stakes (Lucas, 2019b), onto a particular kind of urban texture – one marked by hospitality, organic relations, and community integration. As such, the films demonstrate that platform urbanism, and data circulations in general, "can enact different kinds of values" (Rose et al., 2021: 62), linked for instance to nature and local community (Stabrowski, 2017), beyond their logistical undercurrents. They epitomize a life where "we" (the preferred readers of the adverts) do not have to care much about either technology or logistics. Instead, there is locative guidance to the things that really matter to us. The logistical utopia converges, it seems, with a dream of a restored sense of place.

At the same time, the guidance landscape offers a solution to our human troubles that is reliant not just on mobility, but also on perpetual and automated monitoring. What the films do not show is how people are continuously tracked as they seek out, and are guided to, time-spaces of rest, recreation and play. Likewise, there are no signs of technological friction, brokenness or the type of distress related to logistical labour that we have discussed elsewhere in this book. Symptomatically, in September 2021, a Swedish newspaper, which had tested Lynk & Co's mobility service during the summer period, reported that the "sharable car was not sharable." Just like many other subscribers, the journalists had experienced that the sharing function was actually not available. They had also experienced several other frustrating software problems, for example related to the "hands-free" function for telephone calls.[5]

What the films do not show, either, are the logistical labourers, gig-workers and digital maintenance crews that keep the systems up and running (to the extent they do), or groups in the city that do not have enough resources to make use of the platformed services on offer. As critical urban/digital geographers like Richardson (2015, 2020a), Leszczynski (2016) and Elwood (2021) have recently argued, digital/platform urbanism tends to further marginalize subjects whose abilities to move, act or emplace themselves *in the city they inhabit* are already curbed due to intersecting factors like gender, sexuality, skin colour, and social class. Not only are urban platforms, as a feature of locative guidance, inclined to "routing individuals around 'unsafe' parts of the city in the interests of technologically ameliorating the risks of urban encounter" (Leszczynski, 2016: 1691), there are also parallel systems of digital logistics at play, related to the "smart city," that tend to expose already vulnerable groups like those without shelter to further tracking and control in the name of social initiatives run by municipalities, NGOs or the state (Elwood, 2021). Crucially, as Elwood argues, "the terrain of politics in the 'smart' city is defined not just by these profoundly unequal digital-social-spatial topologies but also by the ideologies that manufacture consent to them" (ibid: 216). The films analysed here, symptomatically, do not show any other class fractions than those possessing the liberty to manage time and space, at least to some degree. They do not show any other bodies than those that are young, fit and capable of moving without much effort (see also Rose et al., 2021). The fact that Voi depicts a woman of colour in their advert is hardly a coincidence (and doing differently would have raised another set of critical questions, of course), but reflects their strategy to associate their brand with equality and security; to inscribe their services as an equally available and empowering element of the urban infrastructure, and thus, by extension, legitimizing the city's new, digital landlords. Hence, as Richardson (2015: 121) argues, "whilst offering an antidote to the narrative of economy as engendering isolation and separation, the sharing economy simultaneously masks new forms of inequality and polarization of ownership." This is exactly what happens in and through the guidance landscape too, in spite of its hospitable and sustainable appearance.

NOTES

1　The study of *Spotted by Locals* was conducted in 2019 (see also Jansson, 2019). As told by the company webpage, as of October 2021 the platform offers "city guides with insider tips by locals in 81 cities" (see https://www.spottedbylocals.com).
2　Information retrieved from the Voi website in April 2021, https://www.voiscooters.com/for-cities.
3　Information retrieved from the Lynk & Co website in April 2021, https://www.lynkco.com/en/membership.
4　For copyright reasons, I am not able to present any images from the films. They were analysed in April 2021. The Voi video was accessed via this link: https://www.voiscooters.com/for-cities. The Lynk & Co video was accessed via this link: https://www.lynkco.com/sv-se/car.
5　See *Dagens Industri*, 6 September 2021, https://www.di.se/bil/delbar-bil-gick-inte-att-dela-lynk-vd-n-vi-tabbade-oss/.

6. Geomedia *as* the human condition

In all its complexity, the human condition is an eternal source of curiosity, contemplation and engagement, even exhaustion. We are all, in different ways, struggling to find some meaning in the things we do, and in the things *done to us*, and get a little bit of recognition from others, maybe even love. At the same time, there is no end to our human shortcomings when it comes to doing what is "good" for ourselves and others. We are vulnerable and exposed to the world, yet at the same time capable of the worst forms of inhuman(e) actions. The shadows of genocides and terror haunt our existence. There is a comic absurdity to it all.

Still, the humanistic perspective of society is grounded in a relatively optimistic view of what humans can achieve. As life continues, there will always be openings onto something new, and new possibilities to "do good" and to make a difference. In this regard, we should be very grateful to have the treasure of expression. As humans, we are able not just to act upon, and with, our life environment but also to *communicate* about, and (re-)imagine, what our individual lives and society at large could be (instead). We can identify this outlook in several of the key theoretical sources that have framed the analyses of this book – notably from the fields of humanistic geography and critical phenomenology. In their spirit, as we have now come to the final parts of the book, I want to contribute a discussion that balances up the critical view of logistical society and its perpetually reinvented forms of exploiting human lives with a reflection on where we may find prospective sources and spaces of human emancipation – in terms of autonomy, security and recognition. Many of the analyses presented in the previous chapters emphasize how logistical accumulation, via the industrial logics of streamability (Chapter 3), transmedia circulation (Chapter 4) and locative guidance (Chapter 5), positions people as logistical labourers, continuously preoccupied with keeping up (with) data streams and maintaining the infrastructures that carry the streams. But this is just one side of the picture. I have also stressed the frictions involved in these processes, including the failures of technology and the everyday resistance people often exert – if capable – in order *not to be steered*, or, at least, to maintain a *sense* of being in command of, and feeling secure in, the environments where they dwell.

What unfolds is a logistical battlefield with increasingly diffuse positions. As I have argued, geomedia is a regime that accentuates the intermediation of humans and their environment in ways that puncture the boundaries of the self and make it increasingly difficult to sort out questions of human agency (questions that have preoccupied philosophers since the dawn of civilization). Geomedia, as characterized in this book, has turned the spotlight onto the fact that, as Peters (2015) argues, media were *always* part of the human condition, only that their saturation into human affairs is now more pervasive, or intrusive, than ever before:

> Media are not just pipes or channels. Media theory has something both ecological and existential to say. Media are more than the audiovisual and print institutions that strive to fill our empty seconds with programming and advertising stimulus; they are our condition, our fate, and our challenge. (Peters, 2015: 52)

What concerns us here, is Peters' very last word. If geomedia, the currently ordering principle of our media environment, also constitutes the human condition, on what grounds and by what means can it be *challenged*? It is not just newborns that are "thrown" into a digitally mediated existence; most of us are (Lagerkvist, 2017). And, to recognize the *captivating* and *entangling* force of geomedia (see Chapter 3), it is perhaps more correct to say that we are "dragged," "drawn" or "lured" into the digital. Whether at work or at school, whether in public or in private, we are turned into data subjects or what I call logistical labourers. As such, we do not just handle streams. *Our lives are streamed*, turned into the raw material of data extraction that, in turn, feeds logistical accumulation.

As Couldry and Mejias argue in their account of the "costs of connection," this implies that social relations are not just "embedded" in the economic system but "*become* the economic system" (Couldry & Mejias, 2019b: 117, original emphasis). The continuous surveillance exercised by the digital (platform) economy constitutes a fundamental "assault on human autonomy" (ibid: 161–163) as it interferes into the "space of the self" (ibid: 164–166) and damages what the authors call the "minimal integrity of human life" (ibid: 153–157; see also Zuboff, 2015). While I am not quite as pessimistic as Couldry and Mejias, I agree with the humanistic premises of their analysis. Their observations should incite us to consider the role of boundaries; not just spatial boundaries but also the boundedness, or "boundlessness," of the self (see also Adams, 2005). Our ability to guard these boundaries – and, to open them up, as we wish – is unevenly distributed. Think of the gig-worker, whose income is unpredictable, yet dependent on permanent connectivity and what Richardson (2020a: 628) calls "coercive flexibility," or the retired person who is dependent on the support from younger family members and friends, that is, "warm experts" (Bakardjieva, 2005), to make digital platforms, and thus life at large, function with a preserved sense of dignity. In the latter case, there is a lack of digital skill. In the former, skills do not help to counter the power of the platform economy. To improve the human condition, I argue, the relations between humans and their social world must be salvaged from the obligatory logistical labour to include forms of *action* that resist further erosion of meaningful boundaries between self and environment, between private and public. Following Arendt's (1958/1998) ideas, it is through such action that human beings can *appear* as humans and stake out new directions for their dwelling.

In this chapter, I want to highlight what I consider to be three important "pillars" for reforming the human condition under geomedia. These pillars, which are extracted from the preceding analyses, can also be interpreted as social forces that, if combined, may shove the trajectories of geomediatization in a more humanistic direction. First, I discuss the possibilities of subverting pre-existing affordances of geomedia in ways that sustain more autonomous forms of communicative action. Not least, this entails a potential shift *from logistical labour to logistical action* and the construction of new *spaces of appearance*. The second pillar concerns the social significance of *place* as a potential shield from the entangling, sometimes oppressive, force of geomedia. As shown in previous chapters, there is no lack of human efforts to resist or withdraw from digital connectivity – efforts that can be read as signs of a widespread longing for *boundedness* and *spaciousness*. This calls for an updated, post-digital version of the humanistic agenda of human geography. Finally, I consider which skills and resources are required to challenge geomedia and among which groups in society we might, and even *should*, expect alternative visions to take shape. I argue, in line with Bourdieusian analyses of mediatization processes, that *cultural capital* has a better chance of contesting geomedia than economic capital, as the latter is by definition inseparable from logistical accumulation. Today, cultural capital is likely to incorporate geomedia-related skills. However, it is vital that such skills not only translate into symbolic violence, as discussed in Chapter 3, but also sustain logistical action. Such a reorientation within the regime of geomedia, I argue, holds political implications that would be beneficial to the human condition.

FROM LOGISTICAL LABOUR TO LOGISTICAL ACTION

Under geomedia, we have all become logistical labourers. This is now part of what it is to be human, at least as long as we also want to enjoy the standard benefits of being members of a modern society. Much of the explanation for this can be traced to the digital platform economy and the competitive advantage given to those industrial actors that are successful in processing and making sense of digital data streams. Therefore, as Couldry and Mejias (2019a, 2019b) argue, these industries – individually and as a complex capitalistic structure – want to capture, or colonize, growing areas of our human lives to extract valuable information. It is a development that by definition turns dwelling into a site of exploited labour. As I have tried to show in this book, however, logistical labour is not limited to the very handling and generation of digital streams (of information and/or data). As long as sensors are not implanted directly into our bodies and not all digital infrastructures are remote controlled, data circulation is as a matter of fact not a self-generating process. Whether we speak of parking apps, smart household equipment, sound systems, or the elementary broadband connection, we have to install them. We must also upgrade and maintain them, not least in order to make different devices and systems work together and to solve problems related to (dis)connection and malfunction. In a wider perspective, we are even obliged to adjust parts of our life environments and everyday routines to make way for new technology. This is not a new phenomenon, of course. What is new, and interesting, is how logistical labour, on each of these levels, saturates expanding areas of our lives and thereby leads to deeper, yet mundane, entanglements with the digital economy.

The flip side of the coin is obviously that we – some of us more than others – find this development meaningful. Geomedia is not a directly oppressive regime, but a regime that continuously adapts to the things that we, as humans, desire the most. It speaks directly to the human desire for social recognition and self-understanding, that is, to *culture*. This is how surveillance and monitoring are legitimized and why people are willing to accept steadily escalating media dependence. This does not make the system less exploitative, but it forces us to abandon an altogether deterministic view of where geomediatization eventually will take us. It may certainly be the case that people sometimes find an immediate satisfaction in being able to manage their hurried lives more efficiently thanks to improved media technology; to find their way near and afar, and to coordinate and orchestrate the flows of money, information and human energies that keep the wheels of modern life turning. Media-related logistical labour and its side effects are in some part the price paid for logistical advantages gained in other realms of life. Still, in a wider perspective, the main attraction is rarely the sophistication of logistical affordances per se, but rather the extended significance of such affordances in the social and cultural integration of society, that is, to sustain the possibility to *appear* as humans to one another and thus gain mutual recognition. This is what humanity boils down to. José van Dijck (2013) dismantles this condition in her account of the culture of connectivity, where she basically argues that it is the human need for recognition and a sense of identity that fuels the connectivity industry and makes platformed sociality possible. The same thing can be said about the entire "quantification sector," whose tentacles extend well beyond social media and into our most mundane activities – the platformization of eating, drinking, shopping, exercising, sleeping, making love, and so forth – as discussed by Couldry and Mejias (2019b). If we are to understand logistical labour, we cannot isolate it analytically from the human capacity and need for communication. Logistical labour is not in and by itself corrosive to communication. It is also *enabling* processes that open up possibilities for communicative action and meaningful human appearance. As Mark Deuze (2011) argues in his account of "media life," people's willingness to embrace and actively explore the affordances of new technology may then be the most efficient way to foster awareness and literacy as to how the systems work and how they can assist in the creation of a more liveable and meaningful life.

This is neither to ignore the intricate weave of exploitation enabled by geomedia, nor to argue that platforms by default, or as such, constitute spaces of appearance. I basically sympathize with scholars like Couldry and Mejias (2019b) in their insistence on the datafied environment *as* the human condition and at the same time *an assault* on what it is to be human in terms of autonomy, morality and justice. As they argue, it is a dangerous illusion to believe that datafication would engender a new type of human autonomy premised on the extension of datafication itself – as seen for example in the Quantified Self movement. However, I would not go as far as to believe that "since we have no choice but to go on acting in a world that undermines the self's autonomy, one consequence is that we may progressively *unlearn* the norms associated with it" (Couldry & Mejias, 2019b: 173, original emphasis). While this becomes a rather speculative issue, and one that depends on which time-frame we apply, in principle, I stick to Arendt's idea that one of the markers of being human is the inevitable capacity to strive for *action*, and as such also to envision change. While history contains numerous examples of how this capacity has been suppressed – examples that have also entailed violence and periods of social "unlearning" – we must acknowledge that geomedia is *not* a regime that directly inhibits appearance, communication and the possibility for action. Rather, it feeds off this human drive. As Maren Hartmann (2021) argues, it has even become a civic challenge to defend the right to *not* communicate (or, to "circulate," for that matter). The possibilities to drastically rethink the system itself are thus built into the regime.

Let me be more precise: geomedia entails the tools – and hitherto unseen connective, representational and logistical affordances – to rethink and challenge logistical accumulation and its social consequences. Logistical accumulation should be our main target of critique. It represents an extreme extension of what Arendt (1958/1998: 320) describes as the "victory of the *animal laborans*" that came to characterize consumer society. The current industrial preoccupation with managing streams for the sake of making streams themselves more expansive, predictable and computable resonates with how Arendt describes the modern shift from a social order that regarded work and the making of durable things as the highest form of activity to an order that was instead concerned with the *processes* of making and the tools that could make these processes more efficient. As a consequence, the ideal member of society was positioned not as a maker but as someone in the business of improving tools to make tools – someone who "only incidentally also produces things" (ibid: 309). Likewise, as logistical labourers, most of the time we are separated from any concrete, durable outcome of our efforts. What we achieve is also what we immediately consume, and to the extent that quantification has become our goal, it implies nothing more than perpetual labour only to reach the "next level" or "milestone," which is basically a way of feeding the system that steers us. Yet, while this means that our tools now *work upon us*, it is *also* true that geomedia constitutes an environment, or an infrastructure, whose resources could be deployed to reform the human condition.

What would it take to reform the human condition? In Arendt's view, the kind of society we should aim for is one that allows for new spaces of appearance to take shape. Such spaces should be understood as public realms where people come together through action and speech. As we discussed in Chapter 2, action is to "begin something new"; it is "not forced upon us by necessity, like labour, and it is not prompted by utility, like work" (Arendt, 1958/1998: 177). At the same time, as Arendt (ibid: 178) explains, without speech, "action would not only lose its revelatory character, but, and by the same token, it would lose its subject, as it were; not acting men but performing robots would achieve what, humanly speaking, would remain incomprehensible." Hence, in the public realm, people disclose themselves to one another *as humans* with a distinct kind of morality and personality rather than as actors with pregiven roles. As so conceived, the space of appearance is by definition marked by plurality rather than sameness. It grants a certain degree of autonomy *and* security to acting subjects. We are not dealing with organized political arenas but *open spaces* that typically precede more purposeful arrangements. Likewise, we are not necessarily dealing with physically bounded places – let alone that the city has historically been a foundation for action among people living together (ibid: 201) – since action "always establishes relationships and therefore has an inherent tendency to force open all limitations and cut across all boundaries" (ibid: 190). This quality implies, as Roger Silverstone (2007) argues, that media hold the capacity to nurture exactly the kind of spaces that the human condition requires. With the development of electronic communication and new platforms for boundless communication the prospects for what Silverstone calls "mediapolis" has multiplied.

The point I want to make here, however, is not directly concerned with the (questionable) qualities of a digital "mediapolis." I agree with Silverstone's vision, as well as with his doubts as to whether the Internet would actually foster the type of hospitality and open-ended plurality to which Arendt refers.

We can see today, 15 years after the publication of Silverstone's *The Media and Morality*, that social media, broadly conceived (and pretty much like society at large), entail promising spaces of appearance – just think of the #metoo movement and other forms of digital activism (see, e.g., Kaun & Uldam, 2018; Sundén & Paasonen, 2020) – as well as a vast realm of "idle talk," "strategic recognition work" (Fast & Jansson, 2019) and outright hostility and defamation that reflects the quantifying logic of streamability that privileges circulation rather than content (and thus also constitutes an inherent threat to the legitimacy of digital activism). However, as I have explored in this book, there is more to geomedia than the communicative spaces opened up by new platforms. When we assess the conditions for emergent spaces of appearance, I argue, we should account not only for connective and representational affordances, which is most often the case when these issues are discussed in media and communication studies, but also for logistical affordances. While it is true, as Silverstone (2007: 42–43) argues, that we should allow for other forms of appearance than speech to be seen as vital parts of "mediapolis," not least the wide spectrum of social performance and imagery through which people (more or less deliberately) express their identities – which is also to problematize Habermas' view of the public sphere – this perspective still excludes many forms of action. Notably, it underplays the role of orientation, coordination and orchestration as foundations of the public realm (whatever shape such a realm takes). If we were to follow the dominant academic discourse on publicness and communicative action, we would run the risk of dismissing a great deal of the recent, logistically biased, media developments as rather useless for enabling meaningful forms of human action. This would be a mistake, I think. While it is beyond the analytical aim of this book, I am convinced that future research should look deeper into how logistical media affordances are enacted as part of actions that bring people and their minds, bodies and hearts closer together in mutual openness. Again, this is to recognize the fundamental role of media as a material substratum of civilization.

In principle, logistical action may challenge logistical accumulation in three ways. The first way, as already indicated, has to do with action emerging out of, or in tandem with, people's engagement with logistical media to form new spaces of appearance. These spaces do not have to be constructed with the strategic goal of subverting the ideology of our logistical society, quite the opposite; to the extent there is a potential for new spaces of appearance there is also an open-ended potential for critique and the manifestation of alternative values and life forms – especially due to the unpredictability of action itself. As discussed in this book, the critical sentiments and revealing experiences of logistical labour (in all its guises) are already in place, which means that even commercial apps like Snapchat and Google Maps that enable people to share their location and thus locate the whereabouts of other people may sustain gatherings that problematize geomedia itself. Similar affordances that promote serendipitous social encounters are typically built into platforms designed for specific businesses or communities, for example in co-working spaces (Fast, forthcoming) or among expats (Polson, 2016a).

The second version of logistical action concerns interventions *into* the logics of streamability in order to disturb logistical accumulation. We may even call this *counterlogistics* (Chua et al., 2018). As discussed in Chapter 2, there are already many examples of organized actions taking aim at algorithmic operations and digital surveillance exercised in the name of the "connectivity industry," the "gig economy," the "smart city," "platform urbanism," and other branches of logistical society (see, e.g., Briziarelli, 2019; Leszczynski, 2020a; Mann et al., 2020; Velkova & Kaun, 2021). While some of these actions, such as outright hacktivism, may lead to short-term disturbances they are rarely sustainable in the long run and can even be dangerous to society if applied on a wider scale, as noted by Couldry and Mejias (2019b: 195). We should rather assess the public significance of this sort of explicit (counter)logistical action, ranging from alternative uses of media infrastructure to public interference into the mediated flows of people, goods and information (as seen especially in public demonstrations and art projects), in terms of its awareness-raising effect (due to publicity). As such, it feeds synergistically into the first type of logistical action, even blurring the boundaries between the two. A good example is provided by Sarah Elwood in her analysis of "glitch politics" and the case of street papers sold at designated public places in cities by non-sheltered, "homeless," people. These papers, and the spaces of appearance to which they give rise, articulate a glitch in the "digital-social-spatial settlements that define urban life in the technocapitalist city" (Elwood, 2021: 218). Not only do they break away from the dominant digital norms and the associated tendencies of socio-spatial sorting and encapsulation; they also open up taken-for-granted arrangements in the city and enable new kinds of encounters to occur across class- and race-related, as well as other, lines of division. In this way, they constitute a logistical intervention into the dominant forms of circulation while at the same time proffering alternative views of what it is, and could be, to dwell in the city beyond the digital norm.

This leads us to the third way of challenging logistical accumulation, which concerns various forms of "disconnection," "non-use" and "media withdrawal." As I have shown in previous chapters, the experience of being steered, guided and nudged to (inter)act with media and the surrounding environment in certain prescribed ways causes ambiguous feelings. There is often a clash between a sense of convenience and mastery of one's life, on the one hand, and a shrinking space for privacy *and* autonomous appearance, on the other. In Arendtian terms, this can be understood as an inner conflict between the gratification-seeking labourer/consumer and the acting human subject. The potential power of this shared human experience must not be underestimated. An increasingly common consequence, as I will discuss in the following section, is that people also under mundane conditions try to break away, if only temporarily, from the logistical machineries that measure, circulate and ultimately guide their lives.

A POST-DIGITAL SENSE OF PLACE

One of the things that I have tried to illuminate in this book concerns the frictions that affect media circulation. The logistical dream of seamless integration of media technology into human affairs – which sometimes reverberates also in media theory – is bound to remain at least partly unrealized. While geomedia implies that many technological features are automated (e.g., self-installing software and automated roaming) and platforms are joined to enable smooth interaction (e.g., in online transactions and platformed services linked to social media accounts), there will always remain issues that cause interruption and delay and thus impede streamability. Besides the fact that connectivity, as Jenny Sundén (2018) argues, always remains in a state of incompleteness, or brokenness, whether due to technological failures and bugs or because of human errors and omittances in handling and maintenance, there are also instances of more deliberate withdrawal from media. This is something we need to acknowledge and reflect upon before jumping to conclusions regarding data colonialism and the ever-expanding exploitation of logistical labour.

While I discussed some examples in Chapter 4, related to people's attempts to disconnect or restrict their digital media use while on vacation, there is today an expanding field of disconnection research looking into a variety of "non-uses," pertaining to different contexts and media types and pursued for different purposes (see, e.g., Jansson & Adams, 2021b). They range from temporary "Facebook vacations," "company switch-offs," and "digital detoxing" intended to bring back a sense of command over one's life (see, e.g., Jorge, 2019; Syvertsen & Enli, 2020; Hartmann, 2021; Hesselberth, 2021), to the revitalization of analogue cultures (see, e.g., Sundén, 2015) and "slow media" (see, e.g., Rauch, 2018) and politically motivated actions and boycotts of certain platforms or technologies (see, e.g., Karppi, 2018). As such, the divisions between "connection" and "disconnection," and between voluntary and involuntary forms of non-use, or reluctant use, are diffuse (see, e.g., Cassidy, 2016; Mannell, 2017, 2019). In a helpful account based on extensive ethnographic data gathered from Australian households over a period of 16 years (2002–2017), Kennedy and colleagues crystallize five types of interstitial practices that are neither use nor non-use. These are called "partial use," "active resistance," "passive neglect," "vicarious use" and "radical use" (Kennedy et al., 2020: 207). They capture, for example, the fact that people often turn off certain features of a device or restrict their usage to specific times and places; exclude particular genres or platforms from their media diet; let others (for example in the household) handle certain types of technology, or connectivity at large, in their place; and sometimes even try to subvert, or retool, the intended functionality of a technology.

Without going into the details of these types, the point here is that our dwelling with media is a continuously fluctuating matter, especially in contexts of co-habitation or co-presence, where "non-use is not a question of individual agency, or lack thereof," but "emerges in relation to the people, practices, and technological population of households" (Kennedy et al., 2020: 236). While there is of course a possibility, at least in principle, to opt out from platforms or "disconnect" altogether from certain technologies, dwelling entails various ways of "not-doing" things (Light & Cassidy, 2014: 1174). In other words, if the social "ongoingness" of dwelling is a precondition and resource for data extraction, it is also the cause of friction and resistance. Dwelling under geomedia, or what has elsewhere been described as "digital wayfaring" (Hjorth & Pink, 2014), is a double nature; harbouring at the same time logistical labour enhancing streamability *and* (more or less) tactical moments of interruption and delay. Furthermore, what happens within the spaces of "the ordinary" may overlap with, and feed into, more explicit movements in society and thus have a wider political import than what immediately meets the eye. In a study of Australian gay men and their uses of the online dating platform Gaydar, for example, Cassidy (2016) found that the participants largely rejected the functionalities and subject positions afforded by the interface because of the platform's conformist and sexualized view of GLBT relations. Due to the lack of alternative platforms, however, these individuals did not opt out but developed tactics to limit their sense of being steered by the platform. Cassidy characterizes this mode of digital (dis)engagement as "participatory reluctance"; "a particular orientation to social media and its assemblage of affordances and associated cultures that further problematizes binarized notions of connection and disconnection" (Cassidy, 2016: 2615; cf. also Kuntsman & Miyake, 2019).

Therefore, *how* does this challenge logistical accumulation? Regardless of what digital "disconnection," "non-use," "withdrawal" or "disengagement" looks like, such practices have two important things in common. First, deliberately or not, there is always some kind of *boundary*, or *shield*, inserted between the self, or the social unit, and the entangling digital environment. Shielding occurs via infrastructural measures (e.g., restricted or discontinued access) or boundary maintaining routines, sometimes manifested as rules (e.g., when and where to use media) and sometimes in relation to physical "containers" and borders (e.g., particularly designated places for media disconnection or non-use). Second, there is always something *removed*, or *excluded*, from the life environment, whether a particular technology, a platform, a functionality, or certain types of information. In this way, as the things excluded tend to be the things people regard as intrusive, distractive, addictive or exploitative (depending on habitus, values and life situation), the lifeworld becomes *less crowded*. Combined, we should think of these measures as a mundane form of logistical action; measures by which logistical labour is overthrown and transformed (at least in part) into a blockage of streamability. It is a way of hampering the exploitative drive towards seamlessness and de-differentiation that the connectivity industry promotes, accelerated by transmedia (see Chapter 4), in order to reclaim a sense of autonomy. Again, while the industry and its logics per se are not always the explicit targets of disconnective practices, the overall thrust of such logistical struggles points us to the enduring power of humanism that Buttimer (1990, 1999) speaks about (see Chapter 2). In dwelling, we find the seeds of a grander movement to restore the human condition, in the words of Couldry and Mejias, as "a zone of open-ended connection and growth" *and* "something that *finds its own limits* as it continuously changes and develops" (2019b: 199, original emphasis).

From this follows some interesting theoretical implications. As I argued at the outset of this book, the rapid expansion of digital geographies – as a research field and a social condition – has led to a dismissal of humanistic perspectives that (due to a well-motivated eagerness to avoid anthropocentrism and spatial romanticism) has also closed off those layers of human experience through which we can begin to understand the deeper consequences of geomedia. In previous chapters, I have addressed the shifting nature of geomediatized environments and landscapes. As we now consider the implications of mundane forms of logistical action, it takes us to issues directly related to the phenomenological construction of *place*. The forms of everyday resistance and tactics that a growing body of research, especially in media studies, has started to scrutinize can only be fully grasped, I argue, if we consider how they are related to people's ordinary desires for a sense of place (see also Jansson & Adams, 2021a). This should not be mistaken for an epistemological or ideological turn to a particular type of place or even to a specific definition of place (e.g., endorsing a certain view of the "home" or the "local"). There is no reason to fall back into the type of non-reflective "sedentary metaphysics" that once saturated phenomenological approaches in human geography (Cresswell, 2006). But under conditions where digital entanglements have become the rule and the handling of transgressive streams is mandatory to dwelling it is obvious, as we saw, that many people feel a strong need to reclaim *boundedness* as well as *spaciousness*. They may even feel a need to shelter themselves from media *in order to* gain more space.

The focus group interviews that frame this book are full of such examples, where people either go to particular places to avoid intrusive media, or, conversely, try to manage connectivity in order to restore or maintain a non-mediat(iz)ed sense of place (for example, in the bedroom or around the dinner table). Often, these dual tendencies coalesce. We could see this in Chapter 4, in the example with Peter who described how he brought a "dumb phone" instead of his ordinary smartphone when going on vacation. There are also descriptions of how *going away*, to places beyond the reach of regular media infrastructures, leads to a sense of inner harmony due to the temporary "de-crowding" or "decluttering" (Newport, 2019), of the lifeworld.

> Mimi: I have a summer cottage in the northern part of [the region] where there is hardly any mobile coverage at all, that's really nice. Really nice.
> Interviewer: How do you feel when you return from there?
> Mimi: It's peaceful. It's possible to listen to the radio, but no TV or nothing. It's rest for the soul, somehow.

Examples like this provide the logical counterpart to Adams' (2005) argument that our globalized, disembedded society is predicated on selves that are increasingly extensible, even boundless. It is indicative that Mimi works as an accountant and runs her own business, which means that her life is deeply mediatized and that the boundaries between work and non-work are porous. Likewise, it is indicative that she takes measures to disentangle, or withdraw, if only for some time from digital infrastructures. We may think of the outcome of such measures – regardless of whether they are as easily identifiable as in this case, or more closely intertwined with dwelling – as a *post-digital sense of place*; a reclaiming of place that challenges the norms and conventions of a digital existence from within (Jansson & Adams, 2021a). Perhaps the most striking example is what Fast (2021) calls "disconnective geomedia," that is, apps like Lock Me Out that are designed to automatically disable certain apps or connectivity altogether when the user (that is, the user's smartphone) is located in specific places (or at specific times) (see also Beattie & Cassidy, 2021). We find important tools for theorizing such new tendencies in the works of Yi-Fu Tuan (1977: 54), who describes the dialectic of boundedness and spaciousness in his book *Space and Place*:

> Space lies open; it suggests the future and invites action. On the negative side, space and freedom are a threat. […] To be open and free is to be exposed and vulnerable. Open space has no trodden paths and signposts. […] Enclosed and humanized space is place. Compared to space, place is a calm center of established values. Human beings require both space and place. Human lives are a dialectical movement between shelter and venture, attachment and freedom.

While we do not have to subscribe to Tuan's view of what is the "normal" or "healthy" balance between boundedness and spaciousness, he brings up issues that should be key concerns in future research on logistical struggles. For example, he discusses how experiences of *crowding* translate into a fractured sense of spaciousness, which, in Arendt's words, refers to a shrinking space for the self to appear through action and speech. Such experiences are not directly correlated with the number of things, people or events filling up the lifeworld, but are also matters of quality. As Tuan (1977: 60) argues, a bustling city may feel more open than a local community marked by fewer but more controlling eyes. Similarly, I argue, forms of mediation that are experienced as surveillant, causing what Leszczynski (2015b) calls "anxieties of control," are likely to trigger human desires to *restore* the ontological moorings of boundedness and spaciousness and, eventually, the preconditions for more open-ended action.

The enduring relevance of humanistic approaches is obvious also in light of the budding sector for "digital wellbeing," "workfulness" and different types of "self-help" – and associated mobile apps – aspiring to assist people in taking (back) control of their digitally entangled lives (see, e.g., Enli & Syvertsen, 2021; Fast, 2021; Karppi et al., 2021). As Enli and Syvertsen (2021) show in an analysis of contemporary self-help literature, there is a predominant drive towards promoting digital disconnection and "detoxing" as a way of *reconnecting* with a more "authentic" self, as well as to the places and persons that anchor the self. Likewise, it is no surprise that an author like Cal Newport, an American computer scientist who has in a series of books championed "digital minimalism" as a pathway to "deep work" and thus a productive life and career, includes "decluttering" as one of the concrete measures for getting rid of unwanted digital disturbances in one's everyday life (notably among knowledge workers) (Newport, 2019). In Newport's view, instead of being perforated by more or less chaotic streams of digital information, life should revolve around productive work and meaningful hobbies, especially those of an analogue nature, such as handicraft. There is indeed a familiar ring to such accounts. They proclaim what seems quite similar to the rekindled sense of place cherished by Tuan and other humanistic geographers in the 1970s (see especially Relph, 1976). However, the current "disconnection turn" (Fast, 2021) is invoked foremost as a means to productivity and individual success, rather than as a form of action that might also challenge the overall system of logistical accumulation. Disconnection is predicated on the fact that connection is the normal state. This means, in turn, that being disconnected and able to control one's boundaries becomes exclusive, even a matter of distinction among the "happy few" – those who can afford to buy into selectively disconnected lifestyles via customized tourism, self-help literature, add-on software, personal coaching, and so forth. As we saw in Chapter 5, the same contradiction is integral to the promotion of digital mobility services. Our analysis highlighted that platform urbanism is largely a matter of legitimizing digital guidance landscapes based on the submission to data extraction and surveillance via representations that bespeak sedentarist ideals of local community, place, the ecological and the human scale. In such discourses, logistical accumulation is annihilated, covered up by the fantasies of a disconnected existence and a more sincere relation to authentic spaces and places of the self.

Clearly, the power of place is both concrete and metaphysical, phenomenological and ideological. Whereas geomedia signifies the collapsing of media into place, the mutual becoming of space and communication, there are forces at play that for better or worse try to reinstate or benefit from such (blurred) divisions and people's desire to handle de-differentiation. This is why we need a strong phenomenological conception of space and place – not to endorse the value of certain spatial arrangements or attachments but to understand what is *at stake* under geomedia. As I will discuss in the final section, this is also the entry point to further inquiries into ordinary logistical expertise as a form of capital in society today.

GEOMEDIA CAPITAL AND THE SPACE OF APPEARANCE

The above observations signal that the possibility of voluntarily withdrawing from media, to negotiate the social and material expectations associated with geomedia, has become something exclusive. To achieve a post-digital sense of place, which I here understand as something that could be beneficial to the human condition if it occurs at a larger scale, demands certain resources – precisely because it is predicated on the digital as our inevitable condition of dwelling. In Bourdieusian terms, we may hypothesize this capacity as a form of capital. The particular resource presented to those who are able not only to master geomedia but also to withdraw from it, granting the subject a sense of boundedness and spaciousness, could even be called *geomedia capital*. It would not function as an efficient form of capital, or as a means of social distinction, if it was just a matter of complex technological and environmental skills. The power of such skills reaches its full potential only as the individual attains the ability to apply the skills also in a *reverse manner*, that is, in opposition to the dominant force of logistical accumulation and thus step out of the bubble of logistical labour to reclaim the autonomy of the self.

My ambition here is not to introduce an elaborated theory of geomedia capital but rather to propose the term as a potential way forward for those wanting to analyse the links between geomediatization and social stratification and, by extension, to consider the prospects of restoring the bedrocks of the human condition across social space. The idea of geomedia capital is simple. A person who has acquired the appropriate skills to master geomedia, that is, to improve and increase the efficiency of streamable environments *and* claim time-spaces of "decolonized" dwelling, is also in a privileged position to gradually exchange this capital into any of the dominant forms of capital that

Bourdieu (1979/1984) identifies, notably cultural or economic capital. This takes us back to the issue of expertise. The skills, or expertise, upon which geomedia capital rests, can be defined in relation to connective, representational and logistical media affordances. Under geomedia, to bring out these affordances to the fullest, one must be familiar with (which is not the same thing as liking) the logics of streamability, transmedia and locative media. As we discussed in Chapters 3–5, logistical expertise has come to play an important role in classifying who is able to stay on par with geomediatization, both in terms of benefitting from logistical media affordances for the sake of orientation, coordination and orchestration (see Chapter 5) and to take the logistical measures needed to construct life environments that are not only adjusted to the demands of streamability but also offer *something else*.

It should be underlined, however, that "digital skills" do not automatically translate into geomedia capital. The equation is much more complex and shaped by social factors. Our digitalized, geomediatized society fosters, or forces, people to develop certain skills at the micro level just to get by in their day-to-day lives. During the COVID-19 pandemic, this force was multiplied due to new and unexpected social conditions that accentuated people's need to upgrade their digital hardware, learn how to master new tools and even redesign their home environment. But this growing capability to communicate, coordinate and make transactions online does not mean that everybody has acquired the same skills or that there has been a general increase in geomedia capital. In most cases it has been a matter of doing what has been necessary, and thus expanding the field of logistical labour. The rapid growth of digital skills has not altered the fact that only very few people can take or leave logistical labour as they wish. Logistical accumulation exploits certain people and certain bodies and minds more than others. This is particularly obvious in the realm of work. While the digital skills required from gig-workers lead to the reproduction of "coercive flexibility," as described by Richardson (2020a), the skills developed among tech-designers in Silicon Valley make their way into digital solutions that ultimately reshape the life forms of millions of people (Wajcman, 2019a). Yet others, especially those in possession of large amounts of cultural and/or economic capital, may have the capacity to resist or negotiate the extent to which they should even make use of digital tools. This means that skills that are forced upon some people, those in disadvantaged positions, may be elective to others.

As Richardson and Bissell (2019) argue, it is important that we study these "geographies of digital skill" more closely to find out how the unevenness of the platform economy plays out at different sites, for example in relation to particular workplaces, and to detect new forms of resistance. It is also vital, I argue, that such analyses take into account the dynamics of social reproduction, especially the role of habitus. Previous research indicates that people with a privileged habitus, that is, coming from more affluent social backgrounds, are better equipped to become ordinary logistical experts and to accumulate geomedia capital (as conceived here). Conversely, given the force of cultural classification, the possession of geomedia capital is then also classified as something desirable, a mark of social status. These mechanisms appear quite clearly in a series of survey studies I have conducted with a group of colleagues, where we applied multiple correspondence analysis to reconstruct Bourdieu's social space and position various practices and experiences of (geo)media in that space. One of these studies (Lindell et al., 2021) demonstrates that so-called conspicuous geomedia practices, referring to how people deploy locative media affordances to express online where they are or have been (e.g., via tagged photo sharing or "check-ins"), tend to reproduce already established positions in social space. People in more privileged social positions are more inclined to make use of these functions and as such also expose their taste for certain places and activities via their postings on social media. In another study (Fast et al., 2021), we found that people possessing larger amounts of cultural and economic capital to a greater degree (stated that they) have established routines for regulating their smartphone use. They are also more inclined to "disconnect" in certain time-spaces, such as in nature or on vacation – practices that indicate a more reflexive relationship to digital media and their affordances (see also Beattie & Cassidy, 2021; Doerr, 2021). Notably, people who are affluent in cultural capital rather than economic capital express a sense of *digital unease* – for example, that they get stressed by their smartphones, feel surveilled and disrupted in their work, and feel that they are using their smartphones too much (Fast et al., 2021) – which underpins various forms of "partial non-use" (Kennedy et al., 2020).

In short, privileged groups are generally *both* avid users and capable of disconnecting at certain times and in certain spaces and are, as such, exploited by logistical labour to a lesser degree. The groups that I have previously termed "ordinary logistical experts" possess the tools that can help them not only to orchestrate and describe the world, but also to avoid certain forms of entanglement, or, at least, to carve out the type of decolonized, interstitial spaces that Couldry and Mejias (2019b) propose as a potential antidote to data colonialism. The question, however, is whether these privileged groups actually pursue any type of action that might pull society in that direction. The future is uncertain, especially since the outcomes of action are not even obvious to the acting subject. As Arendt (1958/1998: 192) puts it, "[a]ction reveals itself fully only to the storyteller, that is, to the backward glance of the historian, who indeed always know better what it was all about than the participants." In our contemporary context, it seems, action grounded in geomedia capital can indeed work in two different directions; either as a way of promoting hospitable spaces of appearance, or, conversely, to exercise symbolic violence, as we saw in Chapter 3. To steer in the former direction, I argue, those in command of geomedia capital must take a socially inclusive stance and act in collaboration with other groups. Spaces of appearance emerge *between* people, as Arendt points out. Likewise, the power of appearance is based on the fact that people *act together*.

What is the way forward? There is certainly a risk that those groups that we might currently identify as ordinary logistical experts, even a logistical elite, especially younger people with educational capital and socio-economic resources, are reluctant to counter logistical accumulation, especially to the extent that geomedia capital is traded for economic rather than cultural capital. It is more realistic to expect that geomedia capital leaning towards the cultural side of social space could fuel progressive developments. After all, this is where we find a more articulated critique of commercial systems and technological solutions that interfere with human autonomy and security (notably in terms of privacy). This is where the drive towards alternative public realms and new spaces of appearance, in arts, politics and social affairs, is at its strongest. I am certainly not suggesting that we should put our hope into the actions of cultural elite persons. That would be to simplify things and to overlook the symbolic violence exercised from such positions. Yet, I believe that cultural capital taken in a wider sense – as progressively broadened cultural horizons and skillsets combining theoretical and practical understandings of the world (not least geomedia) – is a fertile soil for growing forms of action that "force open all limitations and cut across all boundaries" (Arendt, 1958/1998: 190). If we figure cultural capital as *Bildung* and reflexivity, even as *experimentation* (to avoid certain conservative views of knowledge), rather than as the means of symbolic power, it could potentially be *the vanguard of boundless action and a safeguard of the boundaries of the self*.

This fostering of imaginative and experimental thinking around geomedia and its consequences is not easily achieved. There is no reason to expect any simple "trickle-down" process to occur, since cultural capital, like action, discriminates and differentiates. But there is in society one key institution at hand – the educational system (on all levels). This is the institution to work with and through, also via political channels, if we are to grow awareness and foster the skills necessary to problematize and eventually alter logistical accumulation. While this may sound like a commonsensical as well as paternalistic solution, I argue, education should be the epicentre of our emancipatory project. To educate especially younger people about geomedia, to make them capable of stepping out of their digitally entangled life environments, if only temporarily, and see them anew is one of the greatest challenges there are if we want to foster a more humanistic world.

References

Abend, P. (2018). From map reading to geobrowsing: Methodological reconsiderations for geomedia. In Felgenhauer, T., & Gäbler, K. (Eds.) *Geographies of Digital Culture*. London: Routledge.

Abend, P., & Harvey, F. (2017). Maps as geomedial action spaces: Considering the shift from logocentric to egocentric engagements. *GeoJournal, 82*(1), 171–183.

Adams, P. C. (1992). Television as gathering place. *Annals of the Association of American Geographers, 82*(1), 117–135.

Adams, P. C. (2005). *The Boundless Self: Communication in Physical and Virtual Spaces*. New York: Syracuse University Press.

Adams, P. C. (2009). *Geographies of Media and Communication*. Malden, MA: Wiley Blackwell.

Adams, P. C. (2020). Agreeing to surveillance: Digital news privacy policies. *Journalism & Mass Communication Quarterly, 97*(4), 868–889.

Adams, P. C., & Jansson, A. (2012). Communication geography: A bridge between disciplines. *Communication Theory, 22*(3), 299–318.

Adams, P., & Jansson, A. (2021). Introduction: Rethinking the entangling force of connective media. In Jansson, A., & Adams, P. C. (Eds.) *Disentangling: The Geographies of Digital Disconnection*. New York: Oxford University Press.

Adams, P. C., Craine, J., & Dittmer, J. (2014). *The Ashgate Research Companion to Media Geography*. London: Routledge.

Adams, P. C., Cupples, J., Glynn, K., Jansson, A., & Moores, S. (2017). *Communications/Media/Geographies*. London: Routledge.

Adorno, T. (1991). *The Culture Industry: Selected Essays on Mass Culture*. London: Routledge.

Ahmed, S. (2006). *Queer Phenomenology: Orientations, Objects, Others*. Durham: Duke University Press.

Åker, P. (2018). Spotify as the soundtrack to your life: Encountering music in the customized archive. In Johansson, S., Werner, A., Åker, P., & Goldenzwaig, G. (Eds.) *Streaming Music: Practices, Media, Cultures*. London: Routledge.

Andersson, M. (2021). The food courier and his/her mobile phone. In Hill, A., Hartmann, M., & Andersson, M. (Eds.) *The Routledge Handbook of Mobile Socialities*. London: Routledge.

Andrejevic, M. (2007). *iSpy: Surveillance and Power in the Interactive Era*. Lawrence: University Press of Kansas.

Andrejevic, M. (2012). Estranged free labor. In Scholz, T. (Ed.) *Digital Labor: The Internet as Playground and Factory*. London: Routledge.

Andrejevic, M. (2013). The infinite debt of surveillance in the digital economy. In Jansson, A., & Christensen, M. (Eds.) *Media, Surveillance and Identity: Social Perspectives*. New York: Peter Lang.

Andrejevic, M. (2018). Drone cartographies: The operational map. Paper presented at the conference *Sensing Media: Reconfigurations between Technologies, Bodies and Environments*, Siegen, 14–15 June 2018.

Andrejevic, M. (2019). Automating surveillance. *Surveillance & Society, 17*(1/2), 7–13.

Andrejevic, M., & Volcic, Z. (2021). "Smart" cameras and the operational enclosure. *Television & New Media, 22*(4), 343–359.

Andron, S. (2018). Selling streetness as experience: The role of street art tours in branding the creative city. *The Sociological Review, 66*(5), 1036–1057.

Ang, I. (1991). *Desperately Seeking the Audience*. London: Routledge.

Arendt, H. (1958/1998). *The Human Condition*. Chicago: University of Chicago Press.

Ash, J., & Simpson, P. (2016). Geography and post-phenomenology. *Progress in Human Geography, 40*(1), 48–66.

Ash, J., Kitchin, R., & Leszczynski, A. (2018). Digital turn, digital geographies?. *Progress in Human Geography, 42*(1), 25–43.

Ash, J., Kitchin, R., & Leszczynski, A. (Eds.) (2019). *Digital Geographies*. London: Sage.

Bakardjieva, M. (2005). *Internet Society: The Internet in Everyday Life*. London: Sage.

Barns, S. (2020). *Platform Urbanism: Negotiating Platforms Ecosystems in Connected Cities*. Basingstoke: Palgrave Macmillan.

Barthes, R. (1977). *Image–Text–Music*. New York: Hill & Wang.

Baudrillard, J. (1983). *Simulations*. New York: Semiotext(e).

Beattie, A., & Cassidy, E. (2021). Locative disconnection: The use of location-based technologies to make disconnection easier, enforceable and exclusive. *Convergence, 27*(2), 395–413.

Beck, U. (2000). *What is Globalization?* Cambridge: Polity Press.

Beck, U. (2006). *Cosmopolitan Vision*. Cambridge: Polity Press.

Bengtsson, S. (2012). Imagined user modes: Media morality in everyday life. *International Journal of Cultural Studies, 15*(2), 181–196.

Bengtsson, S. (2018). Sensorial organization as an ethics of space: Digital media in everyday life. *Media and Communication, 6*(2), 39–45.

Bengtsson, S., Fast, K., Jansson, A., & Lindell, J. (2021). Media and basic desires: An approach to measuring the mediatization of daily human life. *Communications, 46*(2), 275–296.

Bennett, W. L., & Segerberg, A. (2012). The logic of connective action: Digital media and the personalization of contentious politics. *Information, Communication & Society, 15*(5), 739–768.

Benson, M. (2016). Deconstructing belonging in lifestyle migration: Tracking the emotional negotiations of the British in rural France. *European Journal of Cultural Studies, 19*(5), 481–494.

Berger, J. (1972). *Ways of Seeing*. London: Penguin.

Berger, P., & Luckmann, T. (1966). *The Social Construction of Reality: A Treatise in the Sociology of Knowledge*. London: Penguin.

Berker, T., Hartmann, M., & Punie, Y. (2005). *Domestication of Media and Technology*. Berkshire: Open University Press.

Berlant, L. (2016). The commons: Infrastructures for troubling times. *Environment and Planning D: Society and Space, 34*(3), 393–419.

Bernard, A. (2019). *The Triumph of Profiling: The Self in Digital Culture*. Cambridge: Polity Press.

Berry, D. M. (2011a). *The Philosophy of Software: Code and Mediation in the Digital Age*. Basingstoke: Palgrave Macmillan.

Berry, D. M. (2011b). Messianic media: Notes on the real-time stream. *Stunlaw*, 12 September 2011, http://stunlaw.blogspot.com/2011/09/messianic-media-notes-on-real-time.html (accessed in January 2021).

Berry, D. M. (2012). The social epistemologies of software. *Social Epistemology*, *26*(3–4), 379–398.

Berry, D. M. (2017). Phenomenological approaches to the computational: Some reflections on computation. In Markham, T., & Rodgers, S. (Eds.) *Conditions of Mediation: Phenomenological Perspectives on Media*. New York: Peter Lang.

Blumer, H. (1954). What is wrong with social theory. *American Sociological Review*, 18, 3–10.

Bolter, J. D., & Grusin, R. A. (1996). Remediation. *Configurations*, *4*(3), 311–358.

Bosangit, C., Hibbert, S., & McCabe, S. (2015). "If I was going to die I should at least be having fun": Travel blogs, meaning and tourist experience. *Annals of Tourism Research*, 55, 1–14.

Bosma, J., & van Doorn, N. (forthcoming) The gentrification of Airbnb: Closing rent gaps through the professionalization of hosting. *Space and Culture*.

Bourdieu, P. (1979/1984). *Distinction: A Social Critique of the Judgment of Taste*. London: Routledge.

Bourdieu, P. (1980/1990). *The Logic of Practice*. Cambridge: Polity Press.

Bourdieu, P. (1997/2000). *Pascalian Meditations*. Cambridge: Polity Press.

Boy, J. D., & Uitermark, J. (2017). Reassembling the city through Instagram. *Transactions of the Institute of British Geographers*, *42*(4), 612–624.

Brantner, C., Rodriguez-Amat, J., & Belinskaya, Y. (2021). Structures of the public sphere: Contested spaces as assembled interfaces. *Media and Communication*, *9*(3), 16–27.

Brennen, J. S., & Kreiss, D. (2016). Digitalization. In Jensen, K. B., & Craig, R. T. (Eds.) *The International Encyclopedia of Communication Theory and Philosophy*. Oxford: Wiley. Accessed online in February 2020, https://doi.org/10.1002/9781118766804.wbiect111.

Briziarelli, M. (2019). Spatial politics in the digital realm: The logistics/precarity dialectics and Deliveroo's tertiary space struggles. *Cultural Studies*, *33*(5), 823–840.

Bruns, A. (2008). *Blogs, Wikipedia, Second Life, and beyond: From Production to Produsage* (Vol. 45 of Digital formations). Peter Lang.

Burroughs, B. (2019). House of Netflix: Streaming media and digital lore. *Popular Communication*, *17*(1), 1–17.

Buttimer, A. (1990). Geography, humanism, and global concern. *Annals of the Association of American Geographers*, *80*(1), 1–33.

Buttimer, A. (1999). Humanism and relevance in geography. *Scottish Geographical Journal*, *115*(2), 103–116.

Calhoun, C. (2013). The problematic public: Revisiting Dewey, Arendt, and Habermas. *The Tanner Lectures on Human Values*, University of Michigan, 11 April 2013.

Calvignac, C., & Smolinski, J. (2020). How can the use of a mobile application change the course of a sightseeing tour? A question of pace, gaze and information processing. *Tourist Studies*, *20*(1), 49–74.

Campbell, N. (2005). Producing America: Redefining post-tourism in the global age. In Crouch, D., Jackson, R., & Thompson, F. (Eds.) *The Media and the Tourist Imagination: Converging Cultures*. London: Routledge.

Carducci, V. (2006). Culture jamming: A sociological perspective. *Journal of Consumer Culture*, *6*(1), 116–138.

Carey, J. W. (1989). *Communication as Culture: Essays on Media and Society*. Winchester, MA: Unwin Hyman.
Case, J. A. (2010). *Geometry of Empire: Radar as Logistical Medium*. Unpublished doctoral dissertation. Iowa City: University of Iowa.
Case, J. A. (2013). Logistical media: Fragments from radar's prehistory. *Canadian Journal of Communication*, *38*(3), 379–395.
Cassidy, E. (2016). Social networking sites and participatory reluctance: A case study of Gaydar, user resistance and interface rejection. *New Media & Society*, *18*(11), 2613–2628.
Cassinger, C., & Thelander, Å. (2021). Co-creation constrained: Exploring gazes of the destination on Instagram. In Månsson, M., Buchmann, A., Cassinger, C., & Eskilsson, L. (Eds.) *The Routledge Companion to Media and Tourism*. London: Routledge.
Caulfield, J. (1994). *City Form and Everyday Life: Toronto's Gentrification and Critical Social Practice*. Toronto: University of Toronto Press.
Centner, R. (2008). Places of privileged consumption practices: Spatial capital, the dot-com habitus, and San Francisco's internet boom. *City & Community*, *7*(3), 193–223.
Chadwick, A. (2013). *The Hybrid Media System*. Oxford: Oxford University Press.
Christensen, M., & Jansson, A. (2015). *Cosmopolitanism and the Media: Cartographies of Change*. Basingstoke: Palgrave Macmillan.
Chua, C., Danyluk, M., Cowen, D., & Khalili, L. (2018). Introduction. Turbulent circulation: Building a critical engagement with logistics. *Environment and Planning D: Society and Space*, *36*(4), 617–629.
Chun, W. H. K. (2016). *Updating to Remain the Same: Habitual New Media*. Cambridge, MA: MIT Press.
Chung, N., & Koo, C. (2015). The use of social media in travel information search. *Telematics Informatics*, *2*(2), 215–229.
Clay, P. L. (1979). *Neighborhood Renewal: Middle-Class Resettlement and Incumbent Upgrading in American Neighborhoods*. New York: Free Press.
Cohen, E. (1979). A phenomenology of tourism experiences. *Sociology*, *13*(2), 179–201.
Cosgrove, D. E. (1984). *Social Formation and Symbolic Landscape*. Madison: University of Wisconsin Press.
Cosgrove, D. E. (2006). Modernity, community and the landscape idea. *Journal of Material Culture*, *11*(1–2), 49–66.
Costanza-Chock, S. (2014). *Out of the Shadows, Into the Streets! Transmedia Organizing and the Immigrant Rights Movement*. Cambridge, MA: MIT Press.
Couldry, N. (2017). Phenomenology and critique: Why we need a phenomenology of the digital world. In Markham, T., & Rodgers, S. (Eds.) *Conditions of Mediation: Phenomenological Perspectives on Media*. New York: Peter Lang.
Couldry, N., & Hepp, A. (2017). *The Mediated Construction of Reality*. Cambridge: Polity Press.
Couldry, N., & McCarthy, A. (Eds.) (2004). *MediaSpace: Place, Scale and Culture in a Media Age*. London: Routledge.
Couldry, N., & Mejias, U. A. (2019a). Data colonialism: Rethinking big data's relation to the contemporary subject. *Television & New Media*, *20*(4), 336–349.
Couldry, N., & Mejias, U. (2019b). *The Costs of Connection: How Data Is Colonizing Human Life and Appropriating It for Capitalism*. New York: Stanford University Press.

Cowen, D. (2010). A geography of logistics: Market authority and the security of supply chains. *Annals of the Association of American Geographers*, *100*(3), 600–620.

Cowen, D. (2014). *The Deadly Life of Logistics: Mapping Violence in Global Trade*. Minneapolis: University of Minnesota Press.

Cramer, F. (2015). What is "post-digital"? In Berry, D. M., & Dieter, M. (Eds.) *Postdigital Aesthetics: Art, Computation and Design*. London: Palgrave Macmillan.

Cresswell, T. (2006). *On the Move: Mobility in the Modern Western World*. London: Routledge.

Cresswell, T. (2015). *Place: An Introduction*. 2nd Edition. Malden, MA: Wiley Blackwell.

Cuppini, N. (2017). Dissolving Bologna: Tensions between citizenship and the logistics city. *Citizenship Studies*, *21*(4), 495–507.

Danyluk, M. (2018). Capital's logistical fix: Accumulation, globalization, and the survival of capitalism. *Environment and Planning D: Society and Space*, *36*(4), 630–647.

de Souza e Silva, A. (2006). From cyber to hybrid: Mobile technologies as interfaces of hybrid spaces. *Space and Culture*, *9*(3), 261–278.

Deuze, M. (2011). Media life. *Media, Culture & Society*, *33*(1), 137–148.

Deuze, M. (2012). *Media Life*. Cambridge: Polity Press.

Deuze, M. (2013). *Media Work*. Hoboken, NJ: John Wiley & Sons.

Dickinson, J. E., Hibbert, J. F., & Filimonau, V. (2016). Mobile technology and the tourist experience: (Dis)connection at the campsite. *Tourism Management*, *57*, 193–201.

Dinhopl, A., & Gretzel, U. (2016). Selfie-taking as touristic looking. *Annals of Tourism Research*, *57*, 126–139.

Doerr, N. M. (2021). Digital disconnection as othering: Immersion, "authenticity" and the politics of experience. In Jansson, A., & Adams, P. (Eds.) *Disentangling: The Geographies of Digital Disconnection*. New York: Oxford University Press.

Draper, N. A., & Turow, J. (2019). The corporate cultivation of digital resignation. *New Media & Society*, *21*(8), 1824–1839.

Duncan, J. S. (1990). *The City as Text: The Politics of Landscape Interpretation in the Kandyan Kingdom*. Cambridge: Cambridge University Press.

Eco, U. (1986). *Travels in Hyperreality*. Orlando: Harcourt Brace & Co.

Elliot, A., & Urry, J. (2010). *Mobile Lives*. London: Routledge.

Elwood, S. (2021). Digital geographies, feminist relationality, black and queer code studies: Thriving otherwise. *Progress in Human Geography*, *45*(2), 209–228.

Enli, G., & Syvertsen, T. (2021). Disconnect to reconnect! Self-help to regain an authentic sense of space through digital detoxing. In Jansson, A., & Adams, P. (Eds.) *Disentangling: The Geographies of Digital Disconnection*. New York: Oxford University Press.

Eriksson, M. (2020). The editorial playlist as container technology: On Spotify and the logistical role of digital music packages. *Journal of Cultural Economy*, 415–427.

Eriksson, M., Fleischer, R., Johansson, A., Snickars, P., & Vonderau, P. (2019). *Spotify Teardown: Inside the Black Box of Streaming Music*. Cambridge, MA: MIT Press.

Falkheimer, J., & Jansson, A. (Eds.) (2006). *Geographies of Communication: The Spatial Turn in Media Studies*. Gothenburg: Nordicom.

Fan, D. X., Buhalis, D., & Lin, B. (2019). A tourist typology of online and face-to-face social contact: Destination immersion and tourism encapsulation/decapsulation. *Annals of Tourism Research*, *78*(C), 1. DOI: 10.1016/j.annals.2019.102757.

Fast, K. (2018). A discursive approach to mediatisation: Corporate technology discourse and the trope of media indispensability. *Media and Communication*, *6*(2), 15–28.

Fast, K. (2021). The disconnection turn: Three facets of disconnective work in post-digital capitalism. *Convergence*, *27*(6), 1615–1630.

Fast, K. (forthcoming). Who has the right to the coworking space? Reframing platformed workspaces as elite territory in the geomedia city. *Space and Culture*.

Fast, K., & Jansson, A. (2019). *Transmedia Work: Privilege and Precariousness in Digital Modernity*. London: Routledge.

Fast, K., & Lindell, J. (2016). The elastic mobility of business elites: Negotiating the "Home" and "Away" continuum. *European Journal of Cultural Studies*, *19*(5), 435–449.

Fast, K., & Örnebring, H. (2017). Transmedia world-building: The Shadow (1931–present) and Transformers (1984–present). *International Journal of Cultural Studies*, *20*(6), 636–652.

Fast, K., Jansson, A., Lindell, J., Ryan Bengtsson, L., & Tesfahuney, M. (2018a). Introduction to geomedia studies. In Fast, K., Jansson, A., Lindell, J., Ryan Bengtsson, L., & Tesfahuney, M. (Eds.) *Geomedia Studies: Spaces and Mobilities in Mediatized Worlds*. London: Routledge.

Fast, K., Jansson, A., Lindell, J., Ryan Bengtsson, L., & Tesfahuney, M. (Eds.) (2018b). *Geomedia Studies: Spaces and Mobilities in Mediatized Worlds*. London: Routledge.

Fast, K., Lindell, J., & Jansson, A. (2021). Disconnection as distinction: A Bourdieusian study of *where* people withdraw from digital media. In Jansson, A., & Adams, P. C. (Eds.) *Disentangling: The Geographies of Digital Disconnection*. New York: Oxford University Press.

Fast, K., Ljungberg, E., & Braunerhielm, L. (2019). On the social construction of geomedia technologies. *Communication and the Public*, *4*(2), 89–99.

Featherstone, M. (1991). *Consumer Culture and Postmodernism*. London: Sage.

Feifer, M. (1985). *Going Places*. London: Macmillan.

Ferrero Camoletto, R., & Marcelli, D. (2020). Keeping it natural? Challenging indoorization in Italian rock climbing. *Annals of Leisure Research*, *23*(1), 34–51.

Flaherty, G. T., & Choi, J. (2016). The "selfie" phenomenon: Reducing the risk of harm while using smartphones during international travel. *Journal of Travel Medicine*, *23*(2), 1–3.

Fredman, P., & Tyrväinen, L. (2010). Frontiers in nature-based tourism. *Scandinavian Journal of Hospitality and Tourism*, *10*(3), 177–189.

Freeman, M. (2015). Up, up and across: Superman, the Second World War and the historical development of transmedia storytelling. *Historical Journal of Film, Radio and Television*, *35*(2), 215–239.

Freeman, M., & Gambarato, R. R. (Eds.) (2019). *The Routledge Companion to Transmedia Studies*. New York: Routledge.

Frith, J. (2017). Invisibility through the interface: The social consequences of spatial search. *Media, Culture & Society*, *39*(4), 536–551.

Fuchs, C. (2014). Digital prosumption labour on social media in the context of the capitalist regime of time. *Time & Society*, *23*(1), 97–123.

Gale, T. (2009). Urban beaches, virtual worlds and "the end of tourism". *Mobilities*, *4*(1), 119–138.

Gandini, A. (2021). Digital labour: An empty signifier? *Media, Culture & Society*, *43*(2), 369–380.

Gerbaudo, P. (2012). *Tweets and the Streets: Social Media and Contemporary Activism*. London/New York: Pluto Press.

Gerbaudo, P. (2016). Constructing public space: Rousing the Facebook crowd: Digital enthusiasm and emotional contagion in the 2011 protests in Egypt and Spain. *International Journal of Communication, 10*, 254–273.

Gibson, J. J. (1979/2014). The theory of affordances. In Giesking, J. J., Mangold, W., Katz, C., Low, S., & Saegert, S. (Eds.) *The People, Space and Place Reader*. New York: Routledge.

Giddens, A. (1991). *Modernity and Self-Identity: Self and Society in the Late Modern Age*. Cambridge: Polity Press.

Gillespie, T. (2010). The politics of "platforms". *New Media & Society, 12*(3), 347–364.

Givskov, C. (2017). Growing old with mediatization: Reflexivity and sense of agency. *Nordicom Review, 38*(1), 53–64.

Givskov, C., & Deuze, M. (2018). Researching new media and social diversity in later life. *New Media & Society, 20*(1), 399–412.

Goldenzwaig, G., & Åker, P. (2018). Clouds, streams, materiality: Perceptions of musical value in the age of abundance. In Johansson, S., Werner, A., Åker, P., & Goldenzwaig, G. (Eds.) *Streaming Music: Practices, Media, Cultures*. London: Routledge.

Goods, C., Veen, A., & Barratt, T. (2019). "Is your gig any good?" Analysing job quality in the Australian platform-based food-delivery sector. *Journal of Industrial Relations, 61*(4), 502–527.

Goriunova, O. (2019). The digital subject: People as data as persons. *Theory, Culture & Society, 36*(6), 125–145.

Gran, A. B., Booth, P., & Bucher, T. (2020). To be or not to be algorithm aware: A question of a new digital divide? *Information, Communication & Society*, 1–18.

Gregg, M. (2011). *Work's Intimacy*. Cambridge: Polity Press.

Gregson, N., Crang, M., & Antonopoulos, C. N. (2017). Holding together logistical worlds: Friction, seams and circulation in the emerging "global warehouse". *Environment and Planning D: Society and Space, 35*(3), 381–398.

Gretzel, U., & Yoo, K. H. (2008). Use and impact of online travel reviews. Paper presented at the *Information and Communication Technologies in Tourism* 2008 conference.

Habermas, J. (1962/1989). *The Structural Transformation of the Public Sphere: An Inquiry into a Category of Bourgeois Society*. Cambridge, MA: The MIT Press.

Habermas, J. (1981/1987). *Theory of Communicative Action, Volume Two: Lifeworld and System: A Critique of Functionalist Reason*. Boston, MA: Beacon Press.

Hagen, A. N. (2015). The playlist experience: Personal playlists in music streaming services. *Popular Music and Society, 38*(5), 625–645.

Hagen, A. N. (2016). The metaphors we stream by: Making sense of music streaming. *First Monday, 21*(3).

Hagen, A. N., & Lüders, M. (2017). Social streaming? Navigating music as personal and social. *Convergence, 23*(6), 643–659.

Haldrup, M., & Larsen, J. (2009). *Tourism, Performance and the Everyday: Consuming the Orient*. London: Routledge.

Hannerz, U. (1990). Cosmopolitans and locals in a world culture. *Theory, Culture and Society, 7*(2), 237–251.

Hänninen, R., Taipale, S., & Luostari, R. (2021). Exploring heterogeneous ICT use among older adults: The warm experts' perspective. *New Media & Society, 23*(6), 1584–1601.

Harold, C. (2004). Pranking rhetoric: "Culture jamming" as media activism. *Critical Studies in Media Communication*, *21*(3), 189–211.
Harries, K. (1983/1993). Thoughts on a non-arbitrary architecture. In Seamon, D. (Ed.) *Dwelling, Seeing, and Designing: Toward A Phenomenological Ecology*. Albany, NY: SUNY Press.
Hartmann, M. (2013). From domestication to mediated mobilism. *Mobile Media & Communication*, *1*(1), 42–49.
Hartmann, M. (2021). "Install freedom now!" Choosing not to communicate with digital media at work and home. *Javnost – The Public*, 1–16.
Heidegger, M. (1971). *Poetry, Language, Thought*. New York: Harper & Row.
Hepworth, K. (2014). Enacting logistical geographies. *Environment and Planning D: Society and Space*, *32*(6), 1120–1134.
Hesmondhalgh, D. (2020). Is music streaming bad for musicians? Problems of evidence and argument. *New Media & Society*, *23*(12), 3593–3615.
Hesse, M. (2020). Logistics: Situating flows in a spatial context. *Geography Compass*, *14*(7), e12492.
Hesselberth, P. (2018). Discourses on disconnectivity and the right to disconnect. *New Media & Society*, *20*(5), 1994–2010.
Hesselberth, P. (2021). Retreat culture and therapeutic disconnection. In Jansson, A., & Adams, P. (Eds.) *Disentangling: The Geographies of Digital Disconnection*. New York: Oxford University Press.
Hill, A., Hartmann, M., & Andersson, M. (Eds.) (2021). *The Routledge Handbook of Mobile Socialities*. London: Routledge.
Hill, D. W. (2020). The injuries of platform logistics. *Media, Culture & Society*, *42*(4), 521–536.
Hills, M. (2016). The enchantment of visiting imaginary worlds and "being there": Brand fandom and the tertiary world of media tourism. In Wolf, M. J. P. (Ed.) *Revisiting Imaginary Worlds*. London: Routledge.
Hjorth, L., & Pink, S. (2014). New visualities and the digital wayfarer: Reconceptualizing camera phone photography and locative media. *Mobile Media & Communication*, *2*(1), 40–57.
Holloway, D., & Green, L. (2017). Mediated memory making: The virtual family photograph album. *Communications*, *42*(3), 351–368.
Huang, C. D., Goo, J., Nam, K., & Yoo, C. W. (2017). Smart tourism technologies in travel planning: The role of exploration and exploitation. *Information & Management*, *54*, 757–770.
Hutchby, I. (2001). Technologies, texts and affordances. *Sociology*, *35*(2), 441–456.
Ingold, T. (1993). The temporality of the landscape. *World Archaeology*, *25*(2), 152–174.
Ingold, T. (2000). *The Perception of the Environment: Essays on Livelihood, Dwelling and Skill*. London: Routledge.
Ingold, T. (2008). Bindings against boundaries: Entanglements of life in an open world. *Environment and Planning A*, *40*(8), 1796–1810.
Ingold, T. (2010). Bringing things to life: Creative entanglements in a world of materials. *World*, *44*, 1–25.
Ingold, T. (2011). *Being Alive: Essays on Movement, Knowledge and Description*. London: Routledge.
Innis, H. A. (1951). *The Bias of Communication*. Toronto: Toronto University Press.

Iveson, K., & Maalsen, S. (2019). Social control in the networked city: Datafied dividuals, disciplined individuals and powers of assembly. *Environment and Planning D: Society and Space, 37*(2), 331–349.

Jager, B. (1975). Theorizing, journeying, dwelling. In Giorgi, A., Fischer, C., & Murray, E. (Eds.) *Duquesne Studies in Phenomenological Psychology, Vol. 2.* Pittsburgh, PA: Duquesne University Press.

Jansson, A. (2002). Spatial phantasmagoria: The mediatization of tourism experience. *European Journal of Communication, 17*(4), 429–443.

Jansson, A. (2007a). Texture: A key concept for communication geography. *European Journal of Cultural Studies, 10*(2), 185–202.

Jansson, A. (2007b). A sense of tourism: New media and the dialectic of encapsulation/decapsulation. *Tourist Studies, 7*(1), 5–24.

Jansson, A. (2011). Cosmopolitan capsules: Mediated networking and social control in expatriate spaces. In Christensen, M., Jansson, A., & Christensen, C. (Eds.) *Online Territories: Globalization, Mediated Practice and Social Space.* New York: Peter Lang.

Jansson, A. (2013). Mediatization and social space: Reconstructing mediatization for the transmedia age. *Communication Theory, 23*(3), 279–296.

Jansson, A. (2016a). Mobile elites: Understanding the ambiguous lifeworlds of Sojourners, Dwellers and Homecomers. *European Journal of Cultural Studies, 19*(5), 421–434.

Jansson, A. (2016b). How to become an "elite cosmopolitan": The mediatized trajectories of United Nations expatriates. *European Journal of Cultural Studies, 19*(5), 465–480.

Jansson, A. (2018a). *Mediatization and Mobile Lives: A Critical Approach.* London: Routledge.

Jansson, A. (2018b). Rethinking post-tourism in the age of social media. *Annals of Tourism Research, 69,* 101–110.

Jansson, A. (2019). The mutual shaping of geomedia and gentrification: The case of alternative tourism apps. *Communication and the Public, 4*(2), 166–181.

Jansson, A. (2020). The transmedia tourist: A theory of how digitalization reinforces the de-differentiation of tourism and social life. *Tourist Studies, 20*(4), 391–408.

Jansson, A. (2021). Beyond the platform: Music streaming as a site of logistical and symbolic struggle. *New Media & Society.* Ahead of print, DOI: 14614448211036356.

Jansson, A., & Adams, P. (2021a). A return to place: From digital disconnection to post-digital territoriality. Paper presented at the ECREA pre-conference *Advancing Digital Disconnection Research,* 6 September 2021, Braga, Portugal (online).

Jansson, A., & Adams, P. (Eds.) (2021b) *Disentangling: The Geographies of Digital Disconnection.* New York: Oxford University Press.

Jansson, A., & Klausen, M. (2018). The spreadable city: Urban exploration and connective media. In Archer, K., & Bezdecny, K. (Eds.) *Handbook of Emerging 21st Century Cities.* Cheltenham: Edward Elgar.

Jansson, A., Bengtsson, S., Fast, K., & Lindell, J. (2020). Mediatization from within: A plea for emic approaches to media-related social change. *Communication Theory, 31*(4), 956–977.

Jenkins, H. (2006). *Convergence Culture: Where Old and New Media Collide.* New York: New York University Press.

Jenkins, H., Ford, S., & Green, J. (2013). *Spreadable Media: Creating Value and Meaning in a Networked Culture.* New York: New York University Press.

Johansson, S. (2018a). Online music in everyday life: Contexts and practices. In Johansson, S., Werner, A., Åker, P., & Goldenzwaig, G. (Eds.) *Streaming Music: Practices, Media, Cultures*. London: Routledge.

Johansson, S. (2018b). Music as part of connectivity culture. In Johansson, S., Werner, A., Åker, P., & Goldenzwaig, G. (Eds.) *Streaming Music: Practices, Media, Cultures*. London: Routledge.

Johansson, S., Werner, A., Åker, P., & Goldenzwaig, G. (Eds.) (2018). *Streaming Music: Practices, Media, Cultures*. London: Routledge.

Jorge, A. (2019). Social media, interrupted: Users recounting temporary disconnection on Instagram. *Social Media+ Society*, 5(4), 2056305119881691.

Kanngieser, A. (2013). Tracking and tracing: Geographies of logistical governance and labouring bodies. *Environment and Planning D: Society and Space*, 31(4), 594–610.

Kanngieser, A., Neilson, B., & Rossiter, N. (2014). What is a research platform? Mapping methods, mobilities and subjectivities. *Media, Culture & Society*, 36(3), 302–318.

Karppi, T. (2018). *Disconnect: Facebook's Affective Bonds*. Minneapolis: University of Minnesota Press.

Karppi, T., Chia, A., & Jorge, A. (2021). In the mood for disconnection. *Convergence*, 13548565211034621.

Kaun, A., & Schwarzenegger, C. (2014). "No media, less life?" Online disconnection in mediatized worlds. *First Monday*, 19(11).

Kaun, A., & Uldam, J. (2018). Digital activism: After the hype. *New Media & Society*, 20(6), 2099–2106.

Keightley, K. (2003). Low television, high fidelity: Taste and the gendering of home entertainment technologies. *Journal of Broadcasting & Electronic Media*, 47(2), 236–259.

Kennedy, J., Arnold, M., Gibbs, M., Nansen, B., & Wilken, R. (2020). *Digital Domesticity: Media, Materiality, and Home Life*. New York: Oxford University Press.

Kinder, M. (1991). *Playing with Power in Movies, Television, and Video Games: From Muppet Babies to Teenage Mutant Ninja Turtles*. Berkeley: University of California Press.

Kinkaid, E. (2020). Can assemblage think difference? A feminist critique of assemblage geographies. *Progress in Human Geography*, 44(3), 457–472.

Kinkaid, E. (2021). Is post-phenomenology a critical geography? Subjectivity and difference in post-phenomenological geographies. *Progress in Human Geography*, 45(2), 298–316.

Kirillova, K., & Wang, D. (2016). Smartphone (dis)connectedness and vacation recovery. *Annals of Tourism Research*, 61, 157–169.

Kitchin, R., & Dodge, M. (2011). *Code/Space: Software and Everyday Life*. Cambridge, MA: MIT Press.

Kittler, F. (1985/1990). *Discourse Networks 1800/1900*. Stanford: Stanford University Press.

Kittler, F. (2009). Towards an ontology of media. *Theory, Culture & Society*, 26(2–3), 23–31.

Klausen, M. (2017). The urban exploration imaginary: Mediatization, commodification, and affect. *Space and Culture*, 20(4), 372–384.

Klausen, M., & Møller, K. (2018). Unimaginable homes: Negotiating ageism through media use. In Fast, K., Jansson, A., Lindell, J., Ryan Bengtsson, L., & Tesfahuney,

M. (Eds.) *Geomedia Studies: Spaces and Mobilities in Mediatized Worlds*. London: Routledge.

Kuntsman, A., & Miyake, E. (2019). The paradox and continuum of digital disengagement: Denaturalising digital sociality and technological connectivity. *Media, Culture & Society*, *41*(6), 901–913.

Lagerkvist, A. (2017). Existential media: Toward a theorization of digital thrownness. *New Media & Society*, *19*(1), 96–110.

Lagerkvist, A. (2020). Digital limit situations: Anticipatory media beyond "the new AI era". *Journal of Digital Social Research (JDSR)*, *2*(3), 16–41.

Lapenta, F. (2011). Geomedia: On location-based media, the changing status of collective image production and the emergence of social navigation systems. *Visual Studies*, *26*(1), 14–24.

Larsen, J. (2006). Geographies of tourist photography. In Falkheimer, J., & Jansson, A. (Eds.) *Geographies of Communication: The Spatial Turn in Media Studies*. Gothenburg: Nordicom.

Larsen, J., Urry, J., & Axhausen, K. W. (2007). Networks and tourism: Mobile social life. *Annals of Tourism Research*, *34*(1), 244–262.

Lash, S. (1990). Learning from Leipzig – or politics in the semiotic society. *Theory, Culture & Society*, *7*(4), 145–158.

Lash, S., & Urry, J. (1994). *Economies of Signs and Space*. London: Sage.

Latour, B. (1987). *Science in Action: How to Follow Scientists and Engineers through Society*. Cambridge, MA: Harvard University Press.

Lee, K., & Gretzel, U. (2010). Differences in online travel planning: A rural vs. urban perspective. Paper presented at the 2010 *Travel and Tourism Research Association International Conference*.

Lefebvre, H. (1968/1993). The right to the city. In Ockman, J. (Ed.) *Architecture Culture: A Documentary Anthology*. New York: Rizzoli International Publications.

Lefebvre, H. (1974/1991). *The Production of Space*. Oxford: Blackwell.

Leszczynski, A. (2015a). Spatial media/tion. *Progress in Human Geography*, *39*(6), 729–751.

Leszczynski, A. (2015b). Spatial big data and anxieties of control. *Environment and Planning D, Society & Space*, *33*(6), 965–984.

Leszczynski, A. (2016). Speculative futures: Cities, data, and governance beyond smart urbanism. *Environment and Planning A: Economy and Space*, *48*(9), 1691–1708.

Leszczynski, A. (2020a). Glitchy vignettes of platform urbanism. *Environment and Planning D: Society and Space*, *38*(2), 189–208.

Leszczynski, A. (2020b). Digital methods III: The digital mundane. *Progress in Human Geography*, *44*(6), 1194–1201.

Leszczynski, A., & Crampton, J. (2016). Introduction: Spatial big data and everyday life. *Big Data and Society*, (July–December), 1–6.

Leurs, K. (2014). Digital throwntogetherness: Young Londoners negotiating urban politics of difference and encounter on Facebook. *Popular Communication*, *12*(4), 251–265.

Ley, D. (1978). Social geography and social action. In Ley, D., & Samuels, M. S. (Eds.) *Humanistic Geography: Prospects and Problems*. London: Routledge.

Ley, D. (1981). Cultural/humanistic geography. *Progress in Geography*, *5*(2), 249–257.

Ley, D. (1996). *The New Middle Class and the Remaking of the Central City*. Oxford: Oxford University Press.

Ley, D. (2003). Artists, aestheticisation and the field of gentrification. *Urban Studies*, *40*(12), 2527–2544.

Ley, D., & Samuels, M. S. (1978). Introduction: Contexts of modern humanism in geography. In Ley, D., & Samuels, M. S. (Eds.) *Humanistic Geography: Prospects and Problems.* London: Routledge.

Li, J., Pearce, P. L., & Low, D. (2018). Media representation of digital-free tourism: A critical discourse analysis. *Tourism Management, 69*, 317–329.

Li, Y. (2000). Geographical consciousness and tourism experiences. *Annals of Tourism Research, 27*(4), 863–883.

Light, B., & Cassidy, E. (2014). Strategies for the suspension and prevention of connection: Rendering disconnection as socioeconomic lubricant with Facebook. *New Media & Society, 16*(7), 1169–1184.

Lindell, J. (2016). Communication as spatial production: Expanding the research agenda of communication geography. *Space and Culture, 19*(1), 56–66.

Lindell, J., Jansson, A., & Fast, K. (2021). I'm here! Conspicuous geomedia practices and the reproduction of social positions on social media. *Information, Communication & Society*, 1–20. Ahead of print, DOI: 10.1080/1369118X.2021.1925322.

Lippmann, W. (1922/1961). *Public Opinion.* New York: The Free Press.

Lizardo, O. (2011). Pierre Bourdieu as a post-cultural theorist. *Cultural Sociology, 5*(1), 25–44.

Lo, I. S., & McKercher, B. (2015). Ideal image in process: Online tourist photography and impression management. *Annals of Tourism Research, 52*, 104–116.

Lo, I. S., McKercher, B., Lo, A., Cheung, C., & Law, R. (2011). Tourism and online photography. *Tourism Management, 32*(4), 725–731.

Lovink, G. (2012). *Networks Without a Cause: A Critique of Social Media.* Cambridge: Polity Press.

Lowenthal, D. (1961). Geography, experience, and imagination: Towards a geographical epistemology. *Annals of the Association of American Geographers, 51*(3), 241–260.

Lucas, L. (2019a). "I was not able to go there": Introducing a skills perspective about how tourists navigate in Los Angeles. *Tourist Studies, 19*(3), 357–377.

Lucas, L. (2019b). The skills behind the spatial practices. *Space and Culture, 25*(1), 77–89.

Lüders, M. (2021). Ubiquitous tunes, virtuous archiving and catering for algorithms: The tethered affairs of people and music streaming services. *Information, Communication & Society, 24*(15), 2342–2358. DOI: 10.1080/1369118X.2020.1758742.

Lussault, M. (2007). *L'Homme spatial. La construction sociale de l'espace humain.* Paris: Seuil.

Lussault, M. (2009). *De la lutte des classes à la lutte des places.* Paris: Grasset.

Lussault, M., & Stock, M. (2010). Doing with space: Towards a pragmatics of space. *Social Geography, 5*(1), 11–19.

Lutz, C., Hoffmann, C. P., & Ranzini, G. (2020). Data capitalism and the user: An exploration of privacy cynicism in Germany. *New Media & Society, 22*(7), 1168–1187.

Maasø, A., & Hagen, A. N. (2020). Metrics and decision-making in music streaming. *Popular Communication, 18*(1), 18–31.

MacCannell, D. (1973). Staged authenticity: Arrangements of social space in tourist settings. *American Journal of Sociology, 79*(3), 589–603.

MacCannell, D. (1976). *The Tourist: A New Theory of the Leisure Class.* London: Macmillan.

Magasic, M., & Gretzel, U. (2017). Three modes of Internet connectivity during travel: Remote, transit and residential. Paper presented at the 2017 *ENTER Conference.*

Mains, S., Cupples, J., & Lukinbeal, C. (Eds.) (2015). *Mediated Geographies and Geographies of Media*. Berlin: Springer.

Maltby, S., & Thornham, H. (2016). The digital mundane: Social media and the military. *Media, Culture & Society, 38*(8), 1153–1168.

Mann, M., Mitchell, P., Foth, M., & Anastasiu, I. (2020). # BlockSidewalk to Barcelona: Technological sovereignty and the social license to operate smart cities. *Journal of the Association for Information Science and Technology, 71*(9), 1103–1115.

Mannell, K. (2017). Technology resistance and de Certeau: Deceptive texting as a tactic of everyday life. *PLATFORM: Journal of Media & Communication, 8*(1).

Mannell, K. (2019). A typology of mobile messaging's disconnective affordances. *Mobile Media & Communication, 7*(1), 76–93.

Manovich, L. (2017). *Instagram and Contemporary Image*. Open access book, retrieved from: http://manovich.net/index.php/projects/instagram-and-contemporary-image (accessed 1 December 2021).

Månsson, M., Buchmann, A., Cassinger, C., & Eskilsson, L. (Eds.) (2020). *The Routledge Companion to Media and Tourism*. London: Routledge.

Marwick, A. E. (2015). Instafame: Luxury selfies in the attention economy. *Public Culture, 27*(1), 137–160.

Marwick, A. E., & Boyd, D. (2011). I tweet honestly, I tweet passionately: Twitter users, context collapse, and the imagined audience. *New Media and Society, 13*(1), 114–133.

Marx, K. (1867/1990). *Capital*. London: Penguin Classics.

Mason, K. (2004). Sound and meaning in Aboriginal tourism. *Annals of Tourism Research, 31*(4), 837–854.

Massey, D. (2005). *For Space*. London: Sage.

Matassi, M., Boczkowski, P. J., & Mitchelstein, E. (2019). Domesticating WhatsApp: Family, friends, work, and study in everyday communication. *New Media & Society, 21*(10), 2183–2200.

Maxwell, R. (Ed.) (2016). *The Routledge Companion to Labor and Media*. London & New York: Routledge.

McGuigan, L., & Manzerolle, V. (Eds.) (2014). *The Audience Commodity in a Digital Age: Revisiting a Critical Theory of Commercial Media*. New York: Peter Lang.

McQuire, S. (2011). Geomedia, networked culture and participatory public space. In Hinkel, R. (Ed.) *Urban Interior: Informal Explorations, Interventions and Occupations*. Baunach: Spurbuchverlag.

McQuire, S. (2016). *Geomedia: Networked Cities and the Future of Public Space*. Cambridge: Polity Press.

McQuire, S. (2019). One map to rule them all? Google Maps as digital technical object. *Communication and the Public, 4*(2), 150–165.

McRobbie, A. (2016). *Be Creative: Making a Living in the New Culture Industries*. Cambridge: Polity Press.

Merkel, J. (2018). "Freelance isn't free." Co-working as a critical urban practice to cope with informality in creative labour markets. *Urban Studies, 56*(3), 526–547.

Mezzandra, S., & Neilson, B. (2019). *The Politics of Operations: Excavating Contemporary Capitalism*. Durham: Duke University Press.

Molz, J. G. (2012). *Travel Connections: Tourism, Technology and Togetherness in a Mobile World*. London: Routledge.

Molz, J. G. (2013). Social networking technologies and the moral economy of alternative tourism: The case of couchsurfing.org. *Annals of Tourism Research, 43*, 210–230.

Moores, S. (2012). *Media, Place and Mobility*. Basingstoke: Palgrave Macmillan.

Moores, S. (2018). *Digital Orientations: Non-Media-Centric Media Studies and Non-Representational Theories of Practice*. New York: Peter Lang.

Moores, S. (2020). The everyday skills that get us by: Non-representational theories for a linealogy of quotidian cultures. *European Journal of Cultural Studies*. Ahead of print, DOI: 10.1177/1367549420919866.

Moores, S., & Metykova, M. (2010). "I didn't realize how attached I am": On the environmental experiences of trans-European migrants. *European Journal of Cultural Studies*, *13*(2), 171–189.

Morley, D. (1986). *Family Television: Cultural Power and Domestic Leisure*. London: Routledge.

Morley, D. (2009). For a materialist, non-media-centric media studies. *Television & New Media*, *10*(1), 114–116.

Morley, D. (2017). *Communications and Mobility: The Migrant, the Mobile Phone, and the Container Box*. Oxford: Wiley & Sons.

Morris, J. W., & Powers, D. (2015). Control, curation and musical experience in streaming music services. *Creative Industries Journal*, *8*(2), 106–122.

Mosco, V. (2005). *The Digital Sublime: Myth, Power, and Cyberspace*. Cambridge, MA: MIT Press.

Mostafanezhad, M., & Norum, R. (2018). Tourism in the post-selfie era. *Annals of Tourism Research*, *70*, 131–132.

Munar, A. M., & Jacobsen, J. K. S. (2014). Motivations for sharing tourism experiences through social media. *Tourism Management*, *43*, 46–54.

Munt, I. (1994). The "other" postmodern tourism: Culture, travel and the new middle classes. *Theory, Culture & Society*, *11*(3), 101–123.

Murray, S. (2003). Media convergence's third wave: Content streaming. *Convergence*, *9*(1), 8–18.

Nag, W. (2018). Music streams, smartphones, and the self. *Mobile Media & Communication*, *6*(1), 19–36.

Nagy, P., & Neff, G. (2015). Imagined affordance: Reconstructing a keyword for communication theory. *Social Media+ Society*, *1*(2), 1–9.

Nansen, B., Arnold, M., Gibbs, M. R., & Davis, H. (2009). Domestic orchestration: Rhythms in the mediated home. *Time & Society*, *18*(2–3), 181–207.

Nansen, B., Arnold, M., Gibbs, M., & Davis, H. (2010). Time, space and technology in the working-home: An unsettled nexus. *New Technology, Work and Employment*, *25*(2), 136–153.

Nansen, B., Arnold, M., Gibbs, M., & Davis, H. (2011). Dwelling with media stuff: Latencies and logics of materiality in four Australian homes. *Environment and Planning D: Society and Space*, *29*(4), 693–715.

Nash, C., & Gorman-Murray, A. (Eds.) (2019). *The Geographies of Digital Sexuality*. Singapore: Palgrave Macmillan.

Neilson, B. (2012). Five theses on understanding logistics as power. *Distinktion: Scandinavian Journal of Social Theory*, *13*(3), 322–339.

Newport, C. (2019). *Digital Minimalism: Choosing a Focused Life in a Noisy World*. London: Penguin.

Norris, C. (2016). Japanese media tourism as world-building: Akihabara's Electric Town and Ikebukuro's Maiden Road. *Participations*, *13*(1), 656–681.

Olwig, K. R. (2003). Landscape: The Lowenthal legacy. *Annals of the Association of American Geographers*, *93*(4), 871–877.

Olwig, K. R. (2005). Representation and alienation in the political land-scape. *Cultural Geographies*, *12*(1), 19–40.
Olwig, K. R. (2008). Performing on the landscape versus doing landscape: Perambulatory practice, sight and the sense of belonging. In Ingold, T., & Vergunst, J. L. (Eds.) *Ways of Walking: Ethnography and Practice on Foot*. Aldershot: Ashgate.
Örnebring, H., & Hellekant Rowe, E. (2022). The media day, revisited: Rhythm, place and hyperlocal information environments. *Digital Journalism*, *10*(1), 23–42. DOI: 10.1080/21670811.2021.1884988.
Özkul, D., & Humphreys, L. (2015). Record and remember: Memory and meaning-making practices through mobile media. *Mobile Media & Communication*, *3*(3), 351–365.
Paasonen, S. (2015). As networks fail: Affect, technology, and the notion of the user. *Television & New Media*, *16*(8), 701–716.
Paasonen, S. (2020). *Dependent, Distracted, Bored: Affective Formations in Networked Media*. Cambridge, MA: MIT Press.
Papacharissi, Z. (2016). Affective publics and structures of storytelling: Sentiment, events and mediality. *Information, Communication & Society*, *19*(3), 307–324.
Park, R. E., & Burgess, E. W. (1925/2019). *The City*. Chicago: University of Chicago Press.
Parmett, H. M. (2016). It's HBO: Passionate engagement, TV branding, and tourism in the postbroadcast era. *Communication and Critical/Cultural Studies*, *13*(1), 3–22.
Pauwels, L. (2008). A private visual practice going public? Social functions and sociological research opportunities of Web-based family photography. *Visual Studies*, *23*(1), 34–49.
Peters, J. D. (1999). *Speaking into the Air: A History of the Idea of Communication*. Chicago: University of Chicago Press.
Peters, J. D. (2008). Strange sympathies: Horizons of German and American media theory. In Kelleter, F., & Stein, D. (Eds.) *American Studies as Media Studies*. Heidelberg: Universitätsverlag.
Peters, J. D. (2012). Becoming mollusk: A conversation with John Durham Peters about media, materiality and matters of history. In Packer, J., & Crofts Wiley, S. B. (Eds.) *Communication Matters: Materialist Approaches to Media, Mobility and Networks*. New York: Routledge.
Peters, J. D. (2013). Calendar, clock, tower. In Stolow, J. (Ed.) *Deus in Machina: Religion and Technology in Historical Perspective*. New York: Fordham University Press.
Peters, J. D. (2015). *The Marvelous Clouds: Toward a Philosophy of Elemental Media*. Chicago: University of Chicago Press.
Pigni, F., Piccoli, G., & Watson, R. (2016). Digital data streams: Creating value from the real-time flow of big data. *California Management Review*, *58*(3), 5–25.
Pink, S., Ruckenstein, M., Willim, R., & Duque, M. (2018). Broken data: Conceptualising data in an emerging world. *Big Data & Society*, *5*(1), 1–13.
Pollio, A. (2021). Uber, airports, and labour at the infrastructural interfaces of platform urbanism. *Geoforum*, *118*, 47–55.
Polson, E. (2016a). *Privileged Mobilities: Professional Migration, Geo-Social Media, and a New Global Middle Class*. New York: Peter Lang.
Polson, E. (2016b). Negotiating independent mobility: Single female expats in Bangalore. *European Journal of Cultural Studies*, *19*(5), 450–464.
Polson, E. (forthcoming). From the tag to the #hashtag: Street art, Instagram and gentrification. *Space and Culture*.

Powrie, P. (2005). "I'm only here for the beer": Post-tourism and the recycling of French heritage films. In Crouch, D., Jackson, R., & Thompson, F. (Eds.) *The Media and the Tourist Imagination: Converging Cultures*. London: Routledge.

Pratt, A. C. (2011). The cultural contradictions of the creative city. *City, Culture and Society*, *2*(3), 123–130.

Prey, R. (2020). Locating power in platformization: Music streaming playlists and curatorial power. *Social Media+ Society*, *6*(2), 1–11.

Rauch, J. (2018). *Slow Media: Why Slow Is Satisfying, Sustainable, and Smart*. New York: Oxford University Press.

Reid, J. (2006). *The Biopolitics of the War on Terror: Life Struggles, Liberal Modernity and the Defence of Logistical Societies*. Manchester: Manchester University Press.

Relph, E. (1970). An inquiry into the relations between phenomenology and geography. *Canadian Geographer*, *14*(3), 193–201.

Relph, E. (1976). *Place and Placelessness*. London: Sage.

Richardson, L. (2015). Performing the sharing economy. *Geoforum*, *67*, 121–129.

Richardson, L. (2020a). Platforms, markets, and contingent calculation: The flexible arrangement of the delivered meal. *Antipode*, *52*(3), 619–636.

Richardson, L. (2020b). Coordinating the city: Platforms as flexible spatial arrangements. *Urban Geography*, *41*(3), 458–461.

Richardson, L., & Bissell, D. (2019). Geographies of digital skill. *Geoforum*, *99*, 278–286.

Ritzer, G., & Liska, A. (1997). "McDisneyization" and "post-tourism": Complementary perspectives on contemporary tourism. In Rojek C., & Urry, J. (Eds.) *Touring Cultures: Transformations of Travel and Theory*. London: Routledge.

Rodriguez-Amat, J. R., & Brantner, C. (2016). Space and place matters: A tool for the analysis of geolocated and mapped protests. *New Media & Society*, *18*(6), 1027–1046.

Rose, G. (2010). *Doing Family Photography: The Domestic, the Public and the Politics of Sentiment*. London: Routledge.

Rose, G. (2014). How digital technologies do family snaps, only better. In Larsen, J., & Sandbye, M. (Eds.) *Digital Snaps: The New Face of Photography*. London: Routledge.

Rose, G. (2017). Posthuman agency in the digitally mediated city: Exteriorization, individuation, reinvention. *Annals of the American Association of Geographers*, *107*(4), 779–793.

Rose, G., Raghuram, P., Watson, S., & Wigley, E. (2021). Platform urbanism, smartphone applications and valuing data in a smart city. *Transactions of the Institute of British Geographers*, *46*(1), 59–72.

Rossiter, N. (2014). Logistical worlds. *Cultural Studies Review*, *20*(1), 53–76.

Rossiter, N. (2015). Locative media as logistical media: Situating infrastructure and the governance of labor in supply-chain capitalism. In Wilken, R., & Goggin, G. (Eds.) *Locative Media*. London: Routledge.

Rossiter, N. (2016). *Software, Infrastructure, Labor: A Media Theory of Logistical Nightmares*. London: Routledge.

Ruckenstein, M. (2014). Visualized and interacted life: Personal analytics and engagements with data doubles. *Societies*, *4*(1), 68–84.

Sadowski, J. (2020a). The internet of landlords: Digital platforms and new mechanisms of rentier capitalism. *Antipode*, *52*(2), 562–580.

Sadowski, J. (2020b). Cyberspace and cityscapes: On the emergence of platform urbanism. *Urban Geography*, *41*(3), 448–452.

Sadowski, J., & Bendor, R. (2019). Selling smartness: Corporate narratives and the smart city as a sociotechnical imaginary. *Science, Technology, & Human Values*, *44*(3), 540–563.

Saker, M., & Frith, J. (2018). Locative media and sociability: Using location-based social networks to coordinate everyday life. *Architecture_Media_Politics_Society (AMPS)*, *14*(1), 1–21.

Salazar, N. B. (2012). Tourism imaginaries: A conceptual approach. *Annals of Tourism Research*, *39*(2), 863–882.

Sauer, C. O. (1963). *Land and Life: A Selection from the Writings of Carl Ortwin Sauer*. Berkeley: University of California Press.

Scannell, P. (1996). *Radio, Television, and Modern Life: A Phenomenological Approach*. Oxford: Blackwell.

Scannell, P. (2007). *Media and Communication*. London: Sage.

Schegloff, E. A. (2002). Beginnings in the telephone. In Katz, J. E., & Aakhus, M. A. (Eds.) *Perceptual Contact: Mobile Communication, Private Talk, Public Performance*. Cambridge: Cambridge University Press.

Scholz, T. (Ed.). (2012). *Digital Labor: The Internet as Playground and Factory*. New York: Routledge.

Schutz, A. (1932/1967). *The Phenomenology of the Social World*. Evanston, IL: Northwestern University Press.

Schwarz, K. C. (2021). "Gazing" and "performing": Travel photography and online self-presentation. *Tourist Studies*, *21*(2), 260–277.

Scolari, C. A. (2009). Transmedia storytelling: Implicit consumers, narrative worlds, and branding in contemporary media production. *International Journal of Communication*, *3*, 586–606.

Seamon, D. (1979). *A Geography of the Lifeworld: Movement, Rest, Encounter*. New York: Routledge.

Seamon, D. (2014). Lifeworld, place, and phenomenology: Holistic and dialectical perspectives. Paper presented at the conference *Lifeworlds: Space, Place, and Irish Culture*, Galway, 27–30 March 2014.

Seamon, D. (2018). *Life Takes Place: Phenomenology, Lifeworlds, and Place Making*. New York: Routledge.

Shannon, C. E., & Weaver, W. (1949). *The Mathematical Theory of Communication*. Urbana, IL: University of Illinois Press.

Siegert, B. (2013). Cultural techniques: Or the end of the intellectual postwar era in German media theory. *Theory, Culture & Society*, *30*(6), 48–65.

Siegert, B. (2015). *Cultural Techniques: Grids, Filters, Doors, and Other Articulations of the Real*. New York: Fordham University Press.

Silverstone, R. (2007). *Media and Morality: On the Rise of the Mediapolis*. Cambridge: Polity Press.

Silverstone, R., & Hirsch, E. (Eds.) (1992). *Consuming Technologies: Media and Information in Domestic Spaces*. London: Routledge.

Sin, H. L., & He, S. (2019). Voluntouring on Facebook and Instagram: Photography and social media in constructing the "Third World" experience. *Tourist Studies*, *19*(2), 215–237.

Skeggs, B. (1997). *Formations of Class and Gender: Becoming Respectable*. London: Sage.

Smythe, D. (1981). *Dependency Road: Communications, Capitalism, and Canada*. Norwood, NJ: Ablex Publishing Corporation.

Soriano, C. R. R. (2016). Transmedia mobilization: Agency and literacy in minority productions in the age of spreadable media. *The Information Society*, *32*(5), 354–363.

Stabrowski, F. (2017). "People as businesses": Airbnb and urban micro-entrepreneurialism in New York City. *Cambridge Journal of Regions, Economy and Society*, *10*(2), 327–347.

Steinbock, A. J. (1995). *Home and Beyond*. Evanston, IL: Northwestern University Press.

Stine, K., & Volmar, A. (2021). Infrastructures of time: An introduction to hardwired temporalities. In Stine, K., & Volmar, A. (Eds.) *Media Infrastructures and the Politics of Digital Time: Essays on Hardwired Temporalities*. Amsterdam: Amsterdam University Press.

Strain, E. (2003). *Public Places, Private Journeys: Ethnography, Entertainment, and the Tourist Gaze*. Ithaca, NY: Rutgers University Press.

Striphas, T. (2015). Algorithmic culture. *European Journal of Cultural Studies*, *18*(4–5), 395–412.

Stumpf, T. S., Califf, C. B., & Frye, J. J. (2020). Technological metaworlds in travel. *Information Technology & Tourism*, *22*(2), 273–296.

Sturken, M., & Cartwright, L. (2001). *Practices of Looking: An Introduction to Visual Culture*. Oxford: Oxford University Press.

Sundén, J. (2015). Technologies of feeling: Affect between the analog and the digital. In Hillis, K., Paasonen, S., & Petit, M. (Eds.) *Networked Affect*. Cambridge, MA: MIT Press.

Sundén, J. (2018). Queer disconnections: Affect, break, and delay in digital connectivity. *Transformations*, *3*(1), 63–78.

Sundén, J., & Paasonen, S. (2020). *Who's Laughing Now? Feminist Tactics in Social Media*. Cambridge, MA: MIT Press.

Syvertsen, T. (2017). *Media Resistance: Protest, Dislike, Abstention*. Cham: Palgrave Pivot/Springer.

Syvertsen, T., & Enli, G. (2020). Digital detox: Media resistance and the promise of authenticity. *Convergence*, *26*(5–6), 1269–1283.

Szerszynski, B. (2003). Technology, performance and life itself: Hannah Arendt and the fate of nature. *The Sociological Review*, *51*(2_suppl), 203–218.

Szerszynski, B., & Urry, J. (2006). Visuality, mobility and the cosmopolitan: Inhabiting the world from afar. *The British Journal of Sociology*, *57*(1), 113–131.

Tárcia, L. P. T. (2019). Transmedia education: Changing the learning landscape. In Freeman, M., & Gambarato, R. R. (Eds.) *The Routledge Companion to Transmedia Studies*. London: Routledge.

Tegtmeyer, L. L. (2016). Tourism aesthetics in ruinscapes: Bargaining cultural and monetary values of Detroit's negative image. *Tourist Studies*, *16*(4), 462–477.

Terranova, T. (2000). Free labor: Producing culture for the digital economy. *Social Text*, *18*(2), 33–58.

Thielmann, T. (2007). "You have reached your destination!" Position, positioning and superpositioning of space through car navigation systems. *Social Geography*, *2*(1), 63–75.

Thielmann, T. (2010). Locative media and mediated localities: An introduction to media geography. *Aether: The Journal of Media Geography*, Vol. 5, 1–17.

Thielmann, T., van der Velden, L., Fischer, F., & Vogler, R. (2012). Dwelling in the web: Towards a Googlization of space. *HIIG Discussion Paper Series*, No. 2012-03, https://papers.ssrn.com/sol3/papers.cfm?abstract_id=2151949.

Thorén, C., Edenius, M., Lundström, J. E., & Kitzmann, A. (2019). The hipster's dilemma: What is analogue or digital in the post-digital society? *Convergence*, *25*(2), 324–339.
Thrift, N. (2008). *Non-Representational Theory: Space, Politics, Affect*. London: Routledge.
Tomlinson, J. (1999). *Globalization and Culture*. Cambridge: Polity Press.
Topper, K. (2001). Not so trifling nuances: Pierre Bourdieu, symbolic violence, and the perversions of democracy. *Constellations*, *8*(1), 30–56.
Tuan, Y.-F. (1974). *Topophilia: A Study of Environmental Perceptions, Attitudes, and Values*. New York: Columbia University Press.
Tuan, Y.-F. (1977). *Space and Place. The Perspective of Experience*. Minneapolis: University of Minnesota Press.
Tudor, M. (2018). *Desire Lines: Towards A Queer Digital Media Phenomenology*. Doctoral dissertation, Stockholm, Södertörn University.
Urry, J. (1990/2002). *The Tourist Gaze*. London: Routledge.
Urry, J. (1995). *Consuming Places*. London: Routledge.
Urry, J. (2007). *Mobilities*. Cambridge: Polity.
van Dijck, J. (2008). Digital photography: Communication, identity, memory. *Visual Communication*, *7*(1), 57–76.
van Dijck, J. (2013). *The Culture of Connectivity: A Critical History of Social Media*. Oxford: Oxford University Press.
van Dijck, J., & Poell, T. (2013). Understanding social media logic. *Media and Communication*, *1*(1), 2–14.
van Doorn, N. (2020). A new institution on the block: On platform urbanism and Airbnb citizenship. *New Media & Society*, *22*(10), 1808–1826.
Velkova, J., & Kaun, A. (2021). Algorithmic resistance: Media practices and the politics of repair. *Information, Communication & Society*, *24*(4), 523–540.
Wajcman, J. (2019a). How Silicon Valley sets time. *New Media & Society*, *21*(6), 1272–1289.
Wajcman, J. (2019b). The digital architecture of time management. *Science, Technology, & Human Values*, *44*(2), 315–337.
Wallin, B., Wallin, E. T., & Lorentzen, D. G. (2019). Bokläsning och den svenska bokmarknaden. In Andersson, U., Rönnerstrand, B., Öhberg, P., & Bergström, A. (Eds.) *Storm och stiltje*. Gothenburg: The SOM Institute, University of Gothenburg.
Walters, P., & Smith, N. (forthcoming). It's so ridiculously soulless: Geolocative media, place and third wave gentrification. *Space and Culture*.
Wang, D., Xiang, Z., & Fesenmaier, D. R. (2014). Adapting to the mobile world: A model of smartphone use. *Annals of Tourism Research*, *48*, 11–26.
Webster, J. (2019). Music on-demand: A commentary on the changing relationship between music taste, consumption and class in the streaming age. *Big Data & Society*, *6*(2), 1–5.
Webster, J. (2020). Taste in the platform age: Music streaming services and new forms of class distinction. *Information, Communication & Society*, *23*(13), 1909–1924.
Weltevrede, E., Helmond, A., & Gerlitz, C. (2014). The politics of real-time: A device perspective on social media platforms and search engines. *Theory, Culture & Society*, *31*(6), 125–150.
Werner, A. (2020). Organizing music, organizing gender: Algorithmic culture and Spotify recommendations. *Popular Communication*, *18*(1), 78–90.
Wernick, A. (1991). *Promotional Culture: Advertising and Ideology in Late Capitalism*. London: Sage.

Wexler, P. (1990). Citizenship in the semiotic society. In Turner, B. S. (Ed.) *Theories of Modernity and Postmodernity*. London: Sage.
White, N. R., & White, P. B. (2007). Home and away: Tourists in a connected world. *Annals of Tourism Research, 34*(1), 88–104.
Whiting, R., & Symon, G. (2020). Digi-housekeeping: The invisible work of flexibility. *Work, Employment and Society, 34*(6), 1079–1096.
Wijngaarden, V. (2016). Tourists' agency versus the circle of representation. *Annals of Tourism Research, 60*, 139–153.
Wilken, R. (2018). The necessity of geomedia: Understanding the significance of location-based services and data-driven platforms. In Fast, K., Jansson, A., Lindell, J., Ryan Bengtsson, L., & Tesfahuney, M. (Eds.) *Geomedia Studies: Spaces and Mobilities of Mediatized Worlds*. London: Routledge.
Wilken, R., & Goggin, G. (2015). Locative media – definitions, histories, theories. In Wilken, R., & Goggin, G. (Eds.) *Locative Media*. London: Routledge.
Williams, R. (1961). *The Long Revolution*. Harmondsworth: Penguin.
Williams, R. (1974). *Television: Technology and Cultural Form*. London: Fontana.
Williams, R. (1977). *Marxism and Literature*. Oxford: Oxford University Press.
Williams, R. (1980). *Problems in Materialism and Culture: Selected Essays*. London: New Left Books.
Xiang, Z., Wang, D., O'Leary, J. T., & Fesenmaier, D. R. (2015). Adapting to the Internet: Trends in travelers' use of the web for trip planning. *Journal of Travel Research, 54*(4), 511–527.
Young, L. C. (2015). Cultural techniques and logistical media: Tuning German and Anglo-American media studies. *M/C Journal, 18*(2).
Ytre-Arne, B., & Moe, H. (2020). Folk theories of algorithms: Understanding digital irritation. *Media, Culture & Society, 43*(5), 807–824.
Zeffiro, A. (2012). A location of one's own: A genealogy of locative media. *Convergence, 18*(3), 249–266.
Zehle, S., & Rossiter, N. (2016). Mediations of labor: Algorithmic architectures, logistical media, and the rise of black box politics. In Maxwell, R. (Ed.) *The Routledge Companion to Labor and Media*. London: Routledge.
Zook, M. A., & Graham, M. (2007). Mapping digiPlace: Geocoded Internet data and the representation of place. *Environment and Planning B: Planning and Design, 34*(3), 466–482.
Zuboff, S. (2015). Big other: Surveillance capitalism and the prospects of an information civilization. *Journal of Information Technology, 30*(1), 75–89.
Zuboff, S. (2019). Surveillance capitalism and the challenge of collective action. *New Labor Forum, 28*(1), 10–29.
Zukin, S. (1991). *Landscapes of Power: From Detroit to Disney World*. Berkeley: University of California Press.
Zukin, S. (2008). Consuming authenticity, from outposts of difference to means of exclusion. *Cultural Studies, 22*(5), 724–748.
Zukin, S. (2010). *Naked City: The Death and Life of Authentic Urban Places*. Oxford: Oxford University Press.
Zukin, S., Lindeman, S., & Hurson, L. (2017). The omnivore's neighborhood? Online restaurant reviews, race, and gentrification. *Journal of Consumer Culture, 17*(3), 459–479.

Index

Abend, Pablo 127–8
action 31, 55–7, 90, 155
    boundedness resistance 153, 167
    labour/work distinction 35, 47, 51, 53
    uncertainty of outcomes 166
active life (*vita activa*) 6, 29, 51–2
activeness, locative media 127–8
actor network theory 42
Adams, Paul C. 46, 74–5, 104, 162
affective formations 71, 81
affordances 9–11, 47–8
    activity types relation 52, 56, 57
    dwelling perspective 42–3
    geomedia effects 12–15
    see also connective affordances; logistical affordances; representational affordances
agency 25–6, 42
agricultural goods 16–17
Ahmed, Sara 22
AI (artificial intelligence), power of 20
algorithmic exploitation 68
algorithmic resistance 57
algorithmic steering 77
alternative tourism platforms 134–5, 138–42
"ambient communication" 105
analogue trend 39, 71
Andersson, Magnus 46, 105
Andrejevic, Mark 19–20, 68
Andron, S. 112
anthropocentrism 22, 23–4, 47
appearance, spaces of 153, 156–7, 164–7
apps, problems with 5
Arendt, Hannah 4, 23–4, 27, 29, 31, 35, 47, 50–58, 76, 153, 155–6, 158, 163, 166–7
    The Human Condition 88
armchair travellers 93, 99–100
artificial intelligence (AI), power of 20
audio-streaming 60, 66, 75–6, 78, 85–6

    see also music streaming

back-end streams 12, 62, 65, 67
Barthes, Roland 10
Beck, Ulrich 103
    What is Globalization? 101
Being concept 53
Bennett, W. L. 56
Berger, P. 49
Berkeley School 131
Berlant, Lauren 40
Bernard, Andreas 12–13
Berry, David M. 67–8, 70–71
Bezos, Jeff 87
biases 12–13, 16, 22, 47, 54, 57, 146–8
Birmingham School 25
Bissell, D. 165
boundedness/boundlessness 31, 152, 161–3, 167
Bourdieu, Pierre 25–7, 32, 43, 87, 89, 120, 153, 164–6
Briziarelli, M. 57
Burroughs, B. 62–3
Buttimer, Anne 23, 40, 161

Calvignac, C. 129
capitalism 15–16, 19, 54, 103, 114
captivation 70–74
Carey, James 38
Case, Judd A. 17, 124
Cassidy, E. 160
Cassinger, C. 112
Chicago school 24–5
Chua, C. 69
circulation
    enclosed systems 68–70
    friction in 68–70
    of labour 92
    transmedia 92–115
"click labour" 55
"coercive flexibility" 152, 165

commercial logics 129
communication
    humanistic trait 56, 118
    space relation 7–8, 11, 14
communicative practices 46
connective action 56
connective affordances 9–10, 11, 12–14, 47, 58
connective labour 74–5
connective media 62, 66, 75, 146
connectivity
    culture of 62–3, 154
    networks 12
container technology 69
content packages 70
content streams 12, 64, 65–8
continuous travel planning 99, 100–101
coordination 122–4
Cosgrove, Denis 44, 117, 132–3
cosmopolitanism 101, 141
Couldry, N. 73, 152–5, 158, 161, 166
    The Costs of Connection 22
COVID-19 pandemic 2, 33–4, 45, 92, 109–10, 165
Cresswell, Tim 45
crowding 163
cultural capital 142, 153, 165–6, 167
cultural form, logistical media 119, 130
cultural life 7
cultural techniques 18, 119
culture
    of connectivity 62–3, 154
    of streamability 29, 60–91
Cuppini, N. 147

data colonialism 19, 62
data streams 12, 16, 61, 64–8, 96–7
datafication 55, 155
de-differentiation 92–5, 99–101, 106, 108, 112–14
    in tourism 30, 92–4, 138–9, 142
decapsulation through entanglement 106–9
delimitation competence 120
Deuze, Mark 35–8, 40, 148, 155
"digi-housekeeping" 5, 55
digital captivation 73
digital circulation 68–70
digital data streams 64, 96
digital enclosure 68–70

digital geographies 4, 21–7, 161
digital logistics 17
digital networks, embeddedness 14
digital skills 50, 153, 165
digital subjects, users as 96–7
digital thrownness 32
digital throwntogetherness 32
digital time 5–6
digital unease 166
digital wayfaring 50, 102, 105, 112, 160
digitalization 94, 95, 103, 124
Dinhopl, A. 112
disconnection 107, 159–62, 163–4, 166
distance stake 121
Dodge, M. 14
"drone cartographies" 19
dwelling perspective 29, 33–59
    disconnection 160–61
    exploited labour 154
    landscape 132–3
    logistical expertise 86
    logistical labour 80, 82
    naturalization 85
    space and 119–20
    spatial stakes 121
    streamability 61
    transmedia travel 94, 101–6

e-scooters 1–4, 8, 19, 31, 143–4
ecological bias 147
economic capital 153, 165–6
economic transactions 91
educational system 167
efficiency measurement 118
egocentric navigation 127–8
elemental media 35–8
Elwood, Sarah 149, 158
emancipation 6
emplacement 44–5, 120, 128, 141
    performative labour of 109–14
encapsulation/decapsulation dialectic 106–9
enclosure 68–70
engagement 97
Enli, G. 163
entanglement 70–74, 106–9
environment–landscape link 43, 130–31
environment without objects (EWO) 26
environmental regime, geomedia as 3, 6, 35, 46–50, 63, 130–31

Eriksson, Maria 69
event streamability 64
EWO (environment without objects) 26
expertise 50, 89, 165
　see also logistical expertise
exploitation
　algorithmic 68
　of labour 50, 53, 130, 154
extensibility 74–5, 103–5

fabrication, work as 51, 53
familiarization process 126
Fan, D. X. 107
Fast, Karin 13, 162
Feifer, M. 92
flow management 63, 124
friction 68–70, 74
front-end streams 12, 62, 65–7

gentrification processes 25, 111–13, 140
geomedia
　as human condition 151–67
　as environmental regime 3, 6, 35, 46–50, 63, 130–31
　fields of study 6–11
　logistical expansion 4
　as relational construct 14–15
　triadic view of 47, 50–58
geomedia capital 164–7
geomediatization 14, 43, 73–4, 83–4
"German School" 38
Gibson, James J. 9, 26, 42–3, 47
gifts 89
Givskov, Cecilie 83
glitch politics 158
Goggin, G. 13
Google as elemental media 38
Google Maps 19, 127
Goriunova, O. 97
Gretzel, U. 112
ground signage 109–10
guidance landscapes 30, 116–50

Habermas, Jürgen 56, 157
habitat–habitus link 43
habitus 25, 26, 43
Hagen, A. N. 77
Harries, Karston 41
Hartmann, Maren 155

Harvey, F. 127
Heidegger, Martin 41, 43–5, 119
hexis 26, 43, 120
Hjorth, Larissa 46, 102
holism 24, 40–41
home, working from 33–4
hospitable spaces 134–5, 140
hospitality discourse 117, 136–7
human condition
　geomedia *as* 151–67
　shaping 6, 21–7
humanism 23, 24, 56
humanistic geography 23–5, 40–41, 42
"humanness" 23
Hutchby, Ian 9

image-sharing 107, 110
immediacy 105
immutable mobiles theory 125
industrial goods 16
industrial logics 61–2
information streams 65, 91, 96
infrastructuralism 37, 39
infrastructure 2, 10, 18, 37, 40, 111
Ingold, Tim 25–7, 29, 32, 35, 41–7, 49–51, 58, 82, 86, 104, 119–22, 132
"Instagramism" 113, 139
intentionality 41–2
interpretation 41, 64
itinerary competence 120
Iveson, K. 20

Jager, Bernd 45
Javeus, Johan 33
Jenkins, H. 96
"Jenkins legacy" 99
Johansson, S., *Streaming Music* 77

Karppi, T. 71, 97
Kennedy, J. 159–60
kinetic bias 146
Kinkaid, E. 23–4
Kitchin, R. 14
Kittler, Friedrich 37, 119

labour 18, 50, 54–5, 61
　of circulation 92
　connective 74–5

definitions 52–3
exploitation of 50, 53, 130, 154
of mobility 94
performative 109–14
tourism overlap 94, 100
work/action distinction 35, 47, 51, 53
see also logistical labour
Lagerkvist, Amanda 20
landscape 30–31, 50–51
environment link 43, 130–31
guidance 30, 116–50
as social formation 44, 133
landscaping 117, 130–35
Lash, Scott 15, 17, 92, 95, 113
Economies of Signs and Space 15–16, 93
Latour, Bruno 125
Lefebvre, Henri 8, 44, 89
Leszczynski, Agnieszka 15, 57–8, 149, 163
Ley, David 24–5
Humanistic Geography 23
lifestreaming 67
liminal spaces/events 98, 107
limit stakes 121
Lippmann, Walter, *Public Opinion* 132
localism 44, 140–41
locative guidance 30, 117, 124–31, 134, 141, 147
locative media 13–14, 30, 116–17, 126–8
logistical accumulation 3, 17, 19, 90, 130–35, 155
landscape relation 30–31, 135
logistical labour creation 151
streamability 65, 68
transmedia travel 97, 109–14
logistical action 57, 153–9
logistical affordances 9–14, 38, 47, 116–50
logistical bias 12–13, 16, 47, 57
logistical city 18, 147
logistical devices, humans as 68
logistical expertise 4, 14, 29, 63, 82–91, 165–6
logistical labour 4, 27, 30, 103, 149, 151
logistical action relation 153–9
streamability 63, 74–82
tourism blending with 99
transmedia travel 94, 107

logistical media 10, 17–18, 116–50
logistical society 6, 12, 16–18, 24, 98, 151, 158
logistical struggles 6, 15–21, 29, 128–9
streamability 63, 70, 74, 77, 82
logistics 3, 69, 118
coordination 122–3
spatial stakes 121–2
Lovink, Geert 70
Lowenthal, David 44, 131–2
Lucas, L. 120–22
Luckman, T. 49
Lüders, M. 77, 81
Lussault, Michel 117, 119–20, 122

Maalsen, S. 20
MacCannell, D. 140
machine learning 69
Manovich, L. 113
maps 125, 127
market–place mediation 133
Marx, Karl 52
mass media 36, 38, 95–6, 101
Matassi, M. 73
McQuire, Scott 15, 19
media
boundaries of 36
entanglement 106–7
living in/with 49
as means of communication 7
saturation 152
use of term 118
media action 56
media affordances *see* affordances
media infrastructures 5–6, 37
media labour 53–4
media life 36–40
media studies 20–21, 38, 54
media work 54
mediated simulacra 16
mediatization 16, 39–40
Mejias, U. A. 152–5, 158, 161, 166
The Costs of Connection 22
meshwork 49, 82
metrics competence 120
micro-mobility 1–4, 8, 19
mobile phone use 103
see also smartphones
mobility
labour of 94

place polygamy 102
   as service 134, 136, 142–9
Moores, Shaun 36, 42–3, 46, 103
Morley, David 38
Morris, J. W. 62
movement, digital subjects 97
multi-sited dwelling 99, 101–6
multiplied streams 70
Munt, I. 92
Murray, Simone 64, 68, 96
music, analogue trend 39, 71
music listening 71, 80–81, 84–5
music streaming 60, 69, 74–82
Musk, Elon 87

Nag, W. 76
Nansen, B. 72, 81–2, 85, 123
natural attitude 49
naturalization 85
nature as process 53
navigation systems 3, 53, 57, 122, 124–8, 146, 148
networked spatial information 32
networks
   connectivity 12
   objects relation to 25–6
Newport, Cal 163
newspaper formats 10
non-human bias 22
non-use 159–60

objects
   agency of 42
   networks relation 25–6
   things as 82
Olwig, Kenneth 117, 131–3
online tourism planning 100–101
open environments/spaces 86, 156
orchestration 81–2, 118–24
ordinariness of dwelling 58
ordinary logistical expertise 4, 14, 29, 63, 82–91, 166
organizational gaze 129
orientation 118–24, 125, 128

Paasonen, S. 71, 81
Park, Robert 24
parking apps 4–5, 19
participatory reluctance 160

"perceiving spaces" 20
performative labour 109–14
Peters, John Durham 7, 10, 14, 17, 35–40, 48, 84, 109, 116–18, 125, 152
The Marvellous Clouds 18
phenomenology 21, 42, 161, 164
photography 10, 54
Pigni, Federico 64, 68
Pink, Sarah 46, 102
place
   market mediation 133
   phenomenological construction 161, 164
   post-digital sense of 31, 159–64
   re-connection with 148
   representational affordances 11
   space distinction 7–8
place-contingency, locative media 126–8
place polygamy 101–3, 105
placement stake 121
platform economy 12, 19, 75, 142–9, 165
   guidance provision 14, 117, 129, 133–4, 136
   platform urbanism distinction 136–7, 141
   tourism 110–111, 142
platform urbanism 117, 136–8, 148–9
   affordances 57–8
   "click labour" 55
   as guidance landscape 30, 117, 163
   hospitality discourse 140
   platform economy distinction 136–7, 141
   triadic nature of 134
platforms, streaming 77–8, 84
playlists 61, 69
political landscapes 117, 133
Polson, E. 111, 141
post-digital bias 148
post-digital sense of place 31, 159–64
post-phenomenology 22
post-tourism thesis 30, 92–5, 99, 113
power relations 77, 85–6
Powers, D. 62
prescription 20, 127–8, 133
process
   of making 156
   nature as 53
production

labour as 52–3, 55
   of space 8
properties/things, entanglement 26–7
public sphere 157
"push" technologies 66

quantification 154–6

rational idealism 85
"real people", definition 21
real-time streams 66–7, 70, 72, 96, 103–4, 127
reflexive accumulation 16–17, 142
reflexive attention 82
"reflexive hesitation" 109
Relph, E. 44, 140
rentiers 142
representational action 56
representational affordances 9, 10–14, 47, 54, 94
representational aspects, space 44
representational bias 16, 54
representational goods 15–16
representational practices 43, 111
Richardson, Lizzie 138, 149, 152, 165
Rossiter, Ned 17, 119, 126
   Software, Infrastructure, Labour 18

Sadowski, J. 142
Samuels, M. S. 24
   Humanistic Geography 23
Sauer, Carl, *The Morphology of Landscape* 131
scale 44, 120
Scannell, P. 102
Schegloff, E. A. 103
seaming media 61
Seamon, David 41, 44–5, 58
Segerberg, A. 56
selfie logistics 109–14
selfie spots 109–11, 113, 115, 117
semiotic society 15–17, 93–4
semiotic version, capitalism 15, 54
sequential activities 122
services, mobility 134, 136, 142–9
Shannon, C. E. 36
sharing economy 139, 142–4, 149
shielding 160
Siegert, Bernhard 119

signs 15–16
Silverstone, Roger 38, 156
   The Media and Morality 157
Skeggs, Beverly 25
smart cameras 20
smart cities 14, 136–7, 146, 149
"smart living" 37
smart mobile devices 96
smart tourism technologies 100
"smartness" 85–6
smartphones 3–5, 46, 78–9, 107–8
Smolinski, J. 129
social formation 117, 130–31, 132, 134
social media 58, 96, 107–9
   see also connective media
"socio-spatio-technical relations" 15
software, labour impacts 18
space
   of appearance 56, 153, 156–7, 164–7
   communication relation 7–8, 11, 14
   "doings with" 116–17, 119–20
   landscaping 132
   locative guidance 141
   maps controlling 125
   phenomenological construction 164
   place distinction 7–8
   production of 8
   representational aspects 44
   surveillance 20
spaciousness 31, 153, 161–3
spatial competences 120
spatial ease 126, 129–30, 134–5, 140
spatial media 32
spatial pragmatics 30
spatial stakes 120–23, 125–6
speech 87–8, 90, 156
splicing 64
Stabrowski, F. 137
Stine, K. 5–6
Stolt, Per 60
streamability 12–13, 97, 104, 110, 158
   conceptualizing 64–70
   culture of 29, 60–91
   as mindset 61, 65
streams
   connective labour 75
   detectability 64
   management of 16–17
   measurability 64

modalities 96
    users woven into 67
Stumpf, T. S. 108
Sundén, Jenny 159
surveillance 20, 50, 152
surveillance capitalism 19, 103, 114
symbolic power 85, 89
symbolic violence 82–90, 166–7
Symon, G. 5
Syvertsen, T. 163
Szerszynski, Bronislaw 51–2

taskscapes 50–51, 122
technological trajectories 15
texts and texture 44
texturation 80–82
texture 44, 80–82
Thelander, Å 112
Thielmann, Tristan 14–15, 127–8
things
    entanglement 26–7
    as objects 82
time-spaces
    audio-streaming 60
    of disconnection 145
topophilia 8
tourism 92–115, 120
    alternative platforms 134–5, 138–42
    de-differentiation in 30, 92–4, 138–9, 142
    labour overlap 94, 100
    ubiquity of 99
tourist gaze 112–13
transience of world view 44
transmedia 13, 94–9
transmedia circulation 92–115
transmedia travel 30, 92–115
travel planning 30, 92–115
Tuan, Yi-Fu 8, 44
    Space and Place 162–3

ubiquity of tourism 99
urban landscape 117, 136, 140–41, 143
Urry, J. 17, 92, 95, 102, 113
    Economies of Signs and Space 15–16, 93

van Dijck, José 12, 75, 154
    The Culture of Connectivity 61–2
video-streaming 66
virtual tourists 30, 99–106
vita active (active life) 6, 29, 51–2
vita contemplativia 51
Volcic, Z. 20
Volmar, A. 5–6
"voluntourists" 109

Wajcman, Judy 129
warm experts 83, 87, 89, 152
Weaver, W. 36
web-browsers, "push" technologies 66
Webster, J. 76
Weckert, Simon 57
Weltevrede, E. 66
Whiting, R. 5
Wilken, R. 13
Williams, Raymond 25, 27, 71, 84, 130
work
    dwelling perspective 55
    home office 33–4
    labour/action distinction 35, 47, 51, 53
    logistical labour 90
"world-building" 95

Zuboff, Shoshana 19, 103, 114
Zuckerberg, Mark 87
Zukin, Sharon 117, 133

Printed and bound by CPI Group (UK) Ltd, Croydon, CR0 4YY
13/11/2023
08187638-0003